Association Tax Compliance Guide

SECOND EDITION

JEFFREY S. TENENBAUM

with contributions from

MATT JOURNY
GEORGE CONSTANTINE
LISA HIX
AUDRA HEAGNEY
JANICE RYAN
KRISTALYN LOSON
MEG ROHLFING
MEGAN MANN

association management press®

WASHINGTON, DC

The authors have worked diligently to ensure that all information in this book is accurate as of the time of publication and consistent with standards of good practice in the general management community. As research and practice advance, however, standards may change. For this reason it is recommended that readers evaluate the applicability of any recommendations in light of particular situations and changing standards.

Association Management Press
ASAE: The Center for Association Leadership
1575 I Street, NW
Washington, DC 20005-1103
Phone: (202) 626-2723; (888) 950-2723 outside metropolitan Washington, DC area
Fax: (202) 220-6439
Email: books@asaecenter.org

We connect great ideas and great people to inspire leadership and achievement in the association community.

Keith C. Skillman, CAE, Vice President, Publications, ASAE: The Center for Association Leadership
Baron Williams, CAE, Director of Book Publishing, ASAE: The Center for Association Leadership

Cover and interior design by Troy Scott Parker, Cimarron Design

This book is available at a special discount when ordered in bulk quantities. For information, contact the ASAE Member Service Center at (202) 371-0940. A complete catalog of titles is available on the ASAE website at www.asaecenter.org.

ISBN-13: 978-0-88034-369-5
ISBN-10: 0-88034-369-9

Printed in the United States of America.

10 9 8 7 6 5 4 3 2 1

CONTENTS

ACKNOWLEDGEMENTS

Special thanks to my colleagues George Constantine, Lisa Hix, Audra Heagney, Janice Ryan, Kristalyn Loson, Meg Rohlfing, Megan Mann, and especially, Matt Journy, without whose invaluable assistance and effort this second edition would not have been possible.

1

Tax Exemption for Associations

A. NONPROFIT VS. TAX-EXEMPT STATUS

The terminology used to describe trade and professional associations, as well as charitable organizations (all of which will be referred to as associations in this introduction), often generates much confusion. Consequently, it is useful to clarify two key terms. Associations are generally organized and operated as both nonprofit and tax-exempt entities. Nonprofit status refers to incorporation status under state law; tax-exempt status refers to federal income tax exemption under the Internal Revenue Code (the Code).

It is often assumed that as nonprofit, tax-exempt entities, associations may not earn profits (realize more income than expenditures) and that they need not pay any taxes. Neither conclusion is correct.

Even though they are nonprofit organizations, associations are permitted to generate greater income than expenses and still retain their nonprofit status. As nonprofit organizations, what associations are barred from doing is distributing their net earnings to individuals who control the organizations or are otherwise deemed to be insiders with respect to the organizations (other than as compensation for services actually rendered at prevailing market rates). Similarly, they are barred from accumulating equity appreciation for a private person's benefit. Since nonprofit organizations have chosen to undertake programs to benefit an industry, a profession, or the public rather than private individuals, their earnings must, by law, be dedicated to furthering the purposes for which they were organized. Nonprofit organizations have no shareholders and pay no dividends; all earnings are reinvested in the organization in furtherance of its nonprofit purposes.

Most associations are also tax-exempt entities, but they need not be. Because the requirements for federal income tax exemption are more stringent than those for nonprofit corporation status, there are some associations that are nonprofit corporations but do not qualify for exemption from federal income tax; these are taxable nonprofit corporations. However, these organizations are few and far between. Most nonprofit organizations qualify for federal income tax exemption under one of 25 subsections of section 501(c) of the Code. Most associations are recognized as exempt under sections 501(c)(3) or 501(c)(6), and a smaller number under sections 501(c)(4) or 501(c)(5). In addition, many 501(c)(6) associations form related educational and charitable foundations exempt under section 501(c)(3), political action committees exempt under section 527, and other taxable and tax-exempt affiliated entities.

But what does tax exemption mean? Does it mean that an organization is exempt from all taxes? No. Tax-exempt status means that an organization is exempt from paying corporate federal income tax on income generated from activities that are substantially related to the purposes for which the entity was organized and for which it was granted tax-exempt status in the first place. Organizations that meet the requirements for federal tax exemption can often rely on that status to exempt their income from state corporate income tax. However, it is generally necessary for an organization exempt from federal income tax to apply separately to the applicable state for exemption from state corporate income tax. Thus, for example, revenue derived from programs and activities such as educational conferences and seminars that contribute importantly to the furtherance of an organization's tax-exempt purposes, as defined in its governing documents and Internal Revenue Service (IRS) filings, is exempt from federal (and in many cases state) income tax. The organization does, however, pay corporate federal income tax (at standard corporate rates) on unrelated business income (UBI)—income from a regularly carried on trade or business that is not substantially related to its tax-exempt purposes.

However, most associations that have tax-exempt status do remain subject to a wide variety of other taxes, including federal payroll (Social Security, Medicare, and unemployment) taxes, state and local unemployment taxes, real estate taxes, personal property taxes, sales and use taxes, franchise taxes, and taxes on lobbying activities, among others. Exemptions for certain state and local taxes are provided for charitable organizations in many jurisdictions.

Associations are required to comply at all times with the strict guidelines for both tax-exempt and nonprofit status in order to maintain their favored status under federal and state tax codes and state corporation laws.

B. SECTION 501(C)(6) TAX EXEMPTION

Since 1913, when the first federal income tax laws were enacted in the United States, a trade or professional association has been eligible for tax-exempt status as a "business league" if it is "not organized for profit and no part of the net earnings" "inures to the benefit of any private shareholder or individual." This provision now appears as section 501(c)(6) of the Code.

The Treasury Regulations define a business league as an association of persons (including corporations) having a common business interest. Its purpose is to promote the common business interest and not to engage in a regular business of a kind ordinarily carried on for profit. Its activities are directed to the improvement of business conditions of one or more lines of business rather than the performance of particular services for individual persons or entities.

In its Internal Revenue Manual, the IRS has listed an additional seven requirements that must be satisfied by an organization in order to qualify for exemption under section 501(c)(6).

- It must be an association of persons having some common business interest, and its purpose must be to promote this common business interest. This should be reflected in the organization's governing documents.
- It must not be organized for profit; that is, it should be incorporated as a nonprofit corporation, not as a stock corporation.
- It must be a membership organization and have a meaningful extent of membership support.
- No part of its net earnings may inure to the benefit of any private shareholder or individual (see discussion below in this section).
- Its activities must be directed to the improvement of business conditions of one or more lines of business.
- Its purpose must not be to engage in a regular business of a kind ordinarily carried on for profit, even if the business is operated on a cooperative basis or produces only sufficient income to be self-sustaining.
- The organization's primary activity cannot be the performance of particular services for an individual person or persons.

The requirement that members have a common business interest is generally easily satisfied, as most trade and professional associations are made up of individuals or entities in the same industry or profession. The term "business" is broadly construed, and distinctions between trades, businesses, and professions are not made or observed; provided that all members of the organization have a common business interest in a particular field. However, business will not be considered to include organizations that do not have a trade or occupational purpose or connection. The requirement for commonality is generally satisfied if the members are members of the same industry or profession; or are members of different industries or professions but share common business or professional problems or issues. A section 501(c)(6) organization must also promote the common business interests of its members. Several traditional association activities have been recognized by the IRS as promoting business interests, including industry marketing or advertising designed to encourage the use of the products or services of the industry or profession; trade shows; research; the provision of information about industry business conditions; and legislative activities.

As noted above, to qualify for tax exemption under section 501(c)(6), an organization's activities must be directed to the improvement of business conditions of one or more lines of business, as distinguished from the performance of particular services for individual persons. The IRS defines a line of business as a trade or occupation, entry into which is not restricted by a patent, trademark, or similar device which would allow private parties to restrict the right to engage in the business. A line of business must consist of competitors within a trade, industry, or profession; however, it need not consist of the entire industry or all components of an industry in a particular geographic area. The association's activities must serve the entire line of business, not just the members of the association.

"Particular services" has been defined to include any "activity that serves as a convenience or economy to members in the operation of their business, rather than to promote or improve the industry represented by the association" or any services that are provided to the organization's membership that are in addition to those that are exempt activities funded by dues. The determination is a quantitative one—whether or not the particular service is only incidental or minor compared to the principal purpose or benefits of an activity. Denial of tax-exempt status will only occur if it is concluded that the primary purpose of the organization is the performance of particular services. (See Section II.A.3.) In most cases, the particular services are provided to members of the organization; however, in some instances, tax-exempt status is denied when an organization provides particular services to individuals outside the membership of the organization. The IRS has found that an association is providing a particular service in the following instances: the association is providing a service that relieves its members of obtaining the same service on an individual basis from a nonexempt commercial business; the association is providing a service that is individually tailored for each member of the association; and members are paying an additional fee for the service and the fee varies depending on the member's level of participation in the service.

An organization's satisfaction of the requirements described above will cause the organization to be recognized as an organization exempt from federal income tax under section 501(c)(6). However, an organization's failure to satisfy any of the requirements can be fatal to the organization's ability to obtain or maintain tax-exempt status. The IRS or a court will scrutinize an organization's compliance with section 501(c)(6) requirements when exemption is initially applied for through submission of IRS Form 1024 to the IRS, or later when the tax-exempt status of the organization is reviewed through an IRS examination. (Note that, as discussed in greater detail in this chapter, an application for recognition of exempt status (Form 1024) is not required to be submitted for an organization to have section 501(c)(6) exempt status.)

At the time of application for recognition of exempt status, the IRS will examine whether an entity seeking section 501(c)(6) status complies with and is likely to continue to comply with the applicable requirements. The IRS will examine the association's governing documents (typically the articles of incorporation and the bylaws) to determine whether such documents limit its purposes to one or more exempt purposes, and whether the documents otherwise give rise to cause for concern, such as on private inurement and particular services issues.

In addition, the IRS will examine whether the organization's activities and operations are consistent with the requirements of section 501(c)(6) and applicable Treasury Regulations. The IRS may review websites, brochures, meeting minutes, and other documents as part of its analysis.

1. International Operations

Note that it is permissible for a tax-exempt organization, under section 501(c)(6) or any other section, to conduct part or all of its activities in one or more countries outside of the United States without jeopardizing its tax-exempt status. The IRS takes a global view of tax-exempt organization activities, so neither the geographic location of the activities nor the geographic origin of the funds will have any adverse effect. The nature of the activity is controlling. In other words, so long as the organization conducts its activities in furtherance of its tax-exempt purposes, simply conducting such activities outside of the United States will not risk that status, even if all of its activities are conducted and all of its funds are received in countries other than the United States. However, conduct outside of the United States that is impermissible, restricted, or taxed (e.g., as UBI) under U.S. law will be treated the same when the activities are conducted in foreign countries.

Although income from the conduct of exempt activities abroad will likely be exempt from U.S. federal income tax, depending on the activity and the country in which such activity is conducted, local taxes may apply. Before conducting any significant activity internationally, an association should familiarize itself with the tax treatment of revenue earned in the specific country, whether the income will be subject to double taxation, and whether there are any tax treaties between the United States and the specific country of which the association may be able to take advantage.

Some countries may exempt associations from income or profits tax, but most countries do not have formal tax exemption statutes or regulations similar to the United States. Withholding taxes may be imposed by the host country on transfers or payments from a branch office or subsidiary organization to the parent association, such as withholding of dividends, royalties, and interest. Generally, for a foreign country to impose tax on an entity there must be a "permanent establishment," such as an office with employees and a formal carrying on of business in that country, that provides jurisdiction for tax purposes. Local country laws (and not just those addressing tax matters) should be carefully analyzed and revenue flows properly characterized to ensure tax and legal compliance.

2. Recognition of Tax Exemption

Recognition of tax-exempt status is a function of the IRS, which it exercises by making a written determination (in the form of a "determination letter") that an organization constitutes a tax-exempt entity. However, eligibility for tax-exempt status is different from recognition of that status. Congress, not the IRS, is responsible for the underlying granting of tax-exempt status. Thus, when an organization files an application with the IRS for recognition of its tax-exempt status—using IRS Form 1023 for would-be 501(c)(3) entities and IRS Form 1024 for all other categories of tax-exempt entities—it is requesting the IRS to recognize its tax exemption, not to grant it.

As a general rule, organizations other than 501(c)(3) organizations and employee benefit organizations are not required to secure recognition of tax-exempt status from the IRS through a determination letter in order to be treated as tax-exempt; so long as they meet the qualifications for tax exemption, they will be treated as such. Code section 508(a) states that any organization organized after October 9, 1969, will not be treated as an organization described in section 501(c)(3) unless it has provided notice to the IRS in the manner prescribed by the regulations; the regulations provide that the required notification for recognition of an organization's status as a section 501(c)(3) organization is the Form 1023. Neither the Code nor the regulations provide any similar notification requirement necessary for organizations to be recognized as exempt from income tax under different sections of the Code. Further, the IRS has stated that such organizations generally are not required to notify the IRS that they are seeking exemption, and to obtain recognition of exemption, such organizations may self-certify their exempt status.

In contrast, as described above, organizations seeking recognition under section 501(c)(3), for example, must file Form 1023 with the IRS and receive a favorable determination.

Note that a special streamlined procedure called "group exemption" is available to provide groups of affiliated entities, such as state and local chapters of a national association, with tax exemption on a group basis. (See Section I.D.)

Subject only to the authority of the IRS to revoke a ruling for good cause (see the following paragraph), an organization whose tax-exempt status has been recognized by the IRS can rely on that determination as long as it timely files its annual information returns with the IRS and there are no substantial or material changes in its character, purposes, or methods of operation and no material changes in the law. Until recently, the IRS required an organization to communicate any material changes in its operations through a letter to IRS Exemption Organizations Determinations as soon as possible after the material change occurred or became effective. However, the IRS now instructs organizations to report new, significant program services or significant changes in how it conducts programs on its annual information return (e.g., Form 990). Exempt Organizations Determinations no longer issues letters confirming the tax-exempt status of organizations that report new services or significant changes. However, a substantial change in an organization's purposes or operations may result in modification or revocation of the organization's tax-exempt status upon review of such material changes by the IRS.

Once an association's tax exemption has been recognized by the IRS, the three most significant ongoing threats to the tax-exempt status of a section 501(c)(6) organization are:

- An exempt organization's income may be characterized as unrelated business income when such income is generated from an unrelated trade or business, which is defined as any trade or business, the conduct of which is not substantially related to the exercise or performance by such organization of its exempt functions. The Code defines "trade or business" as "any activity which is carried on for the production of income from the sale of goods or the performance of services," and Treasury Regulations define "regularly carried on" as activities that "manifest a frequency and continuity and are pursued in a manner, generally similar to comparable commercial activities of nonexempt organizations." Significant unrelated business income resulting from activities that do not substantially promote the organization's tax-exempt purposes and mission may ultimately jeopardize an organization's tax-exempt status (unrelated business income must be of such an amount that would cause the IRS or a court to conclude that the primary purpose of the organization was unrelated to its tax-exempt purposes). A more detailed discussion of unrelated business income is included in Chapter II.

- The provision of too many particular services for individuals (again, that amount that would allow the IRS or a court to infer that such services were the primary purpose of the organization rather than exempt purposes) may jeopardize exempt status.

- Inurement of benefit of net earnings of the organization to any private shareholder or individual also gives rise to risk of loss of exempt status. Note that there is no de minimis exception to the prohibition on private inurement.

The Treasury Regulations define the term "private shareholder or individual" to mean "persons having a personal or private interest in the activities of the organization." The prohibition against inurement essentially applies to organization "insiders": its founders, directors, officers, members, donors, and employees. Inurement of benefit involves more than merely activities that are unrelated to the tax-exempt purposes of the organization, and more than the mere performance of particular services for individuals. Proscribed inurement of benefit has three elements:

- distribution of the benefit of the earnings of the organization—the source of the funds is irrelevant, it is the use of the funds that matters;
- such distribution of the benefit or earnings must be to a person having a personal and private interest in the activities of the organization; and
- the inurement must be more than merely incidental to the tax-exempt purposes of the organization—as all legitimate activities of 501(c)(6) organizations provide some indirect benefit to their members, the IRS has recognized that benefit to individuals that is merely incidental to an activity that furthers the tax-exempt purposes of a 501(c)(6) organization will not result in proscribed inurement of benefit.

Generally, private inurement arises where a financial benefit represents a transfer of the organization's financial resources to a private individual or entity because of the individual's or entity's relationship with the organization, and without regard to accomplishing exempt purposes. The IRS has also stated that inurement involves an expenditure of organizational funds resulting in a benefit which is beyond the scope of the benefits which logically flow from the organization's performance of its exempt functions. Payment of reasonable compensation to "insiders" for services performed for the organization by such persons is permissible. Similarly, a section 501(c)(6) organization may make distributions to its members without it being considered inurement if such distributions represent a pro rata reduction in dues, or contributions previously paid to the organization in support of its activities. However, the IRS is likely to find private inurement where a tax-exempt organization pays an unreasonable amount to, or confers disproportionate benefits upon, an individual director or other insider to the organization. For a discussion of private inurement with respect to 501(c)(3) and (c)(4) organizations (the intermediate sanctions law), the general principles of which should provide guidance to 501(c)(6) organizations. (See Section VI.A.)

C. SECTION 501(C)(3) TAX EXEMPTION

1. Benefits of 501(c)(3) Tax Exemption

While 501(c)(6) organizations are exempt from the payment of federal corporate income tax on income from activities substantially related to their tax-exempt purposes, organizations exempt from federal income tax under section 501(c)(3) are able to avail themselves of certain additional advantages available exclusively to section 501(c)(3) organizations.

For instance, only section 501(c)(3) organizations are:

- eligible to receive tax-deductible charitable contributions—section 501(c)(6) organizations can receive dues or other payments that will be deductible to the payor only if they serve a business purpose of the payor;
- eligible to receive private foundation grants without the private foundation having to exercise "expenditure responsibility" (thus significantly facilitating the ability to receive grants from private foundations);
- able to qualify for nonprofit postal permits (enabling utilization of significantly reduced nonprofit postal rates);
- eligible to receive many federal, state, and local government grants;
- eligible for many state and local sales and use, real estate, and other tax exemptions—in many jurisdictions, only certain categories of section 501(c)(3) organizations are eligible for certain state and local tax exemptions;
- eligible to issue tax-exempt bonds, providing for significantly lower financing costs;
- eligible to receive tax-deductible gifts of property;
- able to commence a deferred-giving program through charitable remainder gift arrangements, charitable gift annuities, and pooled-income funds; and
- able to maintain a charitable-bequest program for federal gift and estate tax purposes, whereby individuals are encouraged and enabled to make some provision for support of the organization as part of their estate plan.

Consequently, certain trade and professional associations, where possible, seek federal tax exemption under section 501(c)(3). Other associations, themselves tax-exempt under section 501(c)(6), frequently establish related educational, research, or charitable foundations under section 501(c)(3) in order to take advantage of one or more of the above-described benefits of 501(c)(3) status. (See Section III.F.)

2. Qualifying for and Maintaining 501(c)(3) Tax Exemption

Whether an independent organization is filing for recognition of tax-exempt status under section 501(c)(3) or whether a section 501(c)(6) organization is establishing a related foundation under section 501(c)(3), the standards for obtaining recognition of tax exemption from the IRS are the same in either circumstance. The section 501(c)(3) standards are more rigid than those under section 501(c)(6) and under practically all circumstances require the filing of an application for recognition of tax exemption (Form 1023). Certain organizations, including churches, integrated auxiliaries of churches, and conventions or associations of churches, and any organization that has gross receipts in each taxable year of normally not more than $5,000, may be considered tax-exempt under section 501(c)(3) even if they do not file Form 1023. However, such organizations may still choose to file Form 1023 in order to receive a determination letter that recognizes their tax-exempt status and specifies whether contributions to such organizations are tax deductible. Once an organization obtains written determination from the IRS of its section 501(c)(3) status, the determination will remain in effect as long as it timely files its annual information returns with the IRS and there are no substantial or material changes in the organization's character, purposes, or methods of operation, and no material changes in the law. Organizations should report new, significant program services or significant changes in how it conducts programs on its annual information return (e.g., Form 990). Exempt Organizations Determinations no longer issues letters confirming the tax-exempt status of organizations that report new services or significant changes. However, a substantial change in an organization's purposes or operations may result in modification or revocation of the organization's tax-exempt status upon review of such material changes by the IRS.

Effective Date of Tax Exemption

Most would-be 501(c)(3) organizations that were formed after October 9, 1969, will not be treated as tax-exempt under section 501(c)(3) unless they apply for recognition of tax exemption by filing Form 1023 with the IRS. Such organizations will not be treated as tax-exempt for any period prior to the filing of Form 1023 unless they file the application within 27 months from the end of the month in which they were formed (for nonprofit corporations, this is the date of incorporation). If the organization files the 1023 application within this 27-month period, the organization's tax exemption will be recognized retroactively to the date it was formed. Otherwise, tax exemption will be recognized only for the period following the IRS' receipt of the application. The date of receipt is the date of the U.S. postmark on the envelope in which the Form 1023 is mailed or, if no postmark appears on the envelope, the date the Form 1023 is stamped as received by the IRS. Note that an organization that fails to file a Form 1023 within the required time period may be granted a discretionary extension to file if it submits evidence to establish that it acted reasonably and in good faith and that granting a discretionary extension would not prejudice the interests of the federal government.

Note that an organization (other than a private foundation) that does not normally have more than $5,000 in annual gross receipts is not required to apply for recognition of tax exemption by filing Form 1023. Such organizations will be deemed tax-exempt automatically if they meet the requirements of section 501(c)(3). An organization with gross receipts more than the amounts in the gross receipts test, unless otherwise exempt from filing Form 1023 (such as churches and church-related organizations), must file Form 1023 within 90 days after the end of the period in which the amounts are exceeded.

501(c)(3) Purposes

A nonprofit organization may qualify for exemption from federal income tax under section 501(c)(3) if it is organized and operated "exclusively"(defined by the IRS as "primarily") for charitable, religious, educational, literary, scientific, or certain other purposes (Code section 501(c)(3) also includes testing for public safety, fostering national or international amateur sports competition (but only if no part of its activities involve the provision of athletic facilities or equipment), or the prevention of cruelty to children or animals in its enumerated charitable purposes).

Each of the purposes set forth in section 501(c)(3) encompass a broad range of purposes and activities, which are discussed in further detail below.

Charitable Purposes

The term "charitable" covers a broad range of public purposes, such as relief of the poor; advancement of religion, education, or science; lessening the burdens of government; promotion of health, social welfare, or environmental conservancy; and patriotism.

The charitable activities most frequently engaged in by membership associations include, among others, information dissemination by means of meetings and seminars, publications, websites, films, maintenance of libraries, and the like; research; and the provision of scholarships, stipends, loans, and fellowships, among others.

Educational Purposes

The term "educational" in this context has two basic meanings: (1) an activity relating to the instruction or training of the individual for the purpose of improving or developing his or her capabilities, or (2) the instruction of the public on subjects useful to the individual and beneficial to the community. Advocacy of a particular position or viewpoint may qualify as educational if there is a sufficiently full and fair exposition of the pertinent facts so as to permit an individual or the public to form an independent opinion or conclusion. The mere presentation of unsupported opinion is not considered educational.

The IRS has ruled repeatedly that an organization that educates members of a particular profession or vocational group with respect to information or skills that will make them better practitioners of their professions or vocations can be educational within the meaning of section 501(c)(3). However, to qualify for section 501(c)(3) tax exemption, membership associations must be able to demonstrate that their activities are predominantly educational without any other substantial activities that are not educational or otherwise section 501(c)(3) qualifying activities. The IRS has recognized that a professional society may qualify for exemption under section 501(c)(3) if its purpose is to advance the profession by engaging in exclusively educational activities.

Scientific Purposes

To qualify as a scientific activity, the organization must demonstrate that its research will be carried on in the public interest. Scientific research will be considered to be in the public interest if the results of the research (including any patents, copyrights, processes, or formulas) are made available to the public on a nondiscriminatory basis; if the research is performed for the federal government or a state or local government; or if the research is carried on for one of the following purposes:

- aiding in the scientific education of college students;
- obtaining scientific information that is published in a treatise, thesis, trade publication, or in any other form that is available to the interested public;
- discovering a cure for a disease; or
- aiding a community or geographic area by attracting new industry to the community or area, or by encouraging the development or retention of an industry in the community or area.

For tax-exemption purposes, scientific research does not include activities of a type ordinarily incidental to commercial or industrial operations, such as the ordinary inspection or testing of materials or products, and the designing or constructing of equipment, buildings, etc.

The presentation of meetings and seminars, lectures, debates, websites, films, and the like can qualify as educational activities and perhaps also as charitable activities by reason of the advancement of education. The IRS likewise has recognized research and publication activities as both educational and charitable in nature. The granting of scholarships and similar assistance can qualify as the advancement of education and hence charitable in nature. The foregoing types of activities can, in the appropriate setting, qualify as religious or scientific (as well as charitable) by reason of the advancement of religion or science, the promotion of health, or any of the components of the term "charitable" enumerated above.

In order to qualify for tax exemption under section 501(c)(3), an organization must conduct the qualifying functions described above, and also must:

- be organized and operated exclusively for tax-exempt purposes;
- not have any earnings inure to the benefit of private individuals;
- not carry on substantial activities to influence legislation; and
- not participate in any manner in any political campaign activities.

These requirements are discussed below.

Organizational Test

The requirement that the organization be organized exclusively for tax-exempt purposes means that the articles of organization for the organization, such as articles of incorporation and any amendments thereto, must (1) limit the organization's purposes to one or more of those described above and (2) must not expressly empower the organization to engage in activities that do not further one or more of those purposes, other than as an insubstantial part of its activities. The organizational test may be met if the purposes stated in the articles of organization are so limited by explicit reference to section 501(c)(3).

Note that the requirement that an organization's purposes and powers be limited by the articles of organization will not be satisfied if the limit is contained only in the organization's bylaws or other rules or regulations; it must be contained in the articles of organization. Similarly, signed statements to such effect by the organization's officers will not suffice. In addition, the test will not be satisfied by the fact that the organization's actual operations are in furtherance of one or more of the purposes described above.

Dissolution

In order to satisfy the organizational test, assets of a would-be 501(c)(3) organization must be permanently dedicated to one or more of the purposes described above. This means that should the organization dissolve (or be merged into or consolidated with another entity), its assets must be distributed in furtherance of one or more of the purposes described above, or to the federal government or to a state or local government for a public purpose. If the assets could be distributed to members or private individuals or entities, or for any other purpose, the organizational test will not be met. To establish that an organization's assets will be permanently dedicated to a permissible tax-exempt purpose, the articles of organization must contain a provision ensuring their distribution for such purposes in the event of dissolution. If a named beneficiary is to be the distributee, it must be one that would qualify as tax-exempt under section 501(c)(3) at the time of the dissolution. Since the named beneficiary at the time of dissolution may not be so qualified, may not be in existence, or may be unwilling or unable to accept the assets of the dissolving organization, a provision should be made for the distribution of the assets for one or more permissible tax-exempt purposes in the event of any such contingency.

Operational Test

The operational test examines whether the organization's activities and operations are consistent with section 501(c)(3) and the Treasury Regulations thereunder. The requirement in the operational test that the organization be operated exclusively for tax-exempt purposes has been defined by the IRS to permit a 501(c)(3) organization to engage in some activities that are not related to its tax-exempt purposes (for the purpose of determining whether the operational test is met, "exclusively" has been defined by the IRS as "primarily"). Such unrelated activities will not disqualify the organization from 501(c)(3) status so long as they do not constitute a substantial part of the organization's overall activities. However, income derived from certain unrelated activities may be subject to federal corporate income tax (see Section II).

Private Benefit and Private Inurement

Generally, for an organization to qualify as exempt Section 501(c)(3), it must be both organized and operated exclusively for tax-exempt purposes which provide a public benefit. For purposes of Section 501(c)(3), exempt purposes include religious, charitable, scientific, testing for public safety, literary, or educational purposes. If a substantial amount of an organization's activities are in pursuit of a non-exempt purpose, the organization may not qualify for recognition of tax-exempt status.

Private Benefit

A non-exempt purpose includes any purpose that serves a private interest, rather than a public interest, and is often described as a "private benefit." To be recognized as exempt under Section 501(c)(3), "it is necessary for an organization to establish that it is not organized or operated for the benefit of private interests." Thus, an organization is not operated exclusively for exempt purposes if it serves a private rather than a public interest. Moreover, to the extent that an organization confers a substantial benefit on any private individual or entity, an organization may not be operating exclusively for exempt purposes.

While an organization's conference of substantial private benefit may jeopardize its exempt status, "[o]ccasional economic benefits flowing to persons as an incidental consequence of an organization pursuing exempt charitable purposes will not generally constitute prohibited private benefits." As such, the courts and the IRS have acknowledged that under certain circumstances, private individuals or entities will necessarily benefit when an exempt organization is carrying out its exempt mission. A determination with respect to whether the private benefits resulting from an organization's activities confer an impermissible benefit focuses on whether such benefits are incidental, qualitatively and quantitatively, to the public benefits conferred by the organization.

A private benefit will satisfy the qualitative test as incidental if the benefit is "a necessary concomitant of the activity which public at large; in other words, the benefit to the public cannot be achieved without necessarily benefit certain private individuals." As such, where the IRS determines that it would be impossible for an organization to accomplish its purposes without providing the benefits, the IRS has determined that such benefits were qualitatively incidental to the public benefit. As such, where it would be impossible for an organization to accomplish its purposes without providing the benefits, the IRS has determined that such benefits were qualitatively incidental to the public benefit.

A benefit will be quantitatively incidental only if it is insubstantial when compared with the public benefit conferred. The quantitative standard is thus a comparative standard in which the "substantiality of a private benefit is measured in the context of the overall public benefit conferred by the activity." As such, the acceptable amount of the private benefit will vary in each case "in direct relation to the degree of public benefit derived."

Private Inurement

In addition to the prohibition on private benefit, 501(c)(3) organizations are prohibited from allowing any part of their net earnings to any private individual or shareholder. Private inurement is similar to private benefit, sharing common and often overlapping elements; in fact, the U.S. Tax Court has noted that "the private inurement may be arguably subsumed within the private benefit analysis." However, the private inurement is more limited in the scope of the beneficiaries' relationship to the organization and with respect to the types of benefits resulting in inurement. As private inurement is subsumed by, and a more limited application of, the private benefit doctrine, the IRS has correctly taken the position that "all inurement is private benefit, but not all private benefit is inurement."

The private inurement doctrine is derived from Section 501(c)(3) which provides that, to be recognized as exempt, "no part of the net earnings" of the organization may inure to the benefit of "any private shareholder or individual." The term "private shareholder or individual" refers to persons having a personal and private interest in the activities of the organization. More generally, the private benefit doctrine prohibits a charity from siphoning "its earnings to its founder, or the members of its board, or their families, or anyone else fairly to be described as an insider, that is, as the equivalent of an owner or manager." Thus, unlike the private benefit doctrine, private inurement is only applicable to transactions between a tax-exempt organization and an "insider" (i.e., someone with a close relationship with and/or ability to exert substantial influence over the tax-exempt organization).

While the doctrine of private inurement regulates transactions between tax-exempt organizations and insiders, the private inurement doctrine does not prohibit such transactions. The IRS has written previously: "[t]here is no absolute prohibition against an exempt section 501(c)(3) organization dealing with its founders, members, or officers in conducting its economic affairs." Rather, as noted in the IRS's internal guidance, the private inurement doctrine requires that dealings between a charitable organization and its insiders be reasonable, at arm's length and in good faith, for example, "if an organization pays a reasonable compensation to a founder for services rendered, that is not inurement."

(For a related discussion on "Intermediate Sanctions," see Section V.)

Limitations on Lobbying Activity

An organization will not qualify for tax exemption under section 501(c)(3) if it devotes a substantial part of its activities to lobbying, propaganda, or attempting to influence legislation; exceeding the substantial part limit places an organization at risk of losing its exempt status. Whether an organization's attempts to influence legislation are substantial will be determined by a vague facts and circumstances "substantial part" test, unless an organization elects to have such determination made pursuant to an expenditure test, by filing a section 501(h) election with the IRS. Electing organizations are governed by the expenditure test, a mathematical formula that limits the amount a section 501(c)(3) entity may spend on lobbying activities to precise amounts and provides specific definitions of lobbying. (For a full discussion of these limitations on lobbying activities, see Section IV.C.)

Prohibition on Political Campaign Activities

A section 501(c)(3) organization is prohibited from participating or intervening in any political campaign. A section 501(c)(3) organization will lose its tax-exempt status if it participates or intervenes in a political campaign on behalf of, or in opposition to, a candidate for federal, state, or local office. Unlike the limitations on lobbying activities, the prohibition on political campaign activities is absolute and applies to any such activities, no matter how small. A section 501(c)(3) organization that loses its tax exemption because of excessive lobbying or prohibited political campaign activities cannot then convert to a section 501(c)(4) organization.

3. Public Charity Status

Every organization that qualifies for tax exemption under section 501(c)(3) is deemed to be a private foundation unless it falls into one of the categories specifically excluded from the definition of a private foundation referred to in sections 509(a)(1), (a)(2), (a)(3), and (a)(4). Thus, in effect, the definition divides section 501(c)(3) organizations into two classes: private foundations and public charities.

Organizations that fall into the excluded categories generally are those that either have broad public support or actively function in a supporting relationship to an organization that has broad public support.

Organizations that test for public safety also are excluded from public foundation status.

In addition to meeting the organizational tests required of all charitable organizations, private foundations must satisfy additional organizational rules. This organizational test may be fulfilled by including certain provisions in the governing documents. First, a provision requiring the organization's income for each taxable year to be distributed at such time and in such manner as not to subject the organization to tax must be included. The governing documents must also include a provision that prohibits the foundation from engaging in any act of self-dealing, from retaining any excess business holdings, from making any investments in such manner as to subject the foundation to tax, and from making any taxable expenditures. In addition, private foundations are subject to relatively onerous restrictions on operations and activities, as well as certain taxes, which are not applicable to public charities (e.g., taxes on net investment income; prohibitions on self-dealing; limitations on certain business holdings; proscriptions on certain investments; penalties for certain expenditures, including outlays for legislative, political campaign, and non-charitable purposes; minimum annual payout requirements in furtherance of charitable purposes; and other prohibitions and requirements enforced by a series of excise taxes imposed on the foundation and, in some instances, its managers).

Even if an organization falls within one of the categories of public charities, it generally will still be presumed to be a private foundation unless it provides timely notice to the IRS that it is not a private foundation. This notice requirement generally applies regardless of when the organization was formed. Treasury Regulations define what constitutes timely notice, as well as the consequences of failure to do so. If an organization can show that it reasonably can expect to be publicly supported when it applies for tax-exempt status, the organization will be classified as a publicly supported charity and not a private foundation. Further, beginning with the organization's sixth taxable year, it must establish that it meets the public support test by showing that it is publicly supported on its Form 990.

Generally speaking, a large class of organizations excluded from the definition of a private foundation under section 509(a)(1) and all organizations excluded under section 509(a)(2) depend upon a "public support test." This test is used to ensure a minimum percentage of broad-based public financial support in the organization's total financial support pattern. Note that the descriptions of the categories of public charities set forth below are significantly simplified; the actual tests that must be satisfied in each category contain a variety of limitations (such as limitations on the amount that can be counted from certain donors and grantors toward the public support test), qualifications, and subtests, and are very specific.

There are four categories of public charities (i.e., 501(c)(3) organizations excluded from the definition of a private foundation).

- Section 509(a)(1): organizations such as churches, schools, colleges, universities, hospitals, foundations for state universities, governmental units, and certain publicly supported organizations. A publicly supported organization for purposes of this category means that the organization normally receives at least one-third of its total financial support (computed by means of a four-year average) from the general public and/or government units in the form of gifts, grants, contributions, membership fees, and certain other forms. If an organization fails this test, it may qualify under a "facts and circumstances" test. To be classified as a public charity under this facts-and-circumstances test, the organization must satisfy two requirements. The first is that the organization must derive at least 10 percent of its support from governmental units or from direct or indirect contributions from the general public, or a combination of both. The second requirement is that the organization must be organized and operated so that it will attract further support on a continuous basis; the organization must maintain a fundraising program or carry on programs designed to attract support from governmental units or other charities. Additional facts and circumstances will be evaluated to determine whether the organization is publicly supported, including the actual percentage of support derived from the public or governmental units, the sources of support, the composition of its governing body, and the types of services it provides or the nature of the functions it performs in carrying out its exempt purposes. If the organization normally meets the facts-and-circumstances test by obtaining at least 10 percent of its support from qualified sources and by implementing a program to attract additional support over a five-year period, and other facts and circumstances support public charity status, the organization will be considered a publicly supported charity for the taxable year.
- Section 509(a)(2): organizations that (1) normally receive *at least one-third* of their annual financial support (computed by means of a four-year average) from the general public, governmental units, or certain public charities (in the form of contributions, grants, or membership fees) and/or certain types of gross revenues from related activities (such as program service revenue from the conduct of activities related to the organization's tax-exempt purposes, including but not limited to many educational meeting and conference registration fees, many publication sales, etc.), *and* that (2) normally receive *no more than one-third* of their annual financial support from gross investment income (defined broadly to include interest, dividends, rents, and royalties) and the excess of unrelated business income over the tax imposed on that income. Generally, an organization described in section 509(a)(2) may also fit the description of a publicly sponsored organization under section 509(a)(1). The two

basic differences are that 509(a)(2) organizations may count income for activities directly related to their tax-exempt purposes, and that 509(a)(2) organizations are limited in the amount of gross investment income and unrelated business income they may earn.

- Section 509(a)(3): organizations that qualify as "supporting organizations" in relation to one or more section 501(c)(3), (c)(4), (c)(5), or (c)(6) organizations that themselves meet one of the two above-described public support tests. To qualify as a supporting organization under this category, the organization must:
  (1) be organized and operated exclusively for the benefit of, to perform the functions of, or to carry out the purposes of, one or more section 501(c)(3), (c)(4), (c)(5), or (c)(6) organizations that themselves meet one of the two above-described public support tests;
  (2) be operated, supervised, or controlled by or in connection with one or more such section 501(c)(3), (c)(4), (c)(5), or (c)(6) organizations; and
  (3) not be controlled by any "disqualified persons" other than foundation managers and other than one or more such section 501(c)(3), (c)(4), (c)(5), or (c)(6) organizations.

Each of these tests also has subtests. However, a principal manner in which to satisfy the basic elements of the supporting organization rules is for the officers and/or directors of the supporting organization to be appointed by, controlled by, or share control with the officers and/or directors of the supported organization. This is the principal category under which related foundations of trade and professional associations qualify as public charities. (A more detailed discussion of supporting organizations may be found in Section III.H.)

- Section 509(a)(4): organizations that are organized and operated exclusively for testing for public safety. However, such organizations are limited in their ability to receive charitable contributions or grants from private foundations.

D. GROUP EXEMPTION

1. Overview

A group-exemption letter is a ruling or determination letter issued by the IRS to a "central organization" recognizing on a group basis the federal tax exemption of affiliated "subordinate organizations" on whose behalf the central organization has applied for recognition of tax exemption. (Note that group exemption is only applicable and necessary when the subordinate organizations are separate legal entities.) A central organization is an organization that has one or more subordinates under its general supervision or control. A subordinate organization is a chapter, allied society, or similar unit of a central organization. A central organization may be a subordinate itself, such as a state organization that has subordinate (local) units and is itself affiliated with a national (central) organization.

In the association community, the group-exemption process is most frequently utilized to provide recognition of tax exemption, on a group basis, for state and local chapters of national associations. This relatively simple and cost-efficient procedure permits a central (most frequently, national) organization to obtain similar tax-exempt status for the subordinate organizations (most frequently, chapters) that are affiliated with it and under its "general supervision or control," relieving each chapter in the group from having to file its own tax-exemption application.

The procedures by which a group exemption may be recognized by the IRS require a functioning of the central organization as an agent of the IRS. The central organization is required to continuously evaluate the tax-exempt status of its subordinate organizations to ensure that the tests for tax exemption continue to be met by the subordinates. On an annual basis, the central organization is required to file a current listing of its qualifying subordinate organizations. This listing constitutes an attestation by the central organization that the subordinates continue to qualify as tax-exempt so the IRS need not carry out an independent evaluation as to the tax-exempt status of the organizations.

2. Group Exemption Application Procedure

Provided the central organization has obtained its own recognition of tax exemption, it can apply for a group-exemption letter for its affiliated subordinates under its general supervision or control. The application is made by letter instead of by Form 1023 or 1024.

The letter must be signed by a principal officer of the central organization and must contain certain information about the central organization, such as its employer identification number (EIN), the date of the letter recognizing its tax exemption, and the IRS office that issued it. It also must verify the following information regarding those subordinates to be included in the group exemption.

- They are affiliated with the central organization.
- They are subject to its general supervision or control.
- They are all eligible to qualify for tax exemption under the same paragraph of section 501(c) of the Code, though not necessarily under the same paragraph under which the central organization is tax-exempt.
- They are not private foundations (if the subordinates are claiming section 501(c)(3) status).

- They are all on the same accounting period (fiscal year) as the central organization. This is only necessary if they are to be included in group returns, which is not required (see Section I.D.5.).
- They are organizations that have been formed within the preceding 15 months, but only if they are claiming 501(c)(3) status and seek to be recognized as tax-exempt from their date of creation. A group exemption letter may be issued where one or more subordinates have not been created within the preceding 15 months, so long as all subordinates are willing to be recognized as tax-exempt under section 501(c)(3) only prospectively from the date of application. This 15-month rule does not apply to subordinates seeking tax exemption under any section other than section 501(c)(3); in such cases, the group exemption will be retroactive to the date of creation of the subordinates.

In addition, the application letter must set forth or include as attachments:

- a detailed description of the purposes and activities of the subordinates, including the sources of income and the nature of expenditures;
- a sample copy of a uniform governing instrument (such as model articles of incorporation or bylaws) adopted by the subordinates, or, in its absence, copies of representatives instruments (such instruments must contain the standard IRS-required language for tax-exempt organizations);
- an affirmation that the purposes and activities of the subordinates are as stated in the description of purposes and governing instruments provided;
- a statement that each subordinate to be included in the group exemption has provided written authorization to that effect to the central organization;
- a list of subordinates to be included in the group exemption to which the IRS has previously issued a ruling or determination letter relating to tax exemption;
- if the application involves section 501(c)(3), an affirmation that no subordinate to be included in the group exemption is a private foundation; and
- a list of the names, addresses, and EINs of subordinates to be included in the group exemption.

3. Maintaining the Group Exemption; Events Causing Loss of Group Exemption

The continued effectiveness of a group exemption is based on the following conditions:

- the continued existence of the central organization;
- the continued qualification for tax exemption of the central organization;
- the submission by the central organization of the information required annually (see Section I.D.4. below); and
- the annual filing of the Form 990 (or other appropriate information return) by the central organization if required.

The continued effectiveness of a group exemption as to a particular subordinate is based on these four conditions, as well as on the continued conformity by the subordinate to the requirements for inclusion in a group exemption, the authorization for inclusion, and the annual filing of any required information return for the subordinate. Note that loss of tax exemption by one or more members of the group will not adversely affect the group exemption as it pertains to the other members of the group.

A group exemption no longer has effect, for either a particular subordinate or the group as a whole, when:

- the central organization notifies the IRS that it is going out of existence;
- the central organization notifies the IRS, by its annual submission or otherwise, that any of its subordinates will no longer fulfill the conditions for continued effectiveness, as described above; or
- the IRS notifies the central organization or the affected subordinate(s) that the group exemption will no longer have effect for some or all of the group because the conditions for continued effectiveness of a group exemption (as described above) have not been fulfilled.

When notice is given under any of these three conditions, the IRS will no longer recognize the exempt status of the affected subordinates until they file separate applications on their own behalf or the central organization files complete supporting information for their re-inclusion in the group exemption at the time of its annual submission.

4. Information Required Annually

To maintain a group exemption, the central organization must submit to the IRS annually, at least 90 days before the close of its annual accounting period (fiscal year), the following information:

- all changes (if any) in the purposes, character, or method of operation of the subordinates included in the group exemption;
- a separate list of the names, addresses, and EINs of the affected subordinates for each of the following three categories: (1) subordinates that have changed their names or addresses during the year; (2) subordinates no longer to be included in the group exemption because they no longer exist or have disaffiliated or withdrawn their authorization to the central organization; and (3) subordinates to be added to the group exemption because they are newly organized or affiliated or because they have authorized the central organization to include them during the year (if there were none of the above changes, the central organization must submit a statement to that effect); and
- for new subordinates to be added to the group, the information required to be submitted by a central organization at the outset on behalf of subordinates to be included in the group exemption (as described above) (however, if the information upon which the group exemption was based applies in all material respects to these new subordinates, then a statement to this effect may be submitted instead).

5. Form 990 Filing Requirements and Options

Group exemption does not require that the subordinates file the annual information return (Form 990) in combination with the central organization. Most national trade and professional associations that utilize the group-exemption procedure for state and local chapters require their chapters to file their own Form 990 returns each year (note that most organizations that normally have gross receipts of $50,000 or less must submit Form 990-N for Tax-Exempt Organizations Not Required to File Form 990 or 990-EZ if they choose not to file Form 990 or Form 990-EZ). However, if desired, a group return on Form 990 may be filed by a central organization for two or more subordinates and not all subordinates need be included. In such event, all financial data for the included subordinates is included in the group return. This group return is in addition to the central organization's separate annual return, if required; the central organization's financial data cannot be included in the group return.

It should be noted that the Code provides for the automatic revocation of any tax-exempt organization that does not file the required returns or notice for three consecutive years, and requires the IRS to publish and maintain a list of all such organizations that are so revoked. Many organizations exempt under a group exemption have lost exempt status due to these relatively recent requirements.

II

Unrelated Business Income Tax

A. DEFINITION

Although associations are granted by the Code a general exemption from federal income taxes for income from activities that are substantially related to the purposes for which the association was granted tax-exempt status, they nevertheless are potentially taxable for income derived from unrelated business activities. The Code defines an unrelated trade or business as any trade or business the conduct of which is not substantially related (aside from the need of such organization for income) to the exercise or performance by such organization of its purpose or function constituting the basis for its exemption.

The tax on unrelated business income first appeared in the Code in 1950. Congress' principal purpose in enacting the unrelated business income tax (UBIT) was to provide a level competitive playing field for tax-paying businesses, so that tax-exempt organizations could not use their privileged tax status to unfairly compete with tax-paying businesses in activities unrelated to their purposes. Instead of prohibiting tax-exempt organizations from engaging in any business activities at all (and denying or revoking tax exemption because of such activities), it chose to specifically permit a certain degree of business activity by tax-exempt organizations and tax such income like any other for-profit business. Thus, such business activities are permissible, so long as the activities are not a "substantial part of its activities." The tax applies to virtually all tax-exempt organizations, including associations and their related foundations.

The unrelated business income tax is generally imposed at the federal corporate income tax rates. Deductions are permitted for expenses that are directly connected with the carrying on of the unrelated trade or business. If an organization regularly carries on two or more unrelated business activities, its taxable unrelated business income is the total of gross income from all such activities less the total allowable deductions attributable to such activities.

It is important to note that not all business income is subject to taxation or to limitations: only unrelated business income as defined in the Code. Unrelated business income will only exist if three conditions are satisfied, if any one of the three is not present, then income from the activity will not be taxable. The income must be:

- from a trade or business;
- that is regularly carried on; and
- that is not substantially related to the purposes for which the organization was granted tax exemption.

These conditions are discussed below.

1. Trade or Business

Not all income-generating activities constitute a trade or business. A business is generally an activity carried on for the production of income from the sale of goods or the performance of services. However, the activity need not produce a profit; an activity can be a business even if it loses money. The organization may not have any tax liability from a business operated at a loss, but it is still a business.

One of the most important aspects of the definition of a trade or business is that the income generation must be from an activity. The definition refers to the "sale of goods or the performance of services." What this means is that the organization must take an active role in the generation of the income for the activity to be a business; income from a passive activity is not a business.

Many types of passive income are specifically excluded from the definition of unrelated business income in the Code: dividends, interest, annuities, royalties, and certain rents. These are the types of activities in which the organization simply lets someone else use its money, its property, or its name and receives some payment back for the privilege, without actually becoming involved as an organization. A different set of rules applies if the activity is "debt-financed" (i.e., if the organization uses borrowed money to engage in the activity).

In what is known as the fragmentation rule, activities that are carried on within a larger context of other endeavors, which may or not be related to the organization's tax-exempt purposes, do not lose their identity as trades or businesses. The IRS, therefore, has the authority to "fragment" a tax-exempt organization's various activities into individual parts to identify unrelated business income subject to taxation. For example, if an association solicits, sells, and publishes commercial advertising in its monthly newsletter, the IRS would still view the advertising activity as a trade or business even though the newsletter's subject matter relates to the association's tax-exempt purposes.

2. Regularly Carried On

Even if an activity of a tax-exempt organization constitutes a trade or business, two other factors must be considered to determine if the income generated by the activity constitutes unrelated business income. The first factor is whether or not the business is "regularly carried on."

When determining whether an activity is regularly carried on, the principal factors to examine are: (1) the frequency and continuity with which the activity is conducted; and (2) the manner in which it is pursued. For example, specific business activities of a tax-exempt organization ordinarily will be deemed to be regularly carried on if they manifest a frequency and continuity and are pursued in a manner generally similar to comparable commercial activities of nonexempt organizations. In general, business activities that are engaged in only discontinuously or periodically will not be considered regularly carried on if they are conducted without the competitive and promotional efforts typical of commercial endeavors.

An activity occurring once each year, even if it occurs at the same time every year, may not be considered regularly carried on. For example, the sale of advertising in the program book for an annual fund-raising dinner may not be considered to be regularly carried on. However, in contrast, once-a-year activities have been found to be regularly carried on where the preparation or follow-up stretches over a long period of time (e.g., if the advertising for the program book is solicited for many months prior to the event) may be characterized as regularly carried on. Moreover, an activity occurring only once a year also might be considered regularly carried on if a commercial company performing the same activity would also be active only once a year (e.g., selling Christmas cards in December).

These rules generally permit tax-exempt organizations to carry on occasional fund-raising activities of short duration without paying any UBIT on the profit.

3. Not Substantially Related

Even if an activity constitutes a trade or business that is regularly carried on, it will not be subject to UBIT if it is substantially related to one or more of the tax-exempt purposes of the organization. For an activity to be substantially related, it must contribute importantly to the accomplishment of one or more of the organization's tax-exempt purposes (other than through the production of income to use for tax-exempt purposes). This test requires an organization to examine the relationship between the business activities that generate the income in question and the accomplishment of the organization's tax-exempt purposes.

For most trade and professional associations that are recognized as exempt under section 501(c)(6), the principal tax-exempt purpose is the improvement of the industry or profession's business conditions.

It is important to note that the substantial relationship to the organization's tax-exempt purposes cannot come solely from the organization's need to raise funds. The income received may be vital to an organization's existence, but income production is not enough to save an activity from unrelated business status. Moreover, how the money is used by the organization is similarly irrelevant to the determination of whether a substantial relationship exists.

An activity may be related to one tax-exempt organization's purpose, but not to another's. For example, the sale of primers on the purchase of a new home would not be related to the tax-exempt purposes of an association of automobile manufacturers, but would likely be related to the purposes of an association of home builders.

In the trade and professional association context, an activity will be substantially related if it is primarily directed toward the improvement of its members' business conditions, as opposed to the performance of particular services that provide a convenience or economy to individual members in their businesses. In other words, the activity must benefit members as a whole, rather than as individual entities, to be considered substantially related. In practice, it is often unclear where an association's activity changes from principally benefiting and being directed at the industry as a whole (with incidental benefits to individual members), to principally benefiting and constituting particular services to individual members.

In making this determination, certain key factors are regularly considered by the IRS and the courts:

- the association's intent in performing the activity (i.e., whether or not the association's primary motivation is to generate revenue);
- whether or not the activity is comparable to activities conducted by commercial entities, such as providing standard insurance policies, standard legal and business forms, debt collection (note that if the product or service being provided by the association is commercially available in substantially the same form elsewhere, even if at a higher price, then even though the product or service may be important to the members' businesses, the activity will not be considered substantially related); and
- the uniqueness or distinctiveness of the activity to the association's tax-exempt purposes.

Sometimes an activity that would otherwise be unrelated to an organization's tax-exempt purposes can be modified to make it related. For example, the sale of stationery, serving items, and desk accessories would not normally be related to the tax-exempt purposes of a wildlife conservation society. But because the items were decorated with wildlife drawings and contained or were packaged with a message about wildlife, the activity was found by the IRS to be related to the society's purpose of stimulating public interest in wildlife.

The judgment as to whether an activity is related or unrelated can only be made on a case-by-case basis. Creative planning and restructuring may make it possible to convert an otherwise unrelated activity into a related one.

B. EXCLUSIONS

Even if all three conditions of the UBIT test are satisfied, there are numerous statutory exclusions which can exempt otherwise taxable income from UBIT. Many such exclusions are potentially applicable to trade and professional associations, while many are not. The most relevant exclusions for associations include:

- volunteer labor exception;
- qualified sponsorship payments;
- qualified convention or trade show income;
- dividends, interest, and annuities;
- royalties;
- rents from real property (non–debt-financed); and
- certain capital gains.

These exclusions are discussed below.

1. Volunteer Labor Exception

The Code provides that the term unrelated trade or business does not include a trade or business "in which substantially all the work in carrying on such trade or business is performed for the organization without compensation." This exception, commonly known as the "volunteer labor exception," has been construed to apply only to activities in which (1) the performance of services is a material income-producing factor; and (2) substantially all of the services are performed without compensation. The Code does not provide a definition of compensation for purposes of this exception.

The volunteer labor exception requires that substantially all of the work of the business be performed by volunteers. The question of what constitutes substantially all of the work does not arise if all of the work is performed without compensation. The issue of substantiality arises when a business is conducted in part by volunteers and in part by an organization's paid employees or paid outside parties. In such cases, courts have generally assessed the substantiality of the volunteer effort with reference to the number or percentage of hours worked. While no firm guidelines have ever been set forth regarding exactly what percentage of hours worked constitutes substantially all, IRS and court rulings have generally held that the volunteer exception is available if at least 85 percent of the work is carried on by volunteers; conversely, applicability of the volunteer exception would be questionable if compensated individuals performed more than 15 percent of the work.

2. Qualified Sponsorship Payments

The receipt of "qualified sponsorship payments" by a tax-exempt organization does not constitute the receipt of income from an "unrelated trade or business." In addition, for section 501(c)(3) tax purposes (e.g., public support test), "contributions" include "qualified sponsorship payments" in the form of money, property, or services.

Definition of "Qualified Sponsorship Payment"

A "qualified sponsorship payment" is generally defined as any payment of money, transfer of property, or performance of services by any person (individual or entity) engaged in a trade or business with respect to which there is no arrangement or expectation that the person will receive any substantial return benefit. In determining whether a payment is a qualified sponsorship payment, it is irrelevant whether the sponsored activity is related or unrelated to the recipient organization's tax-exempt purposes. It also is irrelevant whether the sponsored activity is temporary or permanent.

Definition of "Substantial Return Benefit"

A "substantial return benefit" is defined as any benefit other than: (i) goods, services, or other benefits of "insubstantial value" (as described below); or (ii) a "use or acknowledgment" (as described below). Goods, services, or other benefits of "insubstantial value" include benefits with an aggregate fair market value of not more than 2 percent of the amount of the payment. Note that if the fair market value of the benefits exceeds the limits specified above, then (except as provided below) the *entire* fair market value of such benefits, not merely the excess amount, is considered a substantial return benefit, in which case the determination of whether the payment is subject to UBIT is made under existing rules regarding whether income is generated from a trade or business, whether that trade or business is regularly carried on, whether the activity is substantially related to exempt purposes, or is otherwise subject to UBIT.

A substantial return benefit having a fair market value greater than 2 percent of the sponsorship payment may include:

- advertising (as described below);
- providing facilities, services, or other privileges to the sponsor (or persons designated by the sponsor) ; or

- granting the sponsor (or persons designated by the sponsor) an exclusive or non-exclusive right to use an intangible asset (e.g., name, logo, trademark, copyright, patent) of the tax-exempt organization. Note that while payment for providing a sponsor with the right to use such an intangible asset will not constitute a qualified sponsorship payment, it may constitute a tax-free royalty.

Use or Acknowledgment

As stated above, a substantial return benefit does not include a "use or acknowledgment" of the name, logo, or product lines of the sponsor or business in connection with the activities of the tax-exempt organization. Use or acknowledgment does not include advertising (as described below), but may include:

- sponsor logos and slogans that do not contain qualitative or comparative descriptions of the sponsor's products, services, facilities, or company;
- a list of the sponsor's locations (e.g., addresses), telephone numbers, facsimile numbers, or Internet addresses;
- value-neutral descriptions (including displays or visual depictions) of the sponsor's product line(s) or services; and
- sponsor brand or trade names and product or service listings.

Logos or slogans that are an established part of the sponsor's identity are not considered to contain qualitative or comparative descriptions. Mere display or distribution (whether for free or for remuneration) of a sponsor's product by the sponsor or the tax-exempt organization to the general public at a sponsored activity will not be considered an inducement to purchase, sell, or use the sponsor's product and thus will not affect the determination as to whether a payment constitutes a qualified sponsorship payment.

Advertising

"Advertising" is defined as any message or other programming material that is broadcast or otherwise transmitted, published, displayed, or distributed, and that promotes or markets any trade or business, or any service, facility, or product. Advertising includes:

- messages containing qualitative or comparative language;
- price information or other indications of savings or value;
- an endorsement; or
- an inducement to purchase, sell, or use any company, service, facility, or product.

A *single* message that contains both advertising and an acknowledgment is considered advertising. The above rules do not apply to activities conducted by a sponsor on its own (e.g., if a sponsor purchases broadcast time from a television station to advertise its product during commercial breaks in a sponsored program, the tax-exempt organization's activities will not thereby be converted to advertising).

Exclusivity Arrangements

(a) Exclusive sponsor. An arrangement that acknowledges the sponsor as the exclusive sponsor of a tax-exempt organization's activity, or the exclusive sponsor representing a particular trade, business, or industry, generally will not, by itself, result in a substantial return benefit. For example, if, in exchange for a payment, a tax-exempt organization announces that its event or activity is sponsored exclusively by the sponsor (and does not provide any advertising or other substantial return benefit to the sponsor), then the sponsor has not received a substantial return benefit.

(b) Exclusive provider. An arrangement that limits the sale, distribution, availability, or use of competing products, services, or facilities in connection with a tax-exempt organization's activity generally *will* result in a substantial return benefit. For example, if in exchange for a payment, a tax-exempt organization agrees to permit only the sponsor's products to be sold in connection with its event or activity, then the sponsor has received a substantial return benefit.

Allocation of Payment

If there is an arrangement or expectation that the sponsor will receive a substantial return benefit with respect to any payment, then only the portion (if any) of the payment that exceeds the fair market value of the substantial return benefit (determined on the date the sponsorship arrangement is entered into or renewed) will be considered a qualified sponsorship payment. In other words, if, in exchange for a payment to a tax-exempt organization in connection with a sponsored event or activity, the sponsor receives advertising benefits as well as an acknowledgment, then UBIT will be assessed only on the fair market value of the portion allocable to the advertising benefits (subject to the burden of proof described below). However, if the tax-exempt organization fails to establish that the payment exceeds the fair market value of any substantial return benefit, then no portion of the payment will constitute a qualified sponsorship payment. The UBIT treatment of any payment (or portion thereof) that does not constitute a qualified sponsorship payment will be determined by application of the standard UBIT rules and exclusions. For example, payments related to a tax-exempt organization's provision of facilities, services, or other privileges to the sponsor (or persons designated by the sponsor), advertising, exclusive provider arrangements, a license to use intangible assets of the tax-exempt organization, or other substantial return benefits, will be evaluated separately in determining whether the tax-exempt organization realizes any UBI. Note that in many cases, such payments may not result in any UBI to the tax-exempt organization either

(i) because the activity does not constitute a trade or business, (ii) because it is not regularly carried on, or (iii) because one of the UBI exclusions (such as the royalty exclusion) applies—even if the activity is not substantially related to the organization's tax-exempt purposes.

Fair Market Value

The fair market value of any substantial return benefit provided as part of a sponsorship arrangement is the price at which the benefit would be provided between a willing recipient and a willing provider of the benefit, neither being under any compulsion to enter into the arrangement, both having reasonable knowledge of the relevant facts, and without regard to any other aspect of the sponsorship arrangement.

Anti-Abuse Provision

To the extent necessary to prevent avoidance of the "Allocation of Payment" rule described above, where the tax-exempt organization fails to make a reasonable and good faith valuation of any substantial return benefit, the IRS may determine the portion of a payment allocable to such substantial return benefit and may treat two or more related payments as a single payment.

Written Agreements

The existence of a written sponsorship agreement will not be determinative of whether a payment constitutes a qualified sponsorship payment. The terms of the agreement and how it is carried out in practice, not its existence or degree of detail, are relevant to the determination of whether a payment constitutes a qualified sponsorship payment. (See Model Corporate Sponsorship Agreement in Appendix C.)

Contingent Payments

A qualified sponsorship payment does not include any payment the amount of which is contingent, by contract or otherwise, upon the level of attendance at one or more events, broadcast ratings, or other factors indicating the degree of public exposure to the sponsored event or activity. However, the payment may be contingent upon the sponsored events or activities actually being conducted.

Determining Public Support (for 501(c)(3) Organizations)

With respect to section 501(c)(3) organizations, qualified sponsorship payments in the form of money, property, or services will be treated as "contributions" received by the tax-exempt organization for purposes of determining public support to the organization.

Deductibility of Payments by Sponsors

The fact that a payment constitutes a qualified sponsorship payment that is treated as a contribution to the tax-exempt organization does not determine whether the payment is deductible to the sponsor as a business expense or as a charitable contribution.

Exception for Trade Show Activities and Periodicals

The exclusion from taxable UBI for qualified sponsorship payments does not apply with respect to: (i) payments made in connection with qualified convention and trade show activities (which are governed by a separate exception in the Code); or (ii) income derived from the sale of advertising or acknowledgments in periodicals of tax-exempt organizations. For this purpose, the term "periodical" means regularly scheduled and printed material published by or on behalf of the tax-exempt organization that is not related to and primarily distributed in connection with a specific event conducted by the tax-exempt organization.

3. Qualified Convention and Trade Show Income

Code section 513(d) applies to tax-exempt trade and professional associations (whether exempt under section 501(c)(3), (c)(4), (c)(5), or (c)(6)) that regularly conduct trade shows and exhibitions to stimulate interest in an industry's products or services, or that regularly conduct such shows and exhibitions in connection with educational conferences or meetings. Under section 513(d), income from a qualified convention or trade show activity will not be subject to UBIT (whether or not selling or soliciting of orders occurs at the show or exhibition) if the association regularly conducts a qualified convention or trade show (as one of its substantial tax-exempt purposes) that meets all of the following requirements.

- The trade show or exhibition must be regularly conducted by the association in connection with an international, national, state, regional, or local convention, meeting, or show.
- At least one of the purposes of the association in sponsoring the convention or trade show must be:
  - to promote and stimulate interest in and demand for the products and services of the association's industry (or a segment thereof), or
  - to educate the association's members (note that in this context, the education of the association's members must be one of the principal purposes of the convention or trade show; by itself, according to the Treasury Regulations, the display of suppliers' products and services, while useful to members, generally is designed principally to stimulate interest in and sale of suppliers' products and services).

- The convention or trade show must be designed to achieve its purpose through:
  - the character of a significant portion of the exhibits, or
  - the character of conferences and seminars held at the convention or meeting.

This trade show exception, as it is commonly called, exempts virtually all income arising from qualified convention and trade shows, even from "incidental activities" (such as income generated from concession sales) of a kind traditionally carried on at such shows. However, section 513(d) will not provide a UBIT exemption for income from commercial advertising in trade show directories and other convention programs, unless the association: (1) engages in no other commercial advertising activity; (2) only publishes the trade show directory or convention program once a year; and (3) does not solicit such commercial advertising for an extended period of time prior to the trade show or convention.

Finally, the trade show exception does not apply to certain trade shows consisting solely of supplier exhibits—exhibitions involving only goods or services that are supplied to, rather than by, members of the association. A supplier show, by itself, does not constitute a qualified convention or trade show (because it does not stimulate interest in members' products or educate association members through meetings or seminars); however, if it were conducted in connection with a qualified convention or trade show (as defined above), income earned from the rental of exhibit space to suppliers would not be subject to UBIT.

4. Dividends, Interest, and Annuities

Generally, dividends, interest, annuities, payments with respect to securities loans, and other similar income from a tax-exempt organization's ordinary and routine investments is excluded in computing taxable UBI. Deductions directly connected with these types of income are also excluded from such computations. This exception does not apply to unrelated debt-financed income or to interest or annuities received from a controlled subsidiary (see Section III.G.5.).

5. Royalties

Royalties and the deductions directly connected with the royalties are excluded in computing taxable UBI. This exclusion does not apply to royalties received from a controlled subsidiary (see Section III.G.5.). The IRS defines a royalty as any payment received in consideration for the use of a valuable intangible property right, whether or not payment is based on the use made of the intangible property. Payments for the use of trademarks, trade names, service marks, copyrights, photographs, facsimile signatures, and members' names are ordinarily considered royalties. However, payments for personal services provided in connection with the granting of this type of right are not royalties and are taxable UBI.

Therefore, as illustrated in an IRS-provided example, payments for the use of a professional athlete's name, photograph, likeness, and/or facsimile signature are ordinarily considered royalties. However, payments for personal appearances and interviews are not excluded as royalties and must be included as income from an unrelated trade or business.

Endorsements, whereby an association endorses a vendor's product or service, are a rapidly growing area of association activity. Endorsements are a means to (1) generate non-dues revenue from both members and nonmembers; (2) promote the association's name and identity and, by extension, the industry or profession in general; and (3) provide a service (e.g., tailored products and services, discounted rates/fees, etc.) to members.

IRS rulings and court decisions addressing the proper characterization of income from endorsement and licensing arrangements have focused on the role of the association. Very simply, if the association is actively involved in the program that gives rise to the income, other than for the purpose of ensuring proper use of the association's name and logo, then the income will be deemed as having been received as a payment for such active involvement, and not as a royalty. However, if the role of the association can be characterized as passive, the income will generally be excluded from UBIT as a royalty.

A separate issue, but one that is vital to almost every association endorsement program (along with being a profitable source of income in its own right), is income from the rental of association membership mailing lists. Many associations earn considerable income renting (licensing) their mailing lists to suppliers and others who seek to market their products and services to association members. Moreover, an association's endorsement of a vendor's product or service will be significantly less valuable if the vendor cannot use the association's mailing list to promote the endorsed products or services to members of the association.

The endorsement or licensing contract that carries the lowest risk of UBIT liability is one in which the association license(s) its name, logo, and/or mailing list, and exercises quality control rights (and fixes rates and terms of sale for list rentals, if applicable), and nothing more. If administrative and/or marketing services are required, it may be preferable to outsource such services to an unrelated third party, or to the association's taxable subsidiary (with the association and subsidiary entering into separate, independent contracts with the vendor). In a Private Letter Ruling issued to the American Association of Retired Persons (AARP), the IRS validated the use of a wholly owned taxable subsidiary to provide such administrative and/or marketing services, provided it is done on an arm's-length basis (e.g., fair market valuation of the payments to each entity, financial separation, employee time records, etc.).

If such services must be provided by the association directly, the association may draft independent, unrelated contracts to provide for the name, logo, and/or mailing list licensing on the one hand, and the administrative and/or marketing services on the other. Many organizations also provide for licensing and administrative/marketing services within a single agreement. In either case, the fees earned by the association should be clearly delineated pursuant to some fair market valuation. The former should be treated as tax-exempt royalty income; the latter as taxable UBI. (See Model Royalty Agreement for Association Endorsement in Appendix B.) It should be noted that, to date, the IRS has not ruled on a situation in which the marketing and royalty provisions are contained in the same agreement.

The following guidelines should be followed when drafting endorsement or licensing contracts to minimize an association's potential UBIT liability.

- All royalty fees to be earned by the association should be referred to in the contract as royalties and the title of the agreement should state "Royalty Agreement" or "Licensing Agreement."
- The contract should separately list any required duties or activities pursuant to which the association will assist the vendor in the marketing or administration of its products or services, and should indicate that compensation for such services is taxable income (e.g., providing free advertising space in the association's magazine, providing free exhibit space at the association's trade show, drafting and sending letters to the association's members to promote the product or service, processing credit card applications, answering questions about or fielding problems with the product or service). Note that it would not present UBIT risk if the agreement provides for an association staff member or volunteer leader to sign a marketing letter on the association's letterhead stationery that is drafted and paid for by the vendor; this is merely the licensing of intangible property—a name, signature, and letterhead design.
- All marketing and administration of the product or service should be conducted and paid for at fair market rates by the vendor, an unrelated third party, or the association's taxable subsidiary (e.g., the association's regular rates should be paid for advertising space in the association's publications, exhibit booth space at the association's trade shows, etc.). In addition, the association should not share expenses with the vendor.
- It is acceptable, and indeed recommended, that quality-control provisions be included that permit the association to review and approve in advance all marketing materials to protect the association's name and goodwill. It also is acceptable for the association to protect and enhance the value of its intangible property (e.g., using "dummy" names in a mailing list, preparing a rate sheet of mailing list rates and

terms of sale). Note: Under federal trademark law, trademark and service mark holders are obligated to exercise control and supervision over the use of their mark(s) by others.

- Always use gross income as a measurement tool for determining royalty payments. The association should never contract for any percentage of net profits from the activity.
- Avoid the word "agent." The vendor should not be referred to as an agent of the association, nor should the association be referred to as an agent of the vendor.
- The contract should affirmatively state that it is not intended to create a "joint venture" or "partnership" between the parties.
- The program should be referred to as the vendor's program and should never be referred to as a program of the association. For example, the contract should not state: "Vendor is hereby retained to provide services for Association's insurance program." It is the vendor's program, and the association is merely licensing its name, logo, and/or membership mailing list.
- All miscellaneous documents, such as correspondence or board minutes, should be consistent with the contract, and the contract should otherwise be adhered to in practice.

6. Certain Rents from Real Property

Generally, rents from real property are excluded in computing UBIT. Rents from personal property are not excluded. However, special rules apply to mixed leases of both real and personal property. Deductions directly connected with excluded rents also are excluded in computing UBIT. This exception does not apply to:

- rents based on the income or profits derived by any person from the leased property (other than an amount based on a fixed percentage of gross receipts or sales);
- payments for occupying space when personal services also are rendered to the occupant (e.g., renting hotel rooms, renting space in parking lots or warehouses);
- rent received from the lease of debt-financed property (see Section II.C.4.); and
- rents received from a controlled subsidiary (see Section III.G.5.).

7. Certain Capital Gains

Gains or losses from the sale, exchange, or other disposition of property (including any gains from the lapse or termination of options to buy or sell securities) are excluded in computing UBIT, except with respect to:

- property held primarily for sale to customers in the ordinary course of a trade or business;
- stock in trade or other property of a kind that would properly be includible in inventory if on hand at the close of the tax year; or
- cutting of timber that an organization has elected to consider as a sale or exchange of the timber.

This exclusion does not apply to unrelated debt-financed income.

C. SPECIAL UBIT APPLICATIONS

1. Advertising Income

In 1969, Congress amended the tax laws to clarify that tax-exempt organization programs can be segregated into separate portions that are related and unrelated to the organization's tax-exempt functions for taxation purposes. Thus, while the publication of an association's newsletter, magazine, journal, or other periodical is generally considered to be substantially related to the organization's tax-exempt purposes, income from the regular sale of space for advertising in such periodicals is virtually always considered unrelated business income.

The Treasury Regulations specifically provide that the "activities of soliciting, selling, and publishing commercial advertising do not lose identity as a trade or business even though the advertising is published in an exempt organization periodical which contains editorial matter related to the exempt purposes of the organization." The Treasury Regulations dictate a series of complex accounting procedures to determine the UBIT implications of advertising income in periodicals.

As with other unrelated business activity of tax-exempt organizations, for a tax to be imposed on advertising revenues from publications, the advertising activity must be carried on regularly. The law and regulations are not designed to tax advertising revenue from a unique, one-time publication of an association. Likewise, for the periodicals to be considered carried on to produce unrelated business income, an association must intend to realize income from advertising in its periodicals, from other income generated by the periodicals (such as subscriptions), or from both. Association publications that do not contain advertising are not affected by these requirements.

To determine if an association's periodical is subject to UBIT, a series of careful accounting procedures must be followed as dictated by Treasury Regulations. Most important is the allocation of income and costs for a periodical between those related to advertising and those not related to advertising. Income and cost items for the periodical that are related to both advertising and non-advertising aspects must be fairly apportioned. The general rule for taxation of net advertising revenues from association periodicals is that there is no UBIT imposed on a periodical that does not net any overall revenues (including allocable membership dues in revenues). No tax is due if total publication income (circulation income and gross advertising) is no more than total publication costs (readership and direct advertising costs). A complete description of these accounting rules is beyond the scope of this book.

If an association has advertising in more than one periodical, it is permissible to consolidate the publications for computing any UBIT. However, this treatment has to be followed consistently, and IRS approval must be obtained before changing the treatment.

2. Associate Member Dues

Background

The associate member dues issue first arose by way of two 1993 IRS rulings—one issued to a 501(c)(6) professional society and the other to a 501(c)(5) farm organization—concluding that dues paid by the associate members of those organizations were really not tax-exempt dues, but rather were taxable unrelated business income. In the 501(c)(6) ruling, the IRS held that the supplier member dues were essentially purchasing advertising (an unrelated activity), and not much more. In the 501(c)(5) ruling, the IRS held that the dues of nonfarmer associate members were purchasing access to insurance programs (an unrelated activity), and not much more. In both cases, the IRS viewed the associate member dues as merely access charges to gain one or more unrelated benefits. Consequently, the dues were deemed to be taxable income to the organizations and subject to UBIT.

Principal Purpose Test

In 1995, the IRS issued its first precedential guidance in this area, in the form of a Revenue Procedure (Rev. Proc.). This Rev. Proc. established a principal purpose test for determining whether a class of dues income will be subject to UBIT. Specifically, it said that if an associate member category (defined as members who "are accorded less than full or no voting privileges in voting for the directors of the organization") has been formed or availed of for the principal purpose of producing unrelated business income, then dues from associate members will be taxed. The Rev. Proc. defined unrelated business income for these purposes as income from the sale of, or the provision of access to, goods or services produced by an activity that constitutes a trade or business, is regularly carried on, and is not substantially related to the organization's tax-exempt purposes.

On the other hand, if an associate member category has been formed or availed of for the principal purpose of furthering the organization's tax-exempt purposes, then, according to the Rev. Proc., such dues will not be taxable. Finally, the Rev. Proc. said that in applying this standard, the IRS will look to the purposes and activities of the organization rather than of its members (this is an important distinction in the supplier member context). While the Rev. Proc. initially applied to only 501(c)(5) organizations, it was later broadened (through a subsequent Rev. Proc. in January 1997) to apply to 501(c)(6) organizations as well.

In public comments, senior IRS officials have explained this principal purpose test by stating that if there is "real involvement by associate members in exempt function activities, in policy making, in decision making," then the principal purpose of having associate members will be not to generate UBI, and associate member dues will not be taxed. If, however, the IRS determines that the principal purpose for having supplier members, for instance, is merely to raise additional revenue, and there is not the requisite level of involvement in tax-exempt activities, then their dues will be taxable.

Red Flags

If an association has any of the following red flags, its risk of being taxed on its associate member dues income may be increased. However, these red flags are by no means determinative; the presence of one or more of them by no means guarantees the taxation of associate member dues. But if an association's concern about such taxation outweighs the benefits that flow from having these factors present, it may want to consider their elimination.

- Associate members are treated in a materially different manner from regular members.
- The association provides "identifiable economic benefits" to associate members that do not relate to the association's tax-exempt purposes.
- Associate members do not have "full participation" in the association or a right to participate in its "organizational direction," evidenced by the fact that they do not have "meaningful, substantial" voting rights and/or may not hold significant office(s) in the association's elected bodies.
- Associate member solicitation materials predominantly tout access and exposure to potential clients/customers (i.e., the association's "regular" members) or valuable services such as an insurance program.
- There exists a lack of "significant, documented" participation by associate members in the tax-exempt functions of the association (e.g., educational programs, conventions, etc.).
- A high percentage of associate members choose to take advantage of unrelated benefits, or membership survey results exist which point to unrelated benefits as a major motivation for associate members in joining the association.
- Associate member dues are proportionately tied to one or more unrelated benefits (e.g., dues tied to advertising space in association publications).

- Unrelated benefits provided to associate members (e.g., insurance programs) are competitively priced in comparison to market rates for that product or service.
- Associate members pay higher dues than regular members yet receive fewer rights in and benefits from the association.

Tips to Reduce Tax Risk

As noted above, none of these red flags, in and of themselves, should result in the taxation of associate member dues. However, associations wishing to minimize their potential tax liability in this area should consider taking steps, and documenting such steps, to demonstrate how the associate member category has been "formed or availed of for the principal purpose of furthering the organization's tax-exempt purposes."

Regarding specifically what types of factors would reflect the requisite level of associate member involvement in an association's tax-exempt activities, common examples would include:

- involvement by associate members in the association's lobbying activities;
- meaningful voting rights and board representation;
- meaningful participation in the committee process or other governance and policy-making structures; and
- consistent attendance at and participation in educational conferences, seminars, and other activities that support the association's tax-exempt purposes.

Again, contemporaneous documentation (a paper trail) of such participation will be essential to satisfying the IRS.

Associations wishing to minimize their potential tax liability in this area also should take two other important steps:

- review and, if necessary, revise the solicitation materials used to attract associate members to ensure that they reflect a role for associate members in helping to further the organization's tax-exempt purposes, rather than simply touting associate members' access to unrelated benefits (e.g., access and exposure to the association's regular members, various affinity products such as credit cards, hotel, and car rental discounts, and low-rate long-distance telephone service); and
- examine and, if necessary, broaden the association's stated tax-exempt purposes—as reflected in articles of incorporation, bylaws, and IRS filings—to ensure that they encompass a role for associate members in significantly furthering one or more of those purposes.

Any IRS examination will likely include scrutiny of all of these documents.

In summary, the more associate members look like regular members in terms of rights, benefits, and obligations in the association, the more likely the IRS would find that the principal purpose of having associate members is to further the organization's tax-exempt purposes, thereby ensuring continued tax-free treatment of associate member dues income.

3. Group Insurance

Many associations are actively involved in group insurance programs for their members. Association group policies can be tailored to the specific insurance needs and typical losses experienced in the industry or profession represented by the association. The association membership communication channels may provide convenient and economic marketing outlets for insurance programs and may help members keep claims, and thus losses and premiums, to a minimum. As a result, association group insurance sometimes can be made available at premiums that are lower than those for comparable coverage available outside the association.

Associations vary greatly in the extent of their administrative activities connected with group insurance programs. To some extent, state insurance laws may regulate association involvement. Some associations maintain actual insurance operations, including underwriting coverage, drafting and marketing policies, and processing premiums and claims. However, court rulings in this area make clear that this kind of extensive association insurance activity cannot be substantially related to an association's tax-exempt purposes or qualify for royalty treatment, and thus will give rise to UBI.

More common is the association that delegates all or most of the administration of its group insurance plans to an outside commercial insurance carrier, insurance agent or broker, or insurance marketing firm. The outside administrator generally pays the association a percentage of the premiums paid by members. The exempt organization's tax consequences from this activity are not entirely clear, but the IRS position is generally that the revenue from these endeavors is subject to UBIT unless the association remains totally uninvolved (passive) in the administration, marketing, and all other aspects of the insurance program. (See Section II.B.5. for a discussion of the potential passive role of the association in endorsement and licensing arrangements.)

Further, some associations realize no income at all from group insurance programs to which the association's name may be connected for promotional purposes. These associations consider it sufficiently advantageous to ensure that insurance coverage is available to members through the association. Obviously, this type of association involvement in insurance activity is the least questionable from the point of view of taxation because no income is paid to the association, whether from an unrelated business activity or not.

Finally, certain associations have established taxable subsidiaries or group insurance trusts as separate entities to operate the associations' insurance programs. This approach shields the association from UBIT exposure or risk of loss of tax-exempt status (see Section III.H.).

4. Real Estate

UBIT can apply in some circumstances to association rental income or investments that are debt-financed. The two primary types of unrelated business income that can result from association real estate holdings are: (1) rental income when the property is occupied, in whole or in part, by others than the association; and (2) gains realized when the association sells the property.

Generally, a tax-exempt association that holds real estate that (1) is not substantially related to the purposes for which the association was granted tax-exempt status; and (2) was purchased or renovated with borrowed funds, may have its rental income or investment gain subject to UBIT based on the amount of the borrowing the association incurred in making the purchase. This rule has several qualifications and exceptions, discussed below.

For the property to be considered debt-financed, there need not be debt encumbering the property itself. If the real estate is purchased with funds that would otherwise be used for the operating budget, for example, and a loan is used to operate the association, then the real estate will be considered debt-financed.

The income (i.e., rental income, gain on sale) derived from any real estate an association purchases, holds, or sells is not subject to UBIT as long as the property is used substantially (defined as 85 percent or greater) by the association in pursuit of its tax-exempt purposes. This rule applies even if the acquisition or renovation of the property is debt-financed. For example, if an association finances the purchase of a new headquarters building, and if the association occupies 85 percent or more of the building's square footage, then all of the rental income derived from the property (including that received from unrelated tenants such as retail merchants) will be exempt from tax, and all of the gain on sale of the building will be exempt from tax.

If the real estate is debt-financed and less than 85 percent of the building's square footage is occupied by the association (while 15 percent or more is occupied by unrelated tenants), the rental income paid to the association by the unrelated tenants will be subject to UBIT. Of course, such taxable income of the association can be partially or fully offset by the allocable share of allowable deductions, such as depreciation (computed by the straight-line method), interest, utility payments, and other direct expenses.

On the sale of the building, the percentage of any corresponding gains allocable to the association's use of the building will be exempt from tax, while the balance of such gains will be taxable as UBI (subject to any directly connected offsetting expenses such as sales commissions). Under a formula in the Treasury Regulations, this taxable amount will diminish slightly as the mortgage is paid down, but no meaningful reductions will generally occur until the final years of the mortgage term. However, if the mortgage on the property is satisfied in full at least 12 months before the sale of the building, then the property will not be considered to have been debt-financed and there will be no tax on any gains.

D. DEDUCTIONS IN COMPUTING UBIT

The term taxable unrelated business income means the gross income derived from any unrelated trade or business regularly carried on by the tax-exempt organization, less the deductions directly connected with carrying on the trade or business, both computed with the exclusions and modifications discussed above.

If an organization regularly carries on two or more unrelated business activities, its taxable income is the total of gross income from all such activities less the total allowable deductions attributable to all the activities.

1. Deductions for Directly Related Expenses

To qualify as allowable deductions in computing taxable income, the expenses, depreciation, and similar items must qualify as allowable income tax deductions and also must be directly connected with carrying on the unrelated trade or business. To be directly connected with the conduct of an unrelated business, deductions must have a proximate and primary relationship to carrying on that business. Where expenses, depreciation, and similar items are attributable solely to the conduct of an unrelated business, they are clearly proximately and primarily related to that business. However, when facilities or personnel are used both to carry on tax-exempt functions and to conduct an unrelated business, expenses, depreciation, and similar items attributable to the facilities or personnel must be allocated between the two uses on a reasonable basis.

Generally, expenses, depreciation, and similar items attributable to the conduct of a tax-exempt activity are not deductible in computing taxable income from an unrelated business that exploits the exempt activity, because they do not have a proximate and primary relationship to the unrelated business. Therefore, they do not qualify as directly connected with that business. However, these expenses, depreciation, and similar items may be treated as directly connected with the conduct of the unrelated business if all of the following statements are true.

- The unrelated business exploits the tax-exempt activity.
- The unrelated business is a type normally carried on for profit by taxable organizations.
- The tax-exempt activity is a type normally conducted by taxable organizations in carrying out that type of business.

The amount treated as directly connected to the conduct of the unrelated business is the smaller of:

- the excess of these expenses, depreciation, and similar items over the income from, or attributable to, the tax-exempt activity; or
- the gross unrelated business income reduced by all other expenses, depreciation, and all other items that are actually directly connected.

Of special note for associations is the sale of advertising in an association's periodical that contains editorial material related to the association's tax-exempt purposes; this is an unrelated business that exploits an exempt activity—the circulation and readership of the periodical. Therefore, in addition to direct advertising costs, a portion of exempt activity costs (expenses, depreciation, and similar expenses attributable to the production and distribution of the editorial or readership content) can be treated as directly connected with the conduct of the advertising activity. A special set of detailed rules apply to the computation of taxable income from advertising in association periodicals (see Section II.C.1.).

2. $1,000 Deduction

In computing taxable income, an automatic deduction of $1,000 is permitted. However, the deduction is not allowed in computing a net operating loss or the net operating loss deduction. Generally, the deduction is limited to $1,000 regardless of the number of unrelated businesses in which the organization is engaged.

3. Net Operating Loss Deduction

A net operating loss deduction is allowed in calculating UBIT. However, the net operating loss carryback or carryover (from a tax year for which the organization is subject to tax on unrelated business income) is determined without taking into account any amount of income or deduction that has been excluded specifically in computing taxable income. For example, a loss from an unrelated trade or business is not diminished because dividend income was received. Finally, a net operating loss carryback or carryover is allowed only from a tax year for which the organization is subject to tax on its unrelated business income.

4. Charitable Contributions Deduction

An association taxable at corporate income tax rates is allowed a deduction for charitable contributions up to 10 percent of its taxable income computed without regard to the deduction for contributions. Contributions in excess of the 10 percent limit may be carried over to the next five taxable years. A contribution carryover is not allowed, however, to the extent that it increases a net operating loss carryover.

III

Combinations, Affiliations, and Alliances between Nonprofit and For-Profit Entities

In recent years, as associations have searched for additional sources of revenue and new ways to serve members' needs, many have turned to a number of new combinations and partnerships, such as joint ventures with for-profit entities, affiliations with other associations, and creation of for-profit subsidiaries. Joint ventures and the use of related entities are significant planning tools that can be used to preserve tax exemption, generate revenue, limit legal liability, reduce taxable unrelated business income, engage in otherwise prohibited activities, or for other legal, financial, management, or political reasons.

While such arrangements have become more sophisticated over the years, such as the growing use of limited liability companies (LLCs) as the preferred legal form of the venture or subsidiary entity, the underlying concerns with respect to these arrangements remain largely unchanged: (1) whether a tax-exempt organization's participation might adversely affect its tax-exempt status; and (2) whether such participation results in unrelated business income to the tax-exempt organization.

A. OVERVIEW OF JOINT VENTURES

In general, a joint venture is an agreement between two or more entities to undertake a shared objective for the benefit of both parties. There are many specific variations of such relationships. For example, in a commercial co-venture, a nonprofit organization enters into an agreement for a charitable sales promotion with an entity that is regularly and primarily engaged in a trade or business other than raising funds for charities. Commercial co-ventures and similar particular relationships, such as sponsorships, come with their own risks, complications, and compliance concerns. This section is intended to focus on the broader category of joint ventures, which are typically ad hoc, one-time groupings that often concern a single transaction or an isolated enterprise.

In a joint venture, two or more entities lend their efforts, assets, and expertise in order to carry out a common purpose. The associations involved may develop a new entity (such as a limited liability company or a partnership) to carry out the endeavor. Such a new entity may receive tax-exempt status if it is organized and operated for exempt purposes. In most instances, however, associations commit certain resources to a joint venture without forming a new entity. A well-structured joint venture is codified in a written agreement that details the precise obligations and allocation of risk between the associations involved.

With joint ventures and partnerships, an organization's tax-exempt status is put at potential risk through (1) the fact that the organization may no longer be operated principally in furtherance of its tax-exempt purposes (depending upon the express purposes and goals of the partnership, the extent of the organization's control over the partnership or affiliated entity, etc.), and (2) the fact that the organization's assets may be at risk of inuring to the benefit of its for-profit partner(s) (if applicable).

However, an organization's tax exemption generally will not be jeopardized if the organization continues to devote the principal share of its time, expense, and other resources to the furtherance of its tax-exempt purposes. In such event, though, the organization's income from a joint venture or partnership that is not in furtherance of such purposes will be subject to UBIT.

Joint ventures can be permanent, set to expire on a given date or after the accomplishment of a certain goal, or structured with an increasingly overlapping set of commitments and an eye towards an eventual merger. Unless the bylaws of an organization specify otherwise, joint ventures do not usually require the approval of the general membership. A joint venture that is not separately incorporated is usually treated as a partnership for federal income tax purposes. For purposes of the discussion in this section, the term joint venture is used to describe both joint ventures and partnerships between tax-exempt and for-profit entities.

Tax Treatment

As a pass-through entity, a partnership is not itself subject to tax; however, the individual partners are liable for income tax on the partnership income in their separate capacities. In determining their individual income tax liabilities, each partner must separately take into account the distributive share of the partnership's income, gains, losses, etc.

Also, the character of any item of income, gain, loss, deduction, or credit included in a partner's distributive share is determined as if such item were realized directly from the source from which it was realized by the partnership, or incurred in the same manner as it was incurred by the partnership. In other words, if an association is a member of a partnership, it must treat its share of the partnership income in the same manner as if it had directly engaged in the activity that gave rise to the income. Thus, the usual UBIT exclusions (such as for interest and dividend income, royalties, capital gains, and certain real estate rental income) are available even when earned by the partnership.

Finally, a partner's distributive share of income, gain, loss, deduction, or credit generally is determined by the partnership agreement.

Whole and Ancillary Joint Ventures

In a whole joint venture, one or more of the partnering entities contribute all of their assets to the enterprise. Whole joint ventures have, in the past, been a focus of IRS enforcement matters, especially with respect to health care organizations. In particular, the focus has been on joint ventures where a tax-exempt entity transfers, in one form or another, all of its assets to a joint venture with one or more for-profit entities and then continues to operate, to varying extents, for charitable purposes. The IRS has questioned whether these whole joint ventures jeopardize an organization's tax-exempt status. The IRS and the U.S. Tax Court have stated that the key to whether an organization's tax-exempt status is jeopardized by such a joint venture is the operational control of the venture. Operational control means voting control (preferably majority control of the governing body of the venture—veto authority alone has met with skepticism from the IRS and courts) and ensuring through the venture's organizational documents (e.g., LLC or partnership agreement) that the organization's tax-exempt purposes drive all venture decisions (an obligation to put charitable objectives ahead of other objectives).

In addition, even if the tax-exempt organization retains the requisite control over the venture, it is important that the terms do not overly favor the for-profit partner, such as excessive profits paid to the for-profit entity. While for-profit partners rightly expect a return on their investment, that private gain cannot be substantial when compared to the public benefit derived from the venture. This having been said, operational control by the tax-exempt organization remains the key factor in evaluating whether tax exemption is jeopardized by participating in a joint venture involving an organization's entire operations.

What is less clear is whether the same rule applies in the case of joint ventures involving only a portion of the organization's resources, rather than the entire operations of the tax-exempt organization. Associations commonly engage in ancillary joint ventures with other organizations: these are essentially small-scale joint ventures where the enterprise does not become the primary purpose of the organizations involved and the venture is often for a limited duration. Due to the small scale of these ancillary joint ventures, participation is unlikely to jeopardize the association's tax-exempt status. The question in these types of ventures is whether the income from them is subject to UBIT.

UBIT applies to joint venture activities as though the joint venture did not exist. Each portion of the association's joint venture income is tested under the general rules that would apply if the association engaged in the activity directly, (using, for example, the standard three-prong UBIT test and the exclusions for passive income (see Section II.)). In other words, the association must treat its share of the joint venture income in the same manner as if it had conducted the activity in its own capacity.

There have been no cases to date in which the IRS has argued that lack of sufficient control over a partnership or joint venture causes an otherwise related activity to be subject to UBIT. However, IRS officials have indicated publicly that an analysis under the precedent for whole hospital joint ventures could lead to that result. While this remains an open issue, if an association is considering a joint venture with a for-profit partner that is in furtherance of its tax-exempt purposes and it seeks to avoid UBIT, it should attempt to establish operational control over the venture. As stated above, control can consist of a majority of the members of the governing body and/or ensuring through the venture's organizational documents (e.g., LLC or partnership agreement) that the association's tax-exempt purposes drive all venture decisions (an obligation to put tax-exempt objectives ahead of nonexempt ones).

In addition, it is important to ensure that the terms of the joint venture do not overly favor the for-profit partner, such as excessive profits paid to the for-profit entity. An association's partner may be considered an insider, and the IRS closely scrutinizes arrangements between tax-exempt organizations and taxable entities to determine whether the activities contravene the prohibition on private inurement. Thus, an arrangement with a for-profit entity must be entered at arm's length and carefully reviewed to ensure that any benefits to insiders are at or below fair market value. If the income generated by the venture will be subject to UBIT in any event, because the venture consists of providing particular services to members or is not otherwise substantially related to the association's tax-exempt purposes, associations should consider utilizing a taxable subsidiary to hold the ownership interest in the joint venture, as discussed in Section III.G.

B. MERGERS AND CONSOLIDATIONS

Nonprofit associations can fully and completely integrate their programs, functions, and membership through the processes of merger and consolidation. When two nonprofit entities merge, one entity legally becomes part of the surviving entity and dissolves. The surviving corporation takes title to all of the assets, and assumes all of the liabilities, of the non-surviving entity.

Unlike a merger, a consolidation of nonprofit entities involves the dissolution of each of the organizations involved, and the creation of an entirely new nonprofit corporation that takes on the programs, resources, and membership of the former entities. Although the net effect of a merger and consolidation are the same—one surviving entity with all the assets and liabilities of the two previous groups—many associations prefer consolidation over merger because it tends to lend the perception that no organization has an advantage over the other. There is a new corporation which houses the activities of the two and each is dissolved pursuant to the consolidation.

Merger or consolidation of entities with similar exempt purposes may offer a number of benefits to the participating organizations and their members. By merging or consolidating, associations may combine their assets, reduce costs by eliminating redundant administrative processes, and provide broader services and resources to their members. Furthermore, members who paid dues and fees to participate in the formerly separate associations are often able to reduce their membership dues and the costs and time demands of association participation by joining a single, combined organization. Finally, a merger or consolidation may allow associations participating within the same field or industry to offer a wider array of educational programming, publications, advocacy, and other services to a larger constituency in the public arena.

Mergers and consolidations also trigger stringent fiduciary responsibilities for the members of an organization's governing body to ensure that any merger or consolidation is warranted and in the best interests of the organization. Directors and officers may be held personally and individually liable if they fail to act prudently and with due diligence. Due diligence generally requires an organization's governing body to ascertain the financial and legal condition of the organization with which the entity will be merged or consolidated. This includes examination of the other entity's books and records, governing documents, meeting minutes, pending claims, employment practices, contracts, leases, and insurance policies, and investigation into potentially significant financial obligations, such as the funding of retirement programs, binding commitments to suppliers, and the security of investment vehicles.

In addition to conducting routine due diligence reviews, an organization's board of directors must consider the impact of a proposed merger or consolidation on competition within the industry. Federal antitrust laws prohibit mergers or consolidations that may substantially lessen competition in any line of commerce. The U.S. Department of Justice and the Federal Trade Commission may scrutinize any transaction that could lead to price fixing, bid rigging, customer allocation, boycotts, or other anticompetitive practices. However, in practice, mergers and consolidations of nonprofit associations typically do not pose an anticompetitive threat.

Procedural Requirements

To merge or consolidate with another organization, each organization must follow the procedures mandated under the nonprofit corporation law of its state of incorporation, as well as any specific procedures in its governing documents, provided such procedures are consistent with the nonprofit corporation statute. While nonprofit corporation statutes differ by state, the laws governing merger and consolidation of nonprofits typically set forth certain core procedures. The board of directors of each precursor organization must develop and approve a plan of merger or consolidation according to the requirements set forth in the nonprofit corporation statute of the state, or states, where the organizations are incorporated. Typically, the details of the deal between the two organizations are set forth in a merger agreement that is not required to be filed. The plan of merger or consolidation also must be submitted to the voting members, if any, of each organization for their approval. While the conditions for member approval vary from state to state, statutes generally require a vote of two-thirds to effectuate the plan merger or consolidation.

If the merging nonprofits are each tax-exempt under different tax classifications (e.g., a 501(c)(6) and a 501(c)(3)), the resulting merged entity may need to file a new application for federal tax exemption with the IRS. Likewise, a new, consolidated entity must apply to the IRS for recognition of tax-exempt status. On the other hand, where merging entities share the same tax-exempt classification, the tax-exempt status of the surviving organization is typically not affected. Instead, following the merger, all parties to the transaction must notify the IRS of the merger as part of their Form 990 filing obligations and provide supporting legal documentation. Merging entities will be required to file a final Form 990 at the conclusion of the merger; merged entities will report the transaction on their next annual Form 990.

C. ACQUIRING A DISSOLVING ASSOCIATION'S ASSETS

Another way in which associations can combine is through the dissolution and transfer of assets to another target association. This statutory procedure generally involves the adoption of a plan of dissolution and distribution of assets, satisfaction of outstanding liabilities, transfer of any remaining assets to another nonprofit entity, and dissolution.

The dissolving entity will need to adhere to specific statutory procedures. For instance, where the dissolving nonprofit is exempt under section 501(c)(3), the organization must distribute its assets for one or more exempt purposes under section 501(c)(3). A dissolution and transfer of assets is much less onerous for the association that acquires the dissolving entity's assets (the "successor" entity) than a merger or consolidation. Because the successor entity is merely absorbing the assets of another organization, a vote of the membership and accompanying state filings are typically not required for that corporation. Furthermore, receipt of a dissolving nonprofit corporation's assets typically does not affect an organization's tax-exempt status. However, just as with merger or consolidation, a tax-exempt organization must be cautious when taking on programs or activities to ensure that they support its stated tax-exempt purposes. Asset transfer and dissolution may be strategically preferable for combining organizations when one organization is of a much smaller size than the other. In addition, this type of transaction is particularly useful when an organization wishes to acquire the assets of another organization with significant future contingent liabilities, because the successor organization does not, by operation of law, assume the liabilities of the dissolving corporation. Further, the successor organization may seek to limit the liabilities it will assume in a written agreement.

While a successor organization is typically shielded from its predecessor's debts and liabilities, an asset transfer always poses some risk of successor liability, particularly if adequate provision has not been made for pre-existing liabilities. A court may determine that an organization that acquired the assets of a dissolved corporation impliedly agreed to assume the dissolved corporation's liabilities. Alternatively, courts can find that the successor corporation serves as a continuation of the dissolved corporation, that the asset transfer amounts to a de facto merger, or that the transaction was actually a fraudulent attempt to escape liability.

Procedural Requirements

Like a merger or consolidation, an asset transfer and dissolution must follow the applicable state nonprofit corporation laws and each entity's governing documents. The procedure for dissolution and asset distribution is fairly simple for the successor entity, as it will simply be entering into a transaction—albeit a significant one—to acquire assets and absorb members, if any. Member approval by members of the entity acquiring the assets is typically unnecessary unless the organization's bylaws require otherwise. The due diligence requirements imposed on the successor entity are also less stringent.

The process is more complicated, however, for the dissolving entity. In most instances, the nonprofit corporation statute of the dissolving entity's state of incorporation imposes several requirements to effectuate a transfer and dissolution, including the exercise of the same level of due diligence as in a proposed merger or consolidation for the dissolving association's governing body, developing and approving a "plan of dissolution" (or "plan of distribution" according to some states), obtaining member approval of the dissolution plan if needed, and filing requirements. Once the plan of dissolution is executed, the dissolving entity is generally prohibited from carrying on any further business activity, except as is necessary to wind up its affairs or respond to civil, criminal, or administrative investigation.

As part of the asset distribution process, the parties typically execute a written agreement detailing their understanding of the transfer of the dissolving corporation's assets. The parties may utilize such an agreement where they wish to obtain warranties regarding the absence of liabilities to be assumed by the successor corporation; account for any outstanding contractual obligations of the dissolving entity; provide for third-party consents where necessary to transfer any contractual obligations to the successor organization; or detail terms for the integration of the dissolving entity's members. Note that in the event of any breach of warranties by the dissolving corporation, it generally will not be possible for the successor corporation to obtain redress unless the agreement specifically obligates some third party to indemnify the successor corporation, as the dissolving corporation will no longer exist.

D. Federations

A federation is generally an association of associations. Federations are most often structured along regional lines (e.g., a national association whose members are state or local associations). In some cases, a federation consists of special interest groups that represent discrete segments of the industry represented by the "umbrella" association. The national or umbrella association's relationship with its affiliated associations is governed by formal affiliation agreements.

An affiliation agreement is a binding contract that sets forth the nature of the relationship between the parties. Most affiliation agreements include provisions that address the following: term and termination of the relationship; use of the association's intellectual property; the provision of management services; treatment of confidential information; coordinated activities; and tax and/or financial issues, among other provisions. Where an affiliated association fails to adhere to the terms of its affiliation agreement with the national association, the affiliate could lose privileges (e.g., loss of ability to use the association's intellectual property), become disaffiliated, or suffer some other penalty. Similarly, where a national association violates the terms of an affiliation agreement with its affiliate, it may be liable for such breach.

Usually in the federation context, the national association is, for tax and liability purposes, a separate legal entity from its affiliated associations. As is the case with numerous types of closely affiliated entities, there are instances, however, in which the separateness between two entities—even though each entity may have separate corporate and tax statuses—will be disregarded by a court or the IRS, thus creating exposure to potential legal and tax liability to both entities. Specifically, the separateness can be disregarded where the national association so controls the affairs of its affiliates, rendering it an instrumentality of the national association.

There are two primary areas of concern for national associations that are governed by a federated structure. First and foremost, because the national association is primarily (if not completely) comprised of other associations, the income and membership of the national association is generally controlled by its affiliates. Without control over these two vital areas, the national association could be susceptible to secession by an affiliate, resulting in attendant loss of income, or have its power and authority undermined by an affiliate. Second, the federated structure could cause legal or policy problems if factionalism among affiliated associations arose.

Procedural Requirements

Preliminarily, all steps must be taken to form the national association in accordance with applicable state nonprofit corporation (or association) laws. Generally, this requires a minimum of filing articles of incorporation, selecting an initial board of directors, and developing bylaws for the association. Once the association is formed, it should apply to the IRS for recognition of tax-exempt status (note, however, that self-certification is an option available for many non-501(c)(3) entities).

After formation, the national association must execute detailed affiliation agreements with each of its affiliated associations. There are generally no statutory requirements mandating the exercise of due diligence by any entity that chooses to enter into an affiliation agreement. Rather, the relationship is generally governed by the terms of the affiliation agreement and the general principles of contract law.

E. OTHER TYPES OF STRATEGIC ALLIANCES

Mergers, consolidations, acquisitions, and the creation of a federation involve a substantial level of commitment—but associations need not go so far in order to engage in alliances with one another.

Management Company Model

Associations with similar interests can use a management company model to affiliate without going through the process of a merger or consolidation. A common management structure allows the groups to realize the efficiencies of coordinated "back office" operations such as accounting, meeting management, IT, human resources and other supportive functions, possibly utilizing a for-profit affiliate or third party. Although there are mechanisms that could be used to effect the coordinated operations that many associations seek, the idea of affiliating with a for-profit entity is problematic for several reasons, most notably tax law inhibitions on private inurement from a tax-exempt entity and state corporate law restrictions.

The management company model has been used in the past by a number of associations, in which a nonprofit association provides management and staffing for another nonprofit corporate association which is generally within the scope of its exempt purposes.

Association management companies (AMCs) are for-profit entities that manage the day-to-day business of numerous associations. The models vary depending on the resources and needs of the associations, but in almost all settings the AMCs provide the accounting, meeting planning, correspondence, communications, staffing, and office requirements. In some cases, the association will have separate office identity including signage and limited access, while in others there will be common "association offices" with shared employees. These employees are formally employed by the AMC, but essentially report to the boards of the associations.

One critical aspect of this organizational model is that the AMC does not have an ownership interest in the nonprofit associations. They operate under management agreements that typically can be terminated with relatively short notice or at the conclusion of a stated term. The contractual arrangements are based on arm's-length compensation, depending on the services provided.

Partial Asset Purchase or Transfer

Finally, a lesser alternative to dissolution and transfer of all of a nonprofit's assets is a limited asset purchase or transfer from one entity to another. In general, an asset purchase may be advantageous where one nonprofit entity wishes to acquire a discrete property, activity, program, or business unit of another. The directors of both organizations owe their members a significant level of due diligence prior to finalizing the deal, but, depending on the size of the asset transfer, applicable state nonprofit law, and the terms of the transferring organization's governing documents, partial asset transfers typically do not require the approval of an organization's membership. The transfer is executed pursuant to a written asset purchase agreement between the parties.

F. OVERVIEW OF AFFILIATED ENTITIES

In addition to the combinations discussed above, associations can also take advantage of the creation of an array of affiliations and subsidiary entities, as a way to increase revenues, expand activities, and isolate liabilities. These include taxable subsidiaries; related educational, research, or charitable foundations; lobbying affiliates (for purposes of the lobbying limits on 501(c)(3) organizations, the lobbying tax law applicable principally to 501(c)(6) organizations, or the prohibition of lobbying by 501(c)(4) organizations that receive federal grants); group insurance trusts; political action committees; and other affiliated entities. Properly utilized, such affiliated entities can reap enormous benefits for the parent association. However, the legal terrain in which they operate is fraught with traps and pitfalls.

If an association is not prepared to do the detailed record keeping, cost allocation, and other administrative functions necessary to maintain the requisite financial, management, and operational separation, then it should not establish an affiliated entity. It is burdensome to hold separate board meetings; maintain separate financial records, time sheets, and bank accounts; allocate joint program expenses and overhead; observe strict financial separation; and utilize separate letterhead stationery, among other requirements. At the same time, however, there are significant benefits and opportunities to be derived from the creative use of affiliated entities.

Described in the next few sections are several of the most common forms of affiliated entities utilized by associations: taxable subsidiaries, related foundations of 501(c)(6) associations, political action committees, and trusts. While different in form and function from the above entities, association chapters also are discussed. This list is by no means exhaustive. Associations frequently establish a variety of related entities for numerous legal, financial, management, political, practical, and other reasons. However, the general principles discussed below, such as the importance of maintaining separate governance structures and strict financial separation, are for the most part widely applicable to all affiliated organizations and essential to avoiding the legal pitfalls.

G. TAXABLE SUBSIDIARIES

1. Common Reasons for Establishing Taxable Subsidiaries

Exemption-Threatening Activities

If the gross revenue, net income, or staff time devoted to an unrelated business becomes substantial in relation to the tax-exempt function of an organization (thereby jeopardizing its tax-exempt status), the association can "spin off" the activity into a separate but affiliated entity, commonly referred to as a taxable subsidiary. Such a taxable subsidiary will pay income tax on the net income from the activity, but can remit the after-tax profits to the parent (tax-exempt organization) as tax-free dividends.

Providing Administrative or Marketing Services in Connection with Association Products/Services Endorsements

When associations endorse or lend their name to third-party products and services, the income received under such arrangements is usually only exempt from tax to the extent it can be classified as a royalty (payment for the licensing of property such as an association's name and logo). However, if the income is in part a royalty and in part a payment for services (e.g., administrative or marketing services), then the IRS may treat all of the income as unrelated business income. Consequently, to ensure tax-free royalty treatment of endorsement income, some associations do not conduct any services at all in connection with such endorsements, some outsource such services to unrelated third parties, and others conduct such services through their taxable subsidiaries. Under this latter alternative, the association enters into a contract with the vendor for the licensing of its name, logo, and membership mailing list, and the taxable subsidiary enters into a separate contract with the vendor to provide administrative and/or marketing services. The association's income is treated as tax-free royalty income; the taxable subsidiary pays tax on its income (the after-tax profits can then be transferred to the association in the form of tax-free dividends). Associations utilizing such a structure must be careful to ensure: (1) that the amount paid to the association for the right to use its name, logo, and membership list and the amount paid to the taxable subsidiary for marketing services are each at fair market value; and (2) that the arrangement is conducted on an arm's-length basis (e.g., financial separation, employee time records, etc.).

Reducing UBIT and Removing Unrelated Business Information from the Form 990

In some cases, the IRS will only allow a tax-exempt organization to deduct the expenses of the unrelated part of an activity from the income of the unrelated part of an activity. In other words, certain activities (related to an organization's tax-exempt purposes) that generate losses may not be deductible against unrelated business income. For example, advertising income is considered unrelated business income. The IRS applies a complicated formula to determine what expenses of an association's publication can be deducted against the advertising income to compute net taxable income from advertising. In many cases, the formula permits only direct advertising expenses (not other publication expenses) to be deducted from advertising income. This means that a publication as a whole could be losing money, but the tax-exempt organization could be paying substantial income tax on its advertising income, because the expenses that are directly related to the generation of the advertising income are nominal.

If the entire publishing activity is put in a separate taxable entity, all expenses will be deductible from the total revenue generated by the publication to determine whether the publication is operating at a profit or loss. The very same revenue and expenses that can result in significant taxable income when an advertising activity is conducted in a tax-exempt organization can result in little or no taxable income when the entire publishing activity is carried on in a taxable subsidiary.

For political, financial, or other purposes, it may also be desirable for an association to remove some or all unrelated business information from its annual Form 990 returns. In light of the enhanced public disclosure rules (see Section VII) that make it easier for adversarial organizations, members of the media, and other members of the public to obtain copies of associations' Forms 990—but not the tax returns of taxable subsidiaries, which are exempt from the public disclosure requirements—this may be particularly desirable. Note that a section 501(c)(3) organization's Form 990-T (for unrelated business income) is required to be publicly disclosed but a Form 990-T for other types of exempt organizations (including sections 501(c)(4) and (c)(6)) is not a public document.

Protection from Liability

Sometimes new ventures carry potential liability, especially if a product is being sold or other business activity is being undertaken. Common examples include legal claims for breach of contract (including debts), copyright or trademark infringement, defamation, and other tort (injury) claims. Carrying on the activity through a separate legal entity (e.g., taxable subsidiary) can protect the assets of the sponsoring tax-exempt entity from liability, even if the two entities are affiliated.

Segregate Activities Separate from Core Mission

For management, political, legal, or other purposes, it may be advantageous for an association to segregate certain unrelated business activities from its core mission and purposes by transferring the management and operation of such activities into a taxable subsidiary.

2. Choosing the Form of the Subsidiary

In establishing a taxable subsidiary, a parent association may choose from an ever-growing menu of business entities. There are benefits and consequences to the form the taxable subsidiary takes. The most common forms, the C-corporation and the LLC, are discussed below.

C-Corporations

A for-profit subsidiary may be created in the traditional corporate form, called a C-corporation. For-profit business corporations are typically the most common corporate form for taxable subsidiaries of nonprofit organizations. A corporation provides the tax-exempt organization with a shield against liability for the activities of the subsidiary and enables the organization to wholly own the subsidiary by holding all of its stock or to partially own the subsidiary by holding a majority of its stock. The tax-exempt parent may capitalize a corporate subsidiary through a transfer of cash and assets to the subsidiary in exchange for subsidiary stock that is issued. The parent can then receive tax-free dividends on this stock from the subsidiary.

The primary benefit of a corporation in comparison to an LLC or other entity is the ability to raise capital through stock, which tends to be a more convenient and familiar mechanism for potential investors. Limited liability companies do not issue stock. However, the C-corporation form also comes with greater restrictions in terms of governance. As a corporation, the subsidiary would need to comply with the corporate law of its state of incorporation, which requires articles of incorporation, bylaws, a board of directors, and voting procedures. It can be burdensome to hold separate board meetings, maintain separate financial records and time sheets, allocate joint program expenses and overhead, and utilize separate letterhead stationery, among other administrative requirements. In addition, if there will be investors other than the parent exempt organization, there may be costs and delays associated with complying with any applicable securities laws.

LLCs

A limited liability company (LLC) is a type of business entity that, similar to a corporation, shields its owners from legal liability. An LLC has one or more members and is generally governed by an operating agreement. The exempt organization can own the subsidiary as the sole member of the

LLC. Alternatively, if the exempt organization were to conduct its activities in conjunction with another established entity, an LLC may have multiple members. To maintain control over a multiple-member LLC, the exempt organization should be named as the controlling member in the LLC's operating agreement and be provided with a larger share of membership.

LLCs may be disregarded for federal tax purposes, taxed as a partnership, or separately taxed as a corporation. A single-member LLC may be disregarded for federal tax purposes. Disregarded LLCs are considered a branch or division of its member/owner for federal tax purposes. The exempt owner must report the operations and finances on the exempt organization's annual information return as though the activities of the LLC were carried on by the exempt organization itself. Although the member/owner is not liable for legal claims against the LLC, the IRS does attribute the disregarded entity's activities to its exempt owner for purposes of determining whether the exempt owner is in compliance with its tax exemption requirements. Based on this, there is no tax benefit to establishing a disregarded LLC to operate a taxable activity. All net income from the LLC that is passed through to the exempt owner will be subject to tax as unrelated business income. In addition, if the activities of the disregarded LLC are not related to the parent's exempt purposes and are substantial, in comparison to the parent's total activities, such activities could jeopardize the owner's exempt status. Instead, a disregarded LLC is an appropriate choice if the exempt owner is conducting an activity that is related to its exempt purposes but may result in exposure to legal liability. Thus, disregarded LLCs are beneficial where an organization wishes to limit its potential liability for conducting activities which are related to its charitable mission.

An LLC that has more than one member may be taxed as a partnership or as a corporation. The IRS will automatically classify an LLC with a single member as a disregarded entity, and it will classify an LLC with two or more members as a partnership for federal income tax purposes. However, if an LLC wishes to be taxed as a corporation, it must make a specific election to be taxed as a corporation. Once the LLC makes this election, it will be treated as a corporation for tax purposes, and the activities of the LLC will not be attributed to the exempt parent organization for tax purposes. Furthermore, as a separate corporate entity, the separately taxed LLC will also provide a shield from legal liability. Therefore, a separately taxed LLC may be an appropriate corporate form to establish in the event that the nonprofit organization wants to shield itself from both tax and legal liability, but does not want to issue stock.

3. Establishing the Subsidiary

To establish a taxable subsidiary:

- articles of incorporation or other documents are filed with a state government, as required by state law for the type of entity being formed;

- if the subsidiary's principal place of business will be located in a state different than the state of incorporation, then a certificate of qualification to transact business in the other state is obtained from that state's government;
- a federal employer identification number (EIN) is obtained from the IRS (even if the subsidiary will have no employees);
- bylaws are created and approved by the subsidiary's board of directors; and
- a corporate record book and corporate seal are obtained, if applicable.

Certain of these filings are subject to filing fees. The subsidiary must file annual reports with the state in which it is incorporated, as well as with any state(s) in which it has qualified to transact business. Furthermore, the subsidiary must file annual federal and state tax returns and pay annual federal and state taxes, like all other taxable entities, to the extent that it generates taxable income.

A separate bank account, separate financial books and records, separate business stationery, etc., must be established for the subsidiary, and strict financial and operational separation must be maintained (e.g., no commingling of assets, no subsidiary correspondence written on parent letterhead stationery).

In the case of a corporate subsidiary, the board of directors of the subsidiary should be appointed by the parent (i.e., by the parent's board of directors); the subsidiary's officers are then usually appointed by the subsidiary's board. The directors and officers of the subsidiary should be somewhat different from those of the parent (see "Common Directors" and "Shared Officers and Employees" in Section III.G.4.). An initial meeting of the subsidiary's board of directors, separate from a meeting of the parent's board, must be held, and separate minutes must be recorded (although the subsidiary's board can meet on the same date and at the same place as the parent's board, with one meeting immediately following the other).

The subsidiary can have its own employees (as long as withholding and other employer obligations are met) or the parent's staff can work on subsidiary matters with their services in essence leased to the subsidiary (see "Shared Officers and Employees" in Section III.G.4.). In the latter scenario, which is the more common approach (at least initially), the subsidiary must reimburse the parent, at the parent's actual cost (at a minimum), for the staff time (including salary and benefits) that the parent provides.

The subsidiary can be housed in the parent's existing offices, provided that the subsidiary reimburses the parent, at the parent's cost, for its allocable share of rent, office equipment and supplies, utilities, etc. (see "Shared Facilities and Services" in Section III.G.4.).

The parent and the subsidiary should enter into an arm's-length written agreement covering all aspects of the shared facilities, equipment, supplies, services, and employees (see Model Affiliation Agreement between Association and Taxable Subsidiary in Appendix D).

If necessary, the parent's articles of incorporation and/or bylaws should be amended to permit business endeavors or the establishment of a taxable subsidiary by the parent. A business plan, including attention to the details of financial and legal separation between the parent and the subsidiary, should be prepared and approved by the parent's board of directors.

The name of the subsidiary may include the parent's name, but this is not a legal requirement. If the parent's name is included in the subsidiary's name, the terms of a trademark license should be part of the written affiliation agreement discussed above. Although it is not required, the subsidiary may pay the parent, on a regular basis and at fair market value, a royalty for the right to use the parent's name (and logo, if desired).

Once the subsidiary has been established as a separate, taxable entity, distinct from the parent, it can own property, sue or be sued, be taxed, etc. Obligations incurred by the subsidiary will not become the responsibility of the shareholders (if the entity has shareholders) in the event of a default on those obligations by the subsidiary unless:

- the obligations are guaranteed by the parent;
- the parent itself participates in the subsidiary's policy or activity that gives rise to the obligation (in which event both the parent and the subsidiary may be held responsible); or
- a court or the IRS "pierces the corporate veil" between the parent and the subsidiary, finding that they are not separate and distinct entities, but that the subsidiary is an alter ego or mere instrumentality of the parent.

The latter will generally not occur if the entities maintain strict financial, management, and operational separation.

4. Operating the Subsidiary

A tax-exempt organization may form, own, and receive dividends or profits from a taxable subsidiary that operates a commercial business(es), so long as the taxable subsidiary operates separately and apart from the tax-exempt organization and the tax-exempt organization continues to engage in its tax-exempt activities. The separate existence of the subsidiary will not be disregarded for tax purposes where it is organized with the bona fide intention of performing some real and substantial business function. The separate corporate form of the subsidiary will be ignored only if the parent corporation controls the affairs of the subsidiary so pervasively that the subsidiary becomes a mere instrumentality of the parent. Courts have determined that a subsidiary will be deemed the alter ego of its parent only where "the facts provide clear and convincing evidence that the subsidiary is in reality an arm, agent, or integral part of the parent."

IRS rulings in this area also indicate that no one factor determines whether a subsidiary will be respected as a separate entity. Instead, the IRS will consider several different factors and reach a conclusion based on their significance taken together. These include whether a valid business purpose exists for forming the taxable subsidiary; whether the parent is involved in the day-to-day management of the subsidiary's affairs; the extent to which the two entities share directors, officers, and/or employees; and the extent to which the two entities share facilities and services. Each of these factors is discussed below.

Business Purpose

A tax-exempt organization generally can easily establish a legitimate business purpose for forming a taxable subsidiary. A tax-exempt organization's establishment of a taxable subsidiary has been regarded by the IRS as valid whenever the purpose was to: isolate unrelated business activities in order to safeguard the parent's tax-exempt status; limit liability; generate funds to support the parent's tax-exempt activities; or facilitate the management of, and separate accounting for, activities unrelated to the parent's tax-exempt purposes.

General Relationship

Most IRS rulings indicate that, in order for the taxable subsidiary to be treated as a separate entity, the tax-exempt parent organization must not be involved in the day-to-day management of the subsidiary. However, the IRS does permit the parent to establish long-range plans and policies for the subsidiary without jeopardizing the parent's tax-exempt status. In addition, as noted below, the parent may provide substantial support to the subsidiary through the sharing of employees and facilities. However, the distinct separate corporate identity of the subsidiary should be made clear to third parties through, for example, the use of separate business stationery and websites and by the subsidiary entering into contracts in its own name (not that of the parent), and signed by one of its own officers, as an officer of the subsidiary.

Common Directors

Ideally, the board of directors of the taxable subsidiary should consist, as much as possible, of persons who are not directors or officers of the parent, even though the parent would elect all of the board because of its (generally) 100 percent voting stock ownership or other control. The fact that all, a majority, or even a substantial minority of a subsidiary's board are not directors, officers, or employees of its parent is often cited as a positive factor in IRS rulings holding that the subsidiary's activities are not attributable to the parent. Thus, for example, the parent could elect representatives of parent member companies that do not currently sit on the parent's board to fill some of the seats of the subsidiary's board. Further, some overlap is clearly permissible, such as giving the current chairman of the board and president of the parent seats on the subsidiary's board. Indeed, under certain circumstances, it is permissible to have substantial overlap between parent and subsidiary directors. Even if most or all of the subsidiary's directors were directors or officers of the parent, the parent's tax exemption would not be jeopardized so long as other factors indicated that the parent was not involved in the day-to-day management of the subsidiary and dealt with the subsidiary at arm's length.

In any event, the parent's board should limit its discussion of the subsidiary to policy (as opposed to day-to-day management) issues, and the parent's and the subsidiary's boards should hold separate meetings and record separate minutes (although the meetings can be held on the same date and at the same place, with one immediately following the other).

Shared Officers and Employees

A more substantial problem would arise if officers of the parent were also officers of the subsidiary. In that scenario, it is more likely that the subsidiary's activities would be attributed to the parent because the overlap between officers tends to show that the parent is managing the subsidiary on a daily basis (since officers, as opposed to directors, are generally charged with more day-to-day management duties). However, where a majority of the subsidiary's board consists of outside directors (i.e., directors other than officers of the subsidiary), overlap of officers between the parent and the subsidiary has been permitted. In addition, as a practical matter, there is a tradeoff between having common directors and common officers; the less the overlap in one category, the more the overlap may be in the other.

Because business expense deductions, including deductions for salaries, are more valuable to a taxable entity than to a tax-exempt organization, there is an incentive for more of the compensation of nonprofit executives to be paid by the taxable entity and less by the tax-exempt group. But as such compensation shifting is subject to reallocation by the IRS to accurately reflect the income of the organizations involved and to prevent evasion of tax, if there is overlap between paid officers, for example, care should be taken to ensure that compensation received by the parent's officers for services to the parent is paid solely by the parent, and vice-versa.

In addition, compensation from related organizations must be reported on the tax-exempt organization's Form 990 when total compensation paid by all related organizations to an officer, director, or key employee of the filing organization exceeds $10,000. A related organization is any entity that (directly or indirectly) owns or controls, or is owned or controlled by, the filing organization, or that supports or is supported by the filing organization. For these purposes, "owns" means holding (directly or indirectly) more than 50 percent of the voting membership rights, voting stock, profits interest, or beneficial interest. "Control" means that:

- more than 50 percent of the filing organization's officers, directors, or key employees are also officers, directors, or key employees of the second organization being tested for control;
- the filing organization appoints more than 50 percent of the officers, directors, or key employees of the second organization; or
- more than 50 percent of the filing organization's officers, directors, or key employees are appointed by the second organization.

Finally, a related organization includes a "supporting" or "supported" organization, whether or not any elements of ownership or control are present.

In contrast to overlapping officers and directors, sharing of employees between the parent and the subsidiary is less of a problem. In a number of situations, the IRS has ruled favorably where the subsidiary contracted with the parent to lease all or some of the parent's employees to the subsidiary for particular services. Charges for any such contract employees must be at arm's length, for example, based on reimbursement of the allocable share of their actual salaries and benefits. This type of reimbursement arrangement generally results in lower payroll taxes than having each employee employed part-time by two separate employers.

It is critical for shared employees to keep detailed, contemporaneous time records of their work for each corporation to substantiate the allocation of costs. If possible, shared employees should be paid at the identical rate when working for the parent or the subsidiary. This would negate any perception that one entity was subsidizing the other, thus demonstrating the absence of an arm's length relationship. Parent and subsidiary employees may participate in the same health and benefits plans if the costs borne by each corporation are proportionate to the respective time worked for each corporation.

Shared Facilities and Services

The parent and subsidiary may share office space, equipment, supplies, and facilities so long as reimbursement is calculated on an arm's-length basis. For example, the parent may sublease office space to the subsidiary at its cost (i.e., pass-through of a pro-rata share of the parent's actual lease payments). A requirement in the sublease agreement that the subsidiary insure its portion of the premises against risk of loss or damage would be a positive factor in demonstrating an arm's length relationship.

The parent also may share equipment, telephones, and supplies with the subsidiary, so long as the costs are allocated fairly and accurately, based on actual usage. Additionally, the parent may provide administrative, data processing, or other nonmanagement services to the subsidiary so long as the fees charged for such services are based on their fair market value.

The parent and the subsidiary should enter into an arm's-length written agreement covering all aspects of the shared facilities, equipment, supplies, services, and employees. (See Model Affiliation Agreement between Association and Taxable Subsidiary in Appendix D.) The agreement should, of course, be adhered to strictly in practice. It is critical that strict financial separation be maintained (i.e., separate financial books and records, separate bank accounts, separate tax returns, and avoidance of any commingling of assets).

If, in the future, the subsidiary's activities grow to the stage where the subsidiary would require significant use of one or more parent employees, it is generally recommended that one or more individuals be made employees of the subsidiary, not the parent. This would help to minimize any risk of jeopardizing the parent's tax-exempt status.

Active Parent Participation in Subsidiary Activities

In addition to the mere instrumentality doctrine, whereby the parent may be held responsible for all of the actions of its subsidiary due to the exercise of excessive parental control over the subsidiary, a parent also can be held responsible for a particular policy or activity of its subsidiary if the parent itself participates in the development or execution of such policy or activity. The parent's liability generally will depend upon the extent of its participation in the policy or activity. In this circumstance, the mere instrumentality rule is unnecessary. The parent will be held responsible for its own participation and the consequences of such participation. This principle has general applicability to association relations with any separate entity, whether or not affiliated, owned, or otherwise related.

5. Taxation of Payments from Subsidiary to the Parent

The discussion above concerned the organizational and operational rules that a parent and its subsidiary must follow to protect the parent's tax-exempt status. The discussion below now turns to the question of whether funds or assets received by the parent from the subsidiary would be characterized as unrelated business income that would be subject to tax.

As stated above, a tax-exempt organization may engage in incidental business activities unrelated to the purposes for which it was granted tax exemption; however, the net income derived from such activities may be subject to tax. The net unrelated income is taxable if the activities constitute a trade or business that are conducted on a regular basis and are not substantially related to the performance (i.e., do not contribute importantly to the accomplishment) of the organization's tax-exempt purposes. Finally, regardless of whether an activity is substantially related to tax-exempt purposes, certain types of passive income are generally excluded when calculating UBIT, including dividends, interest, annuities, royalties, and certain rents.

However, the otherwise-applicable passive income exclusion is not applicable when interest, annuities, royalties, and certain rents are received by a tax-exempt organization from a controlled subsidiary. Code section 512(b)(13) provides that although such interest, annuities, royalties, and certain rents are generally excluded from tax when received by an exempt organization, that exclusion will not apply (and such payments from the subsidiary to the parent tax-exempt organization will be taxable): (1) when the tax-exempt parent owns more than 50 percent, directly or indirectly, of the voting power or value of the subsidiary's stock; and (2) to the extent that the payments reduce the net unrelated income, or increase the net loss, of the subsidiary. This special rule does not apply to dividend distributions from the subsidiary to the tax-exempt parent.

Applying these rules to the common example of a section 501(c)(6) association that establishes a taxable subsidiary, it is useful to identify the various forms of potential payments from the subsidiary to the parent. As noted above, with regard to dividends paid by the subsidiary to the parent, because section 512(b)(13) does not apply to dividend distributions, and because dividends are excluded from UBI as passive income, dividends paid by the subsidiary can be received tax-free by the parent.

With regard to payments by the subsidiary to the parent for administrative services and the leasing of employees, such payments would not qualify as excludable passive income, nor would they usually qualify as payments for services that are substantially related to the performance of the parent's tax-exempt purposes. As such, such payments would be UBI to the parent. However, all or substantially all of such income received by the parent might be offset through the allocation of corresponding costs (deductions reflecting the parent's actual expenditures), resulting in no UBIT liability for the parent.

With regard to payments by the subsidiary to the parent for rent for shared office space and equipment, while rents for such property are often excludable from UBI as passive income, because of the application of section 512(b)(13), if the parent maintained more than 50 percent control of the subsidiary, such rents would be UBI to the parent. However, as explained above (with regard to payments for services and staff), the rental income from the subsidiary for shared office space and equipment is subject to deductions available to the parent, thereby reducing UBIT liability for the parent.

Of course, payments from the subsidiary should be set on an arm's-length basis at fair market value.

If the subsidiary begins to earn considerable net income, it may elect to have dividends paid up to the tax-exempt parent. Dividend payments are excluded from taxation to the parent; such payments are not deductible to the subsidiary. In addition, if the subsidiary were not a controlled entity (i.e., if the parent owned, by vote or value, directly or indirectly, 50 percent or less of the subsidiary's stock), other forms of payments to the parent, like royalty payments, generally would be deductible to the subsidiary and tax-free to the parent. From a practical perspective, however, parent tax-exempt organizations generally insist on holding more than 50 percent of their subsidiaries' stock, and the anti-avoidance constructive ownership rules make prior options, such as second-tier subsidiary ownership, no longer available.

H. AFFILIATIONS WITH OTHER NONPROFITS

In addition to taxable subsidiaries, an association might also consider affiliation agreements or other relationships with other nonprofit entities in order to move certain activities that might be outside their own exempt purposes into a different entity. Affiliation can also be helpful in expanding the geographic focus of the organization, adding additional resources and programs, and finding other fundraising opportunities.

1. Related Foundations

Overview

"Related foundation" is a term typically used to describe an educational, research, or charitable foundation—recognized as exempt under section 501(c)(3) of the Code—that has some affiliation with a trade or professional association, generally through a shared name or acronym, overlapping boards of directors, power to appoint directors, shared office space and employees, and the like. The reason trade and professional associations establish related foundations is to avail themselves of certain advantages available exclusively to section 501(c)(3) organizations.

For the most part, only section 501(c)(3) organizations are eligible to receive tax-deductible charitable contributions; receive many federal and state government grants; receive grants from private foundations without the foundation having to exercise "expenditure responsibility" (thereby facilitating significantly the ability to receive such grants); and qualify for nonprofit postal permits (enabling utilization of significantly reduced nonprofit postal rates). Organizations tax-exempt under section 501(c)(6), on the other hand, can receive dues or other payments that will be deductible to the payor only if they serve a business purpose of the payor and limited by applicable rules related to the association's lobbying and political activities. In addition, only 501(c)(3) organizations:

- are eligible for many state and local sales and use, real estate, and other tax exemptions (in many jurisdictions, only certain categories of 501(c)(3) organizations are eligible for certain state and local tax exemptions);
- eligible to issue tax-exempt bonds (providing for significantly lower financing costs);
- eligible to receive tax-deductible gifts of property;
- able to commence a deferred giving program with the ability to enter into charitable remainder gift arrangements, provide charitable gift annuities, and have a pooled income fund; and

- able to maintain a charitable bequest program for federal gift and estate tax purposes (whereby individuals are encouraged and enabled to make some provision for support of the organization as part of their estate plan).

The funds raised by a related foundation must be used for educational, charitable, or scientific purposes, but very often, the parent association is already carrying on significant educational, charitable, or scientific activities that can be shifted to the related foundation. To qualify for tax exemption as a section 501(c)(3) organization, the related foundation must be organized and operated for educational, charitable, scientific purposes, or other qualifying purposes.

A related foundation may engage in many activities that benefit the industry or profession represented by the parent association as long as that benefit is merely incidental to the foundation's achieving a broader public benefit. Activities like publishing, putting on education seminars and conferences, research, grant making, and the offering of scholarships are examples of activities that related foundations will frequently conduct. The related foundation's activities can be funded by gifts, grants, and program service revenue (e.g., publication sales and conference registration fees).

It is important to note that educational activities need not be educational to the entire public; they can educate a special segment of the public, such as members of a particular trade or profession. However, the educational programs carried on by the related foundation cannot be limited to members of the parent association (the programs can focus on the interests of such members, but access cannot be restricted to association members).

The Operational Relationship

As with any relationship an association maintains with an affiliated entity, strict financial, management, and operational separation must be maintained between an association and its related foundation at all times. This should start, as should all relationships between associations and affiliated entities, with a written affiliation agreement that codifies the relationship between the two organizations. Such a document can and should provide a blueprint for the association and foundation staff and leadership to follow to maintain the requisite separation. It also will serve as the first line of defense in the event the separate corporate existence of the organizations is challenged by the IRS or in court. (See Model Affiliation Agreement between Association and Related Foundation in Appendix E.)

The separate corporate existence of the related foundation will be disregarded by the IRS or the courts—with tremendous adverse consequences for the association, foundation, and foundation donors—if the parent association controls the affairs of the related foundation so pervasively that the foundation becomes a "mere instrumentality" of the parent. This will occur if "the facts provide clear and convincing evidence that the [foundation] is in reality an arm, agent, or integral part of the parent [association]." As discussed previously in this chapter, IRS rulings and court cases in this area also indicate that no one factor determines whether an affiliated entity will be respected as separate. Instead, the IRS and the courts will consider several different factors and reach a conclusion based on their significance taken together. These include whether a valid purpose exists for forming the affiliated entity; whether the parent is involved in the day-to-day management of the affiliate's affairs; the extent to which the two entities share directors, officers and/or employees; and the extent to which the two entities share facilities and/or services.

However, unlike an association's relationship with a taxable subsidiary or other types of affiliated entities, when the affiliated organization (i.e., related foundation) is considered a "supporting organization" under the Code (which most are), a degree of control by the parent association is not only permitted, but is required. In practical terms, while this does not obviate the need to maintain strict financial and operational separation between the entities, it usually means a close relationship and perhaps some overlap between the two boards. As the Code requires (in the case of a supporting organization) that the related foundation be "operated, supervised or controlled by or in connection with" the parent association, the IRS cannot credibly contest the presence of some common directors and officers. Nonetheless, this is a narrow and often ambiguous line that must be carefully negotiated.

In addition to the mere instrumentality doctrine whereby the parent association may be held responsible for all of the actions of its related foundation due to the exercise of excessive parental control over the foundation, a parent association also can be held responsible for a particular policy or activity of its related foundation if the parent itself participates in the development or execution of such policy or activity. The parent association's liability generally will depend upon the extent of its participation in the policy or activity. In this circumstance, the mere instrumentality rule is unnecessary. The parent association will be held responsible for its own participation and the consequences of such participation. This has general applicability to association relations with any separate entity, whether or not affiliated or otherwise related.

Supporting Organizations

In order for the related foundation to qualify as a public charity and achieve the tax benefits accompanying that status, most related foundations established by associations qualify as "supporting organizations." Under Code section 509(a)(3), a supporting organization is an entity which operates exclusively for the benefit of, to perform the functions of, or to carry out the purposes of one or more public charities, and is not controlled directly or indirectly by one or more disqualified persons, other than foundation managers and other than one or more public charities. Supporting organizations fall into one of three categories: 1) organizations operated, supervised, or controlled by one or more public charities (Type I); 2) organizations supervised or controlled in connection with one or more public charities (Type II); or 3) organizations operated in connection with one or more public charities (Type III). Typically, Type I supporting organizations are directly controlled by the parent, in that the parent holds the right to appoint a majority of the supporting organization's board. In the Type II scenario, the supporting organization often shares a majority of its board members with the other organization. Type III supporting organizations have a more informal relationship with the entity they support, as they are operated "in connection with" that entity and there is usually no formal control arrangement.

A section 501(c)(4), (c)(5), or (c)(6) organization, which would qualify as a "publicly-supported charity" under section 509(a)(1) or (a)(2) if it were a section 501(c)(3) organization, is permitted to establish a supporting organization. This means that a related foundation will qualify as a supporting organization if its parent association "normally" receives (i) at least one-third of its total annual revenue from government grants and/or contributions made directly or indirectly from the general public, or (ii) more than one-third of its total annual revenue from government grants, contributions, membership fees, and program service revenue (i.e., from activities related to its tax-exempt functions) and no more than one-third of its total annual revenue from gross investment income, rents, royalties, and taxable unrelated business income. Most associations satisfy the requirements of the latter test.

As noted above, depending on the type of supporting organization, some level of control is required under the Code in order to qualify. As Code section 509(a)(3) requires that the related foundation be "operated, supervised or controlled by or in connection with" the parent association, the IRS cannot credibly contest the presence of some common directors and officers.

2. Political Action Committees

The nature and extent of allowable trade and professional association participation in the federal election process is governed by both federal election and tax laws. Code section 527(f) imposes a tax (at the highest corporate rate, currently 35 percent) on the lesser of an association's direct political expenditures (called exempt function expenditures) and its investment income. Exempt function expenditures are defined as those expenditures made for the purpose of "influencing or attempting to influence the selection, nomination, election, or appointment of any individual to any federal, state, or local public office, or office in a political organization, or the election of Presidential or Vice Presidential electors, whether or not the individuals or electors are selected, nominated, elected, or appointed." Moreover, federal election law prohibits corporations, including associations, from making contributions to or certain coordinated expenditures in support of federal candidates for public office. (FECA does not regulate state or local political activity.) Associations may make unlimited independent expenditures in federal elections, and there is an additional limited exception for partisan political communications made by an association to its members.

Thus, while it is illegal for incorporated associations to use their own funds to make contributions to federal candidates (certain states do permit incorporated associations to use their own funds to contribute to state and local candidates), FECA sanctions the sponsorship by incorporated associations of affiliated (connected) political action committees (also referred to as "separate segregated funds") to solicit funds and make contributions to candidates for federal office.

PACs, which are subject to Code section 527 and are referred to for tax purposes as "political organizations," are not subject to tax on their exempt function expenditures (as defined above) or their exempt function income. PACs are subject, however, to tax on their nonexempt function expenditures and nonexempt function income, if any. Exempt function income includes all amounts received from the following sources (to the extent they are separately segregated only for use as an exempt function): (1) contributions of money or property; (2) membership dues or assessments; (3) proceeds from political fundraising or entertainment events; (4) proceeds from most sales of political campaign materials; and (5) proceeds from bingo games.

Finally, federal election law permits association funds to be used to establish, administer, and solicit contributions from association members for affiliated PACs that direct the funds to federal candidates (so-called soft costs or indirect expenditures). (Note that only association members may be solicited for contributions to an affiliated PAC, and special rules apply where the members are not individuals, such as corporations.) Election law also permits association funds to be used to make partisan political communications to association members (e.g., communications that urge support for or opposition to particular candidates for federal public office). Such association expenditures, which are permitted under federal election law, are not currently taxable under section 527. Note, however, that all such amounts generally must be included in the association's lobbying tax/membership dues nondeductibility calculations, as such expenditures generally will constitute costs in support of participation or intervention in a political campaign on behalf of (or in opposition to) a candidate for public office (see Section IV.A.1.).

PACs are required to file regular reports with the Federal Election Commission. In addition, PACs must file Form 1120-POL with the IRS, and pay the associated tax, for any year in which a PAC incurs any nonexempt function expenditures over $100 or receives any nonexempt function income over $100, subject to certain deductions. Tax-exempt organizations that are not political organizations must file Form 1120-POL with the IRS, and pay the associated tax, for any year in which it incurs any exempt function expenditures over $100, either directly or indirectly through another organization, subject to certain deductions. Note that the amount of such taxable exempt function expenditures by a non-political organization cannot exceed the amount of the organization's net investment income (defined broadly). In essence, non-political organizations (such as associations) are taxed on expenditures that would be nontaxable if made by a political organization (such as a PAC).

The rules governing political activity by both political organizations (such as PACs) and non-political organizations (such as associations) are provided in federal as well as state election and tax laws and regulations. These rules, including those concerning the organization and operation of PACs, are complex, and the sanctions for their violation can be severe.

3. Trusts

A trust is a separate legal entity that is not incorporated. It can be taxable or tax-exempt. It is most often used when the sponsoring organization wants to emphasize a fiduciary responsibility running from the persons in charge of the particular activity to those who will benefit from it. By far, the most common use of trusts in the association arena is in connection with insurance programs. Many association-sponsored insurance programs are carried on through taxable trusts that are legally separate from the sponsoring organization. The trustees hold the premium funds and insurance policies in trust for the benefit of the insureds.

One benefit of using a trust to conduct an insurance program is that courts have sanctioned the application of the conduit theory of taxation to insurance trusts. This means that the premium dollars that flow from the insureds through the trust to the insurance company are not treated as taxable income to the trust. Only administrative fees and investment earnings are taxable to the trust. Although the conduit theory is theoretically applicable to corporations, it has not been as commonly applied to corporations as it has been to trusts. Most sponsoring organizations choose to take the safer approach and utilize a trust structure when they plan to rely on the conduit theory of taxation.

4. Chapters

National associations frequently establish or encourage the establishment of regional, state, and local chapters (or other subdivisions) to carry out their mission at the local level. Similarly, many state associations often do the same with respect to local chapters (or other subdivisions). However, the legal form and structure of such chapters, and their relationship with the central organizations, can vary. Use of the term "chapter" does not necessarily connote any particular legal form or structure.

Some associations establish chapters as mere local offices of the national (or state) association. Under this scenario, the chapters are all part of a single legal entity. The income and expenses of all chapters are consolidated with the central organization and treated as one entity. The assets and liabilities of the chapters similarly are the assets and liabilities of the entire legal entity, including the central organization. This structure is less frequently utilized in the association community for the principal reason that the central organization is liable for all acts and omissions of the chapters.

A more common structure is whereby the chapters are separate legal entities—often as incorporated organizations; sometimes as unincorporated associations—but are affiliated with the central organization in some manner. Under this structure, the assets and liabilities of each chapter generally remain their own. In most circumstances, the central organization will not be liable for the acts and omissions of its chapters. Chapters can be required to apply for tax exemption on their own (if such application is necessary and advisable), or they can achieve tax exemption through a group exemption maintained by the central organization (see Section I.D.). Similarly, chapters can be required to file their own annual information returns (if such returns are required), or a group return can be filed for all chapters covered by a group exemption (see Section I.D.5.).

Under this structure, because the chapters are separate legal entities, it is important for the central organization to exercise certain controls and limits on chapter activities (without the chapters becoming mere instrumentalities of the central organization, thereby risking a piercing of the corporate veil between the central organization and its chapters). Consequently, it is advisable for the central organization to enter into a written affiliation agreement with each of its chapters that codifies the nature of the relationship; imposes controls and limits on chapter activities and governance; provides a limited, revocable license for the chapter to use the central organization's name; and defines conditions under which the affiliation may be revoked, among other provisions (see Model Chapter Affiliation Agreement in Appendix F). As part of such an affiliation agreement, it also is advisable to require the chapters to adopt model articles of incorporation and/or bylaws provided by the central organization, and to require central organization approval prior to any subsequent amendments to such documents by the chapters.

IV

Lobbying and Political Activities

A. OVERVIEW OF LOBBYING TAX LAW FOR 501(C)(6) ENTITIES

1. Nondeductibility of Membership Dues to 501(c)(6) Entities Engaged in Lobbying and Political Activities

Associations exempt under section 501(c)(6) that engage in lobbying and political activities are subject to special notice, reporting, and tax obligations under sections 162(e), 6033(e), and applicable Treasury Regulations.

Section 162(e) disallows taxpayers from deducting expenses incurred in connection with federal and state lobbying or in connection with any political campaign intervention activities as ordinary and necessary business expenses. Tax deductibility also is disallowed by this law for a portion of membership dues paid to an association if the association spends more than minimal amounts on those activities.

Under section 6033(e), an association that incurs lobbying and political expenditures must advise members at the time of dues assessment or payment what portion of their dues is nondeductible, and it must annually report to the IRS regarding lobbying and political expenditures and dues nondeductibility. As an alternative to notifying members of dues nondeductibility, an association can pay at the end of the year a flat 35-percent proxy tax on its annual lobbying and political expenditures.

2. In-house Lobbying Exception of $2,000

The exception for minimal lobbying expenditures is narrowly tailored. It exempts associations from the dues nondeductibility (or proxy tax) provisions only if in-house expenditures on direct lobbying are $2,000 or less annually. Direct lobbying expenditures include expenditures incurred in connection with attempting to influence certain public officials with regard to federal or state legislation or federal executive branch actions (see Section IV.B.1. below for a more detailed description of each of these categories of lobbying). In determining whether the association has in-house expenditures under the $2,000 threshold, the association must include costs for staff time and materials, but is not required to include any general overhead costs. Amounts paid to engage outside lobbyists or lawyers, dues or other payments made to other organizations that lobby, grassroots lobbying expenditures, political expenditures, and foreign lobbying expenditures do not qualify for this $2,000 exception; any amount of such expenditures triggers the dues nondeductibility (or proxy tax) provisions.

3. Determination of Lobbying and Political Expenditures

The key to a section 501(c)(6) association's compliance with the lobbying tax law is to determine the association's nondeductible lobbying and political expenditures under Code section 162(e), which will affect the amount of either members' dues that is non-deductible or the proxy tax. The categories of lobbying and political activities that are nondeductible under Code section 162(e) and other information necessary to make such determinations are described in greater detail in Section IV.B. below.

4. "Paid" Volunteers

The costs of "paid" volunteers to associations are allocated to whomever makes the payments. If the association pays the volunteers (such as reimbursing them for their travel and other expenses), the costs are attributed to the association. If the volunteers' employers pay them (such as for salaries as well as their expenses), the costs are attributable to the employers, not to the association.

5. Cost Allocation Methods

Treasury Regulations provide detailed guidelines for allocating an association's costs to lobbying, including three illustrative, but not mandatory, cost allocation methods. The regulations also expressly permit the use of any reasonable cost allocation method. To be reasonable, the method must (1) be consistently applied; (2) allocate a proper amount of costs to lobbying activities (including labor costs, general and administrative costs, and outside third-party costs); and (3) be consistent with the specific rules provided in the regulations for de minimis activities. Of particular note is a de minimis rule that staff time spent on lobbying activities may be considered zero if it is less than 5 percent of that person's total overall time (although employees' direct contact lobbying time (defined to include meetings, telephone conversations, letters, and other similar means of communication) may not be apportioned to the 5 percent). Note also that if an association uses either the "Ratio" or the "225% Gross-Up" cost allocation method set forth in the regulations, then it may treat as zero the lobbying labor hours of staff engaged in secretarial, clerical, support, or other administrative activities that do not include significant judgment with respect to lobbying.

6. Membership" Dues and Similar Amounts

Once lobbying expenditures and the additional costs are determined, they are allocated to dues income from association members to determine the percentage of members' dues that are nondeductible, or, alternatively, they provide the basis for the 35 percent proxy tax. The IRS has offered these definitions with respect to dues and similar amounts to which lobbying expenditures are allocated.

- *Annual dues:* The amount an organization requires a person, family, or entity to pay to be recognized by the organization as a member for an annual period.
- *Similar amounts:* (1) voluntary payments made by persons, families, or entities; (2) assessments made by the organization to cover basic operating costs; and (3) special assessments imposed by the organization to conduct lobbying activities. Note that voluntary payments are not limited to those from members, but special assessments are limited to those made for lobbying activities.
- *Member:* Not limited to those with voting rights in the organization.

7. Reporting to the IRS

An association must report annually to the IRS the total amount of lobbying and political activities expenditures incurred by the association and the total amount of dues and similar income received by the association to which the lobbying expenditures are allocable. Lobbying expenditures incurred in a year are allocated against dues and similar income received during the same year. If lobbying expenditures exceed dues and similar income, the excess is carried forward to increase dues nondeductibility for future years.

8. Notification to Members

In addition to IRS reporting, the association must advise members (and other contributors) of dues nondeductibility. The association must provide a notice to each person, family, or entity making payments of dues or similar amounts at the time of assessment or payment (e.g., on the dues invoice, on a dues receipt) of the portion of the dues or similar amounts that the association reasonably estimates will be nondeductible as ordinary and necessary business expenses due to lobbying and political expenditures. The notice must be in a conspicuous and easily recognizable format. If included on a dues invoice or other solicitation, the lobbying nondeductibility notice should be combined with a statement that contributions to the association are not tax deductible as charitable contributions, as described in Section VII.B.1.

9. Underestimation and Overestimation of Lobbying Expenditures

If the dues nondeductibility amount for which notice is provided proves to be too low, the association must pay the 35-percent proxy tax on the deficiency balance or seek IRS permission to carry forward the underestimated amount to future years' nondeductibility notices. With respect to overestimated lobbying expenditures, the legislative history to the Omnibus Budget Reconciliation Act of 1993 (the Act by which Congress created section 6033(e) requiring associations to either provide notice to members of dues nondeductibility or pay the proxy tax) directs the Treasury Department to issue regulations governing the treatment of associations that incur actual lobbying expenditures below the estimated amount. To date, such regulations have not been proposed or issued.

10. Elective Proxy Tax

As an alternative to disclosing what portion of dues is nondeductible because of lobbying expenditures, the association may elect to pay a proxy tax on the total amount of its lobbying expenditures (up to the amount of dues and similar payments received by the association) during the year. Any excess of lobbying expenditures over dues and similar payments is carried forward to the next year. The proxy tax is payable at the highest corporate income tax rate of 35 percent and reportable on Form 990-T, otherwise used as a tax return for unrelated business income taxation.

11. Relationship to Tax on Political Activities

In addition to being nondeductible, political activity expenditures incurred by associations are taxable. As described below in Section IV.D.3, Code section 527(f) imposes a tax at the highest corporate rate (currently 35 percent) on either the amount of the association's political expenditures or the amount of the association's net investment income during the tax year, whichever is less.

When calculating and reporting to the IRS the percentage of member dues that are nondeductible under Code section 6033(e), the association does not include any amounts on which tax is imposed by reason of Code section 527(f). In other words, if the association is required to pay tax on political activity expenditures, those expenditures are not required to be treated as nondeductible by the association's members.

12. Relationship to Lobbying Disclosure Reporting

In addition to tracking and reporting lobbying activities for tax purposes, associations that engage in lobbying are required to track and report their lobbying activities under applicable federal, state, and local lobbying disclosure laws. For example, at the federal level, registration and reporting is governed by the Lobbying Disclosure Act (LDA). Under the LDA, an association must register as a lobbyist employer if one employee (or more) spends more than 20 percent of his or her time on federal lobbying activities. When registered, the association must submit quarterly reports to Congress regarding its lobbying activities, including the amount spent on lobbying.

LDA definitions of lobbying differ significantly from the lobbying definitions found in the Code (whether those applicable to section 501(c)(6) associations under section 162(e) described below in Section IV.B. or those applicable to 501(c)(3) associations that make the so-called 501(h) election described below in Section IV.C.). For example, unlike applicable Code definitions, the LDA applies only to federal lobbying; state and grassroots lobbying activities are not included. Additionally, the LDA applies to a broader swath of federal executive branch lobbying than does the Code.

To simplify an LDA-registered association's record keeping, the LDA permits the association for most LDA reporting purposes to track and report its lobbying activities and expenses for its quarterly reports to Congress using applicable tax code definitions instead of the LDA definitions. If an association elects to use the tax code definitions for LDA reporting, it must do so consistently for all LDA reports covering a full calendar year. The association must also report all expenses that fall within the applicable tax code definition of lobbying, including for state and grassroots lobbying, even though such activities are not considered lobbying under the LDA. Associations that choose to report using the tax code definitions and that have significant expenses on state and grassroots lobbying may therefore end up over-reporting their actual federal lobbying expenses as defined by the LDA. Associations that are sensitive to such over-reporting may prefer to forgo the administrative simplification of tracking and reporting under the tax code alone and instead track and report such activities and expenses separately under each set of applicable definitions.

B. DETERMINING 501(C)(6) LOBBYING EXPENDITURES UNDER CODE SECTION 162(E)

1. Categories of Nondeductible Lobbying and Political Activities

Code section 162(e) defines five categories of lobbying and political activities for which expenditures may not be deducted as ordinary and necessary business expenses.

- *Influencing legislation:* any attempt to influence legislation through communication with (1) any member or employee of Congress; (2) any member or employee of a state legislature; or (3) any federal or state government official or employee who may participate in the formulation of legislation.
- *Grassroots lobbying:* any attempt to influence the general public, or segments thereof, with respect to elections, legislative matters, or referenda. This includes urging association members to engage in grassroots lobbying.
- *Communications to covered federal executive branch officials:* any direct communication with a covered federal executive branch official in an attempt to influence the official actions or positions of such official, including regulatory, administrative, or any other official actions or positions. Covered federal executive branch officials include:
  - the President;
  - the Vice President;
  - any employee of the White House Office of the Executive Office of the President;
  - the two most senior officers of each of the other agencies in the Executive Office of the President (e.g., Office of Management and Budget, United States Trade Representative, Council of Economic Advisers, National Security Council);
  - any individual (and his or her immediate deputy) serving in a position in level I of the Executive Schedule (e.g., Secretary of Commerce, Secretary of Labor, other cabinet secretaries); and
  - any other individual (and his or her immediate deputy) designated by the President as having Cabinet-level status (i.e., White House Chief of Staff; Ambassador to the United Nations, Council of Economic Advisers Chairman, Office of National Drug Control Policy Director, and Environmental Protection Agency Administrator). All other federal executive branch officials and employees are not covered under this category (e.g., Food and Drug Administration Commissioner, Federal Trade Commissioners, Assistant Attorney General for Antitrust).
- *Political activities:* any activity that constitutes participation or intervention in any political campaign on behalf of (or in opposition to) any candidate for public office at the federal, state, and/or local level. (Note that campaign contributions made by an association's affiliated PAC are considered to be made by a separate entity under the tax laws, and thus do not count toward the association's calculation of nondeductible expenditures.) However, the administrative costs incurred by the association to maintain and solicit contributions

to the PAC are expenditures incurred by the association and must be included. This also includes any costs incurred by the association to make partisan political communications to its members.

- *Supporting activities:* any research, preparation, planning, and coordination (including deciding whether to make a lobbying communication) engaged in for a purpose of making or supporting a lobbying communication or political activity (as defined above) is treated as carried out in connection with such communication or activity. In other words, the time spent on any background activity engaged in for a purpose of supporting future planned lobbying communications or political activities also must be counted.

In addition, no deduction is allowed under Code section 162 for expenses incurred in connection with international lobbying.

2. Definitions: Influencing Legislation and Related Terms

Treasury Regulations provide a definition of the term "influencing legislation," as well as relevant related terms.

- *Influencing legislation:* (1) any attempt to influence any legislation through a lobbying communication; and (2) all activities, such as research, preparation, planning, and coordination (including deciding whether to make a lobbying communication), engaged in for a purpose of making or supporting a lobbying communication, even if not yet made.
- *Attempt to influence legislation:* the making of a lobbying communication and all activities such as research and preparation engaged in for a purpose of making or supporting a lobbying communication.
- *Lobbying communication:* any communication (other than that compelled by subpoena or otherwise compelled by federal or state law) with any member or employee of a legislative body or any other government official or employee who may participate in the formulation of legislation that (1) refers to specific legislation and reflects a view on that legislation; or (2) clarifies, amplifies, modifies, or provides support for views reflected in a prior lobbying communication.
- *Legislation:* any action with respect to acts, bills, resolutions, or other similar items by a legislative body. Legislation includes a proposed treaty that requires Senate ratification from the time the president's representative begins to negotiate with the prospective parties to the treaty.
- *Specific legislation:* among other things, this includes a specific legislative proposal that has not been introduced in a legislative body.

- *Legislative body:* Congress, state legislatures, foreign legislatures, and other similar governing bodies, excluding local councils (and similar governing bodies) and executive, judicial, or administrative bodies.

Lobbying or Education?

The regulations explicitly reject the creation of a distinction between influencing legislation and educating legislators; the same basic rules and definitions outlined above apply in determining whether or not educating a legislator constitutes influencing legislation in a given circumstance.

Balanced Analysis of Legislation

The regulations explicitly reject an exception from lobbying for presenting a balanced analysis of the merits and defects of legislation, and they clarify that a view on legislation can be reflected implicitly; support or opposition to legislation does not have to be explicitly stated.

3. Purpose for Engaging in an Activity

The regulations provide that an attempt to influence legislation means a lobbying communication and all activities such as research and preparation engaged in *for a purpose* of making or supporting a lobbying communication. The purpose test looks to the original intent for engaging in a given activity to determine whether it will be deemed a lobbying activity, in whole or in part. Because purpose is essentially a state of mind and a subjective judgment, it is often difficult to prove or disprove through documentation. Recognizing the difficulty of quantifying purpose, the regulations provide a list of facts and circumstances to be considered in making the purpose determination. The purpose or purposes for engaging in an activity are to be determined based on all the facts and circumstances, including, but not limited to:

- whether the activity and the lobbying communication are proximate in time;
- whether the activity and the lobbying communication relate to similar subject matter;
- whether the activity is performed at the request of, under the direction of, or on behalf of a person making the lobbying communication;
- whether the results of the activity are also used for a nonlobbying purpose; and
- whether, at the time the association engages in the activity, there is specific legislation to which the activity relates.

4. Multiple-Purpose Activities

If an association engages in an activity for both lobbying and nonlobbying purposes, it must treat the activity as engaged in partially for a lobbying purpose and partially for a nonlobbying one. The division of the activity must result in a reasonable allocation of costs (e.g., staff time) to lobbying. An allocation will not be reasonable if it allocates to lobbying (1) only the incremental costs (e.g., staff time) that would not have been incurred but for the lobbying purpose; or (2) an amount based solely on the number of purposes for engaging in that activity without regard to the relative importance of those purposes. The regulations state that as long as the relative importance of the various purposes is reflected, the allocation need not be precise.

5. Activities Having No Lobbying Purpose

The regulations provide that the following activities may be treated as having no lobbying purpose:

- determining the existence or procedural status of specific legislation, or the time, place, and subject of a legislative hearing on specific legislation;*
- preparing routine, brief summaries of specific legislation;*
- performing an activity required by law;
- reading any publications available to the general public or viewing or listening to other mass media communications; and
- merely attending a widely attended speech.

6. Communications with Members

If an association communication urges members, either explicitly or implicitly, to contact their legislators concerning a specific piece of legislation (e.g., a legislative action alert), the cost of the communication must be treated as lobbying. Communications that merely inform members about the details or status of legislation do not have to be treated as lobbying, if the communication can be considered a routine, brief summary of legislation or its status, *and* if the association has not yet evidenced a purpose to influence that legislation (either through association staff or members acting on the association's behalf). However, once such a lobbying purpose is evidenced by the association, all subsequent (but not prior) communications to members on that issue, even those that merely provide routine, brief summaries of the legislation or its status, must be treated as lobbying. As with any activity, if the communication (e.g., newsletter) has

* Note that the first two activities above apply only if they occur *before* the association evidences a lobbying purpose with regard to the specific legislation at issue.

nonlobbying purposes as well (as many do), then a reasonable allocation of costs may be made between the lobbying and nonlobbying purposes.

7. De Minimis Rules for Labor Hours

The regulations provide two de minimis rules for disregarding certain minimal amounts of association staff time spent on lobbying activities:

- An association may treat time spent by staff on lobbying activities as zero if less than 5 percent of the employee's total overall time is spent on lobbying activities. Reasonable methods may be used to determine if lobbying time constitutes less than 5 percent of an employee's total time. However, any time spent by any association employee on direct contact lobbying (including the allocable travel time related to the direct contact lobbying) may not be excluded under the de minimis rule. Notwithstanding direct contact lobbying, the de minimis rule may still exclude other time spent by that employee on nondirect contact lobbying if it is less than 5 percent of his or her total time. Direct contact lobbying is defined as a meeting, telephone conversation, letter, or other similar means of communication with a federal or state legislator or covered federal executive branch official that otherwise qualifies as a lobbying activity (e.g., reflects a view on specific legislation). The regulations specify that a person who engages in research, preparation, or other background activities related to direct contact lobbying is not engaged in direct contact lobbying.
- An association may treat as zero the lobbying labor hours of staff engaged in secretarial, clerical, support, or other administrative activities that do not involve significant judgment with respect to lobbying. Note, however, that this de minimis rule is *only* available when used in connection with either of two of the specified cost allocation methods set forth in the regulations, the "Ratio" method and the "225% Gross-Up" method.

C. OVERVIEW OF 501(C)(3) LOBBYING RESTRICTIONS

To maintain their 501(c)(3) tax-exempt status, these organizations must avoid all political campaign activities and must keep lobbying within permissible limits. While there is an absolute prohibition on 501(c)(3) organizations participating or intervening in any political campaign on behalf of or in opposition to candidates for public office, 501(c)(3) organizations can engage in a relatively significant amount of lobbying activity if carefully conceived and managed.

1. The Lobbying Election

The definition of activities considered to constitute lobbying, as well as the extent to which a 501(c)(3) organization may conduct such activities before incurring penalties, varies depending on whether the organization has chosen to make the lobbying election under section 501(h) of the Code. Most informed 501(c)(3) organizations that lobby choose to make the election, and, consequently, are governed by a special "expenditures" test, rather than the "substantiality" test governing non-electors.

In stark contrast to the very vague and sparse rules governing non-electors, the expenditures test provides mathematical methods to concretely determine the extent to which an electing organization may engage in lobbying without incurring penalty taxes or losing 501(c)(3) status. Congress enacted the expenditures test and related rules found in Sections 501(h) and 4911 of the Code to relieve the uncertainty of the substantiality test. The substantiality test prohibits lobbying from becoming a substantial part of a (non-electing) 501(c)(3) organization's activities—with very little guidance as to what constitutes lobbying, what constitutes a substantial part, and with no lesser penalty for violation other than revocation of tax exemption.

Other key advantages of electing are:

- the numerous exceptions provided for what is considered lobbying;
- the imposition of penalty taxes for excessive lobbying instead of the immediate loss of tax exemption;
- a safe harbor (margin for error) for organizations that exceed the lobbying limits in a given year;
- an exclusion for lobbying time donated by volunteers (including board members); and
- a lower IRS audit risk.

The lobbying election is made by filing, at any time, the simple one-page Form 5768 with the IRS. Note that the lobbying election is not available to 501(c)(3) "supporting organizations" that derive their public charity status through their support of a 501(c)(4), (c)(5), or (c)(6) organization that itself meets one of the public support tests. The following rules and definitions apply only to 501(c)(3) organizations that make the lobbying election.

2. Definition of Lobbying

To be considered lobbying, a communication must refer to and reflect a view on specific legislation, which includes legislation that has been introduced in a legislative body (federal, state, or local) and a specific legislative proposal that the organization either supports or opposes, whether or not it has been introduced. Actions by executive, judicial, or administrative bodies (e.g., regulations) are excluded from the definition of lobbying. Lobbying may either be direct or grassroots. Grassroots lobbying is more limited than direct lobbying.

Direct lobbying is any attempt to influence legislation through communication with any member or employee of a legislative body, or with any other government official who may participate in the formulation of the legislation, if the principal purpose is to influence legislation. The communication must refer to specific legislation and reflect a view of the legislation. A communication made to the general public on the subject of a public referendum, ballot initiative, or similar election will be considered direct lobbying if the communication reflects a view on the subject of the vote. Direct lobbying also includes communications by an association to its members directly encouraging them to engage in direct lobbying. When directed solely to members, a communication is not lobbying if it only indirectly encourages members to engage in lobbying.

Grassroots lobbying is defined, except with regard to a limited category of mass media communications (for which specific rules apply), to include only those communications to the general public that (i) refer to specific legislation; (ii) reflect a view on that legislation; *and* (iii) encourage the recipient to take action with respect to such legislation (this third element is often referred to as a "call to action"). It includes communications to members directly encouraging them to urge nonmembers to lobby. An organization generally engages in grassroots lobbying when, directly or through its members, it urges that the public contact legislators, or provides the public with the address, telephone number, or electronic mail address, etc., of a legislator or a petition or tear-off postcard, or even merely identifies legislators who will vote on a particular matter.

For both direct and grassroots lobbying, all costs of researching, preparing, planning, drafting, reviewing, copying, publishing, and mailing a direct or grassroots lobbying communication (including amounts paid as current or deferred compensation for employees' services attributable to these activities) must be counted as lobbying expenditures. The allocable portion of administrative, overhead, and other general expenses attributable to these activities also must be treated as lobbying expenditures. However, if the primary purpose for incurring an expenditure is a nonlobbying purpose (and if the fruits of the expenditure are, in fact, used for such nonlobbying purpose), then no portion of the expenditure needs to be allocated to lobbying. See Section IV.C.5. below for a discussion of the use of nonlobbying material in connection with a subsequent lobbying communication.

3. Exclusions from Definition of Lobbying

Certain activities are excluded from the definition of lobbying for organizations that make the section 501(h) election.

- Lobbying does not include providing technical assistance or advice to a governmental body or committee in response to its unsolicited written request. Note there are two caveats: (1) the request must come from the governmental body or committee, and cannot be merely from an individual member of that body or committee; and (2) the response must be made available to every member of the requesting body or committee.

- Lobbying does not include self-defense activities—communications with legislators concerning decisions that may affect the organization's existence, powers and duties, 501(c)(3) status, or deductibility of contributions.
- Lobbying does not include making available the results of nonpartisan analysis, study, or research (defined as a full and fair exposition of a particular subject that may advocate a view) so long as the presentation of the relevant facts is sufficient to enable readers to reach independent conclusions (e.g., presenting information on both sides of a legislative controversy in a balanced and objective manner). Note there are two caveats: (1) grassroots lobbying communications that directly encourage action do not qualify under this exception; and (2) in order to take advantage of this exception, distribution of studies, reports, etc., may not be limited to, or directed toward, persons interested solely in one side of a particular issue.
- Lobbying does not include examining and discussing broad social, economic, and similar policy issues whose resolution would require legislation—even if such legislation is pending—as long as the organization's discussion does not address the merits of the specific legislation.
- Lobbying does not include communicating with a government official or employee, other than (1) a communication with a member or employee of a legislative body when the communication would otherwise constitute lobbying, or (2) a communication with the principal purpose of influencing legislation.
- Lobbying does not include communications between an organization and its members (broadly defined) about pending or proposed legislation, unless the communications directly encourage the members to attempt to influence legislation (or directly encourage the members to urge nonmembers to attempt to influence legislation). This exclusion will apply as long as a majority of the communication's recipients are members.

Subsequent Use Rule

In certain narrowly defined circumstances, the subsequent *grassroots* lobbying use of "advocacy communications or research materials" (materials that refer to and reflect a view on specific legislation but do not directly encourage recipients to take action with respect to the legislation) may cause the original expense incurred in developing the materials to be treated as a grassroots lobbying expenditure. This could occur most frequently with respect to certain nonpartisan analysis, study, or research reports that are initially created without any accompanying call-to-action messages, but are later used in connection with grassroots lobbying communications. In such event, the "subsequent use" rule may convert the original expense (in its entirety) into a grassroots lobbying expenditure. However, there are two broad safe harbors in which the subsequent use rule will not apply—one relates to the primary purpose of the original materials and the other relates to the timing of the subsequent use.

Under the primary purpose safe harbor, the subsequent use rule will not apply if the organization can demonstrate that the primary purpose of the original materials (i.e., the primary purpose for incurring the original expense) was a nonlobbying purpose. Where the organization makes a substantial distribution of the materials in their nonlobbying form either prior to or contemporaneous with the grassroots lobbying distribution, the IRS will presume a nonlobbying primary purpose. In the case of "nonpartisan analysis, study, or research," whether the distribution is substantial will depend upon the particular facts and circumstances, including normal distribution patterns of similar materials. In the case of other "advocacy communications or research materials," the non-lobbying distribution must be at least as extensive as the grassroots lobbying distribution.

Under the timing of subsequent use safe harbor, the determinative factor is the amount of time between when the organization paid the original expenses and when the subsequent use occurred. All expenses paid more than six months before the subsequent use are protected from the application of the subsequent use rule.

The subsequent use rule will not cause any communications or research materials to be considered *direct* lobbying communications.

4. Limitations on Permissible Lobbying

Under the expenditures test, an organization can quantify exactly how much lobbying it may engage in each year. A sliding scale specifies the amount an organization may expend on all lobbying activities in relation to the amount it spends on most of its other activities (i.e., expenditures in furtherance of the organization's tax-exempt purposes). Under section 4911(c)(2) of the Code, the maximum allowable annual lobbying is the sum of:

> 20 percent of the first $500,000 of an organization's exempt purpose expenditures, plus
>
> 15 percent of the second $500,000 of such expenditures, plus
>
> 10 percent of the third $500,000 of such expenditures, plus
>
> 5 percent of the remainder of such expenditures, with a cap of $1 million in annual lobbying expenses.

On top of this cap, there is a further restriction that an organization may not spend more than 25 percent of its permitted lobbying total on grassroots lobbying.

It is important to note that lobbying expenditures include, among other things, the value of the allocable portion of staff time attributable to lobbying; such salary allocations must be substantiated through the use of time records (see below).

If annual limits are exceeded, a 25-percent excise tax is imposed on the amount of excess lobbying expenditures (i.e., 25 percent times the greater of the amount by which lobbying expenditures exceeded the allowable total limit or by which grassroots lobbying expenditures exceeded the allowable grassroots limit).

An organization's 501(c)(3) status will be revoked only if the sum of total lobbying expenditures or total grassroots lobbying expenditures over a four-year period exceeds 150 percent of the four-year sum of the maximum permissible amounts—a considerable safe harbor. Note that a 501(c)(3) organization that loses its tax exemption because of excessive lobbying or prohibited political campaign activities cannot then convert to a 501(c)(4) organization.

Because the extent of an electing organization's lobbying is measured only by expenditures (and not, for example, by time expended), lobbying efforts by members (volunteers), including unpaid officers and directors, on behalf of an association and for which the association incurs no expense are not subject to any limitation and are not counted toward the association's lobbying totals. If the association incurs expenses (e.g., travel expenses) in connection with its members' lobbying efforts, only those expenses (and nothing more) will be counted toward its lobbying totals.

Affiliated Organizations

The expenditures test contains methods of aggregating the lobbying expenditures of related organizations in order to prevent the creation of numerous entities to avoid the lobbying limitations. Where two or more section 501(c)(3) organizations are members of an affiliated group and at least one of the members has made the 501(h) election, the calculations of lobbying and exempt purpose expenditures must be made by taking into account the expenditures of the entire group. If these expenditures exceed the permitted limits, each of the electing member organizations must pay a proportionate share of the penalty excise tax, with the non-electing members (if any) treated under the substantiality test.

Generally, two organizations are deemed to be affiliated where (1) one organization is bound by decisions of the other on legislative issues pursuant to its governing instruments (e.g., articles of incorporation, bylaws); or (2) the governing board of one organization includes enough representatives of the other (an "interlocking governing board") to cause or prevent action on legislative issues by the first organization. Where a number of organizations are affiliated (such as in the case of certain association-chapter structures), all of them are treated as one group of affiliated organizations. However, if a group of autonomous organizations controls an organization but no single organization in the controlling group alone can control that organization, the organizations are not considered an affiliated group by reason of the interlocking directorates rule.

5. Lobbying Records and Cost Allocation

Under section 501(h), detailed disclosure as part of the annual Form 990 filing and thorough record keeping are required. It is the responsibility of the association to maintain documentation of its direct and grassroots lobbying expenditures. If an activity has mixed (direct and grassroots) lobbying or both lobbying and nonlobbying aspects, the association will be expected to allocate the expenditures, pursuant to the rules set forth below. Employee time records, financial reports, invoices from outside suppliers (e.g., printing bills), postage receipts, and other documentation of expenditures should identify those spent on direct and grassroots lobbying, and should allocate expenditures for mixed lobbying (direct and grassroots) and mixed purpose (lobbying and nonlobbying) activities.

As stated in Section IV.C.2. above, all amounts paid or incurred for, or in connection with, direct and grassroots lobbying communications—including amounts paid or incurred as current or deferred compensation for employees' services attributable to lobbying, as well as the allocable share of overhead expenses attributable to lobbying—are included within the organization's total "lobbying expenditures."

A mixed grassroots and direct lobbying communication must be treated as a grassroots communication except to the extent that the organization demonstrates that the expenditure was incurred "primarily" for direct lobbying purposes, in which case a reasonable allocation must be made between the direct and grassroots lobbying purposes served by the communication.

For lobbying communications that also serve bona fide nonlobbying purposes, there are two alternate allocation rules. Which rule is used depends upon whether the communication is sent primarily to members or nonmembers. The rules are generally more favorable for member communications.

For communications that are sent primarily to bona fide members (i.e., communications sent to more members than nonmembers), the organization must make a reasonable allocation between the amount expended for the lobbying purpose and the amount expended for the nonlobbying purpose. Including as a lobbying expenditure only the amount expended for the specific sentence or sentences that encourage the recipient to action is not considered a reasonable allocation.

For communications that are not sent primarily to bona fide members, all costs attributable to the lobbying portion and to those parts of the communication that are on the same specific subject as the lobbying message must be included as lobbying expenditures. Whether a portion of a communication is on the same specific subject as the lobbying message will depend upon the surrounding facts and circumstances. In general, a portion of a communication will be on the same specific subject as the lobbying message if that portion discusses an activity that would be directly affected by the legislation that is the subject of the lobbying message. Moreover, discussion of the background or consequences of either the legislation or of an activity directly affected by the legislation also will be considered to be on the same specific subject as the lobbying communication.

A transfer of money or property by a 501(c)(3) organization to an individual or entity will be treated as a lobbying expenditure if it is earmarked for that purpose. A transfer of money or property by a 501(c)(3) organization for less than fair market value to a non-501(c)(3) organization that lobbies will be treated as a lobbying expenditure unless it is a "controlled grant" or unless certain other exceptions apply. Also see Section IV.C.6. below regarding transfers by private foundations to 501(c)(3) public charities that lobby.

Relationship to Lobbying Disclosure Act Reporting

As described above in Section IV.A.12., associations that engage in lobbying are required to track and report their lobbying activities under applicable federal, state, and local lobbying disclosure laws in addition to tracking and reporting lobbying activities for tax purposes. At the federal level, registration and reporting is governed by the Lobbying Disclosure Act (LDA). LDA definitions of lobbying differ significantly from the lobbying definitions found in the Code.

To simplify an LDA-registered section 501(c)(3) association's record keeping, the LDA permits the association for most LDA reporting purposes to track and report its lobbying activities and expenses for its quarterly reports to Congress using applicable tax code definitions instead of the LDA definitions of lobbying. The considerations involved in choosing to report under the tax code are similar to those discussed above with regard to section 501(c)(6) organizations. If an association elects to use the tax code definitions for LDA reporting, it must do so consistently for all LDA reports covering a full calendar year. The association must also report all expenses that fall within the applicable tax code definition of lobbying, including for state and grassroots lobbying, even though such activities are not considered lobbying under the LDA. Associations that choose to report using the tax code definitions and that have significant expenses on state and grassroots lobbying may therefore end up over-reporting their actual federal lobbying expenses as defined by the LDA. Associations that are sensitive to such over-reporting may prefer to forgo the administrative simplification of tracking and reporting under the tax code alone and instead track and report such activities and expenses separately under each set of applicable definitions.

6. Private Foundations

Organizations with section 501(c)(3) status that are private foundations are subject to excise tax on any amounts paid or incurred (i) in an attempt to influence legislation, or (ii) in an attempt to influence the outcome of any public election or to carry on certain voter registration drives. The definition of lobbying, and the exceptions thereto, are similar to the definitions and exceptions described above. As long as a private foundation does not earmark a grant for lobbying, it may make a general purpose grant to a section 501(c)(3) public charity that lobbies without incurring penalty tax liability. A private foundation also may make a grant to support a specific public charity project that includes lobbying, as long as the grant is not earmarked for lobbying and as long as it is not larger than the amount budgeted by the grantee for the non-lobbying portion of the project.

7. Conclusion

Associations exempt from tax under section 501(c)(3) must keep lobbying activities within specified limits. Grassroots lobbying is limited more than direct lobbying. To avoid incurring liability for excise taxes or loss of tax-exempt status, care should be taken to ensure compliance with the expenditures test under section 501(h) and to enable such associations to take advantage of the opportunities provided by these rules.

Due to the numerous exclusions from the definition of lobbying for section 501(c)(3) organizations, it is frequently possible, if properly planned and structured, for section 501(c)(3) organizations to conduct all desired government affairs activities within the confines of the 501(c)(3) structure. This option should be thoroughly explored before any significant structural changes are made to an organization—such as the establishment of an affiliated section 501(c)(4) or (c)(6) organization—for the purpose of conducting lobbying activities.

D. POLITICAL ACTIVITIES—TAX LIMITATIONS, LIABILITY, AND REPORTING

1. Section 501(c)(3) Ban on Political Activities

The Code absolutely prohibits 501(c)(3) organizations from engaging in political campaign intervention. Prohibited political campaign intervention includes any activities in support of or opposition to any candidate for elective public office at any level of government (federal, state, or local).

The ban prohibits section 501(c)(3) organizations from, for example, endorsing candidates or making other public statements of support or opposition to a candidate for office, or from sponsoring a federal or state political action committee. Distributing, or even in some cases linking to, statements prepared by others that favor or oppose candidates for elective office also constitutes prohibited campaign intervention. A section 501(c)(3) organization furthermore may not allow a candidate to use the organization's facilities, staff, or other resources (whether monetary or in-kind).

The primary consequence under the Code of engaging in prohibited political campaign intervention is loss of the organization's section 501(c)(3) tax-exempt status. In addition, the IRS may impose excise taxes on the organization, and, in some cases, impose those excise taxes on responsible individual organization managers.

Much has been made of the U.S. Supreme Court's January 2010 *Citizens United v. Federal Election Commission* decision overturning many restrictions on corporate political activities under federal and state campaign finance laws. Specifically, it allowed corporations to make independent expenditures in support of or in opposition to candidates. *Citizens United* did not, however, change the tax code: 501(c)(3) organizations remain prohibited from funding or otherwise engaging in activities in support of or opposition to any candidate for elective public office.

A variety of nonpartisan election-related activities may be conducted by section 501(c)(3) organizations notwithstanding the Code's ban on political campaign intervention. Permissible activities include nonpartisan and unbiased efforts to provide voter education and encourage voter participation in the electoral process (e.g., hosting voting registration drives or candidate appearances or debates; publishing voter guides or candidate questionnaires). Organizations may also continue to discuss and engage in advocacy on policy issues of interest to the organization. Consulting counsel prior to engaging in election-related activities is recommended, as the line between prohibited and permissible activities can be easily crossed if not carefully planned and executed according to IRS guidelines.

Although section 501(c)(3) organizations are prohibited from directly engaging in political campaign intervention activities, a section 501(c)(3) organization is permitted to establish an affiliated 501(c)(4), (c)(6), or other tax-exempt affiliate to carry on lobbying and political campaign activities in which the 501(c)(3) may not directly engage.

2. Section 501(c)(6) Limitation on Political Activities

A section 501(c)(6) organization may engage in political campaign activities in support of or opposition to candidates for elective office without jeopardizing its 501(c)(6) tax-exempt status so long as political campaign activity is not the organization's "primary" activity.

The tax code and regulations do not address how to determine the threshold for when an association's political activity becomes its primary activity. Some practitioners have suggested that "primary" means something less than 50 percent of activities as measured by expenditures, while others have suggested considerably lower or alternative non-expenditure based thresholds. Until additional guidance is provided by Congress or the IRS, whether the primary activity line has been crossed will likely be determined on the facts and circumstances of each case, taking into consideration factors like the nature of all the association's various activities, the resources used in conducting the activities, the time devoted to the activities by employees and volunteers, the purposes furthered by the activities, and the amount of funds received and devoted to particular activities.

The nature and extent of allowable association political campaign activities is governed not only by the tax code but also by campaign finance laws at the federal, state, and local levels of government. Under the Federal Election Campaign Act (FECA) and the campaign finance laws of many states, corporations (which include most associations) are prohibited from using their general treasury funds to make contributions directly to candidates or political committees. FECA expressly allows corporations to participate in federal elections by sponsoring a separate segregated fund (commonly referred to as a political action committee or PAC) through which the association can collect contributions from eligible individuals and distribute funds directly to federal candidates and committees, subject to applicable contribution limits. Sponsorship of a federal or state PAC is permissible political campaign activity for a section 501(c)(6) association under the tax code (though not for a section 501(c)(3) organization). PACs and their tax treatment are described in further detail in Section III.H.2.

After the Supreme Court's 2010 decision in *Citizens United*, discussed above in Section IV.D.1., corporations are now permitted to use general treasury funds to expressly advocate the election or defeat of clearly identified candidates for elective office, provided the communications are made independently of any such candidate (so-called "independent expenditures"). Before *Citizens United*, associations could engage in these types of communications only through a PAC. Although now permitted under campaign finance law, an association interested in directly funding independent expenditures must nonetheless remain careful that political activity does not become the association's "primary" activity to avoid jeopardizing the association's section 501(c)(6) tax-exempt status.

If an association intends to be heavily involved in making independent expenditures in connection with federal elections, it may consider forming an affiliate independent expenditure-only committee or "Super PAC." A Super PAC is generally subject to the same registration and reporting requirements applicable to a regular PAC under federal campaign finance and tax laws, but unlike a regular PAC, a Super PAC may not make contributions directly to candidates. Instead, the Super PAC may raise and spend unlimited amounts from donors (including corporations) on independent expenditure communications.

As discussed in Section IV.A. above and Section IV.D.3. below, expenditures incurred by an association for political activities are nondeductible as ordinary and necessary business expenses under Code section 162(e), and may be taxable under Code section 527(f).

3. Tax on Political Activities Expenditures and Reporting Requirements

As described above in Section IV.A.12., political activity expenditures incurred by associations are taxable. Under Code section 527(f), an association is taxed at the highest corporate rate (currently 35 percent) on either the amount of the association's political expenditures or the amount of the association's net investment income during the tax year, whichever is less.

Taxable political expenditures include expenditures for influencing or attempting to influence the selection, nomination, election, or appointment of any individual to any federal, state, or local public office or office in a political organization, or the election of Presidential or Vice-Presidential electors. If an association sponsors a PAC organized and operated under applicable federal or state campaign finance laws, the PAC's receipts and disbursements are not included in the association's political expenditures for purposes of the Section 527(f) tax. For tax purposes, the PAC is recognized as a separate political organization. Other costs that are not currently taxable include costs incurred by the association to administer an affiliated PAC and expenditures on partisan political communications to association members to the extent such costs are allowable under applicable federal and state campaign finance laws. (Additional information regarding applicable tax and campaign finance laws governing PACs is discussed in Section III.H.2.)

An association must file Form 1120-POL with the IRS and pay any associated tax for any year in which the association incurs taxable political expenditures and has net investment income over $100. (Form 1120-POL is discussed in greater detail in Section VII.A.4.)

V

Intermediate Sanctions

In addition to the private benefit and private inurement prohibitions, which may result in the revocation of an organization's tax-exempt status, the Code allows the IRS to protect an exempt organization's assets from being used for the benefit of the individuals in control by imposing an excise tax (referred to commonly as "intermediate sanctions") on certain individuals who receive excessive benefits. The intermediate sanctions law penalizes insiders of section 501(c)(3) and 501(c)(4) organizations, and those nonprofit managers cooperating with them, who get more out of an organization than they put in. The sanctions are "intermediate" in that they allow the IRS to penalize private inurement through excise taxes without revoking an organization's tax-exempt status.

A. APPLICABILITY

The direct applicability of the intermediate sanctions law is limited to section 501(c)(3) and 501(c)(4) organizations. However, associations exempt from federal income tax under sections 501(c)(5) and 501(c)(6) should be familiar with the law for two principal reasons. First, an association with a related educational or charitable foundation or other affiliated section 501(c)(3) or 501(c)(4) organization may be considered a "disqualified person" for purposes of assessing the excise taxes, which could cause the association itself to be subject to potential excise taxes in the event of "excess benefit transactions" (see Section V.B.).

Second, section 501(c)(5) and 501(c)(6) organizations are subject to the same prohibition on private inurement as their 501(c)(3) and 501(c)(4) brethren (see Section I.B.). Consequently, the guidelines imposed by the intermediate sanctions law as to who is a disqualified person, what constitutes an excess benefit transaction, and how to establish a presumption of reasonableness with respect to compensation arrangements and property sales or rentals, should be considered by section 501(c)(5) and 501(c)(6) organizations in light of the statutory and regulatory prohibition on private inurement. Doing so should help ensure that compensation practices and property sales and rentals will withstand IRS scrutiny.

B. OVERVIEW

An excess benefit transaction is any transaction in which a section 501(c)(3) or 501(c)(4) organization provides an economic benefit to a disqualified person that has a greater value than the reciprocal value received from the person. This includes providing compensation to a person in excess of the value of the services rendered and selling or renting property to a person for less than the property's fair market value. The excess benefit equals the amount by which the value of the benefit received by the disqualified person exceeds the value of the consideration received by the organization.

Intermediate sanctions may be imposed on individuals who receive an excessive benefit from a section 501(c)(3) or 501(c)(4) organization and on any organization manager who knowingly and willfully participated in the transaction. There are two types of excise taxes that may be imposed on disqualified persons who receive an excess benefit. First, there is an "initial tax" that is equal to 25 percent of the excess benefit. In addition to the "initial tax," the person must correct the transaction by undoing the transaction to the greatest extent possible—this is usually accomplished by returning the excessive amount of the benefit received from the organization. If the excess benefit transaction is not corrected before the earlier of the date on which the IRS deficiency notice is mailed for the 25-percent tax or the date on which the 25-percent tax is assessed, the IRS may impose an "additional tax." The "additional tax" is equal to 200 percent of amount of the excessive benefit received by the disqualified person. If the second-tier tax is assessed, the person will be liable for both the 25-percent tax and the 200-percent additional tax. However, if a person is subject to the "additional tax" they will no longer be required to correct the transaction.

In addition to taxing the person who received the excessive benefit, the intermediate sanctions impose a tax on organizational managers who knowingly, willfully, and without reasonable cause participate in the excess benefit transaction. The tax on the organization managers is equal to 10 percent of the excess benefit, but no more than $20,000 for any single transaction. All organization managers subject to intermediate sanctions are jointly and severally liable for the total amount of the tax.

C. DISQUALIFIED PERSONS

A disqualified person is defined as someone who, at any time during the five years preceding an excess benefit transaction, was in a position to exercise substantial influence over the affairs of the organization.

If an individual is a disqualified person, then certain related parties are also considered disqualified persons. These include spouses, brothers or sisters, spouses of brothers or sisters, direct ancestors, direct descendants and their spouses, and corporations, partnerships, and trusts in which the disqualified person has more than a 35-percent interest.

D. SPECIFICALLY INCLUDED

Certain individuals within an organization are specifically deemed to be disqualified persons. These include any individual who serves as a voting member of the governing body of the organization; any individual who has the power or responsibilities of the president, chief executive officer, or chief operating officer of an organization; and any individual who has the power or responsibilities of treasurer or chief financial officer of an organization.

E. SPECIFICALLY EXCLUDED

An employee of the organization is not considered a disqualified person if he or she meets all of the following criteria:

- The person receives less than $80,000 of direct or indirect benefits from the organization for the year (adjusted for inflation);
- The person is not a member of a specifically included category (like those described above); and
- The person is not a substantial contributor to the organization.

F. SUBSTANTIAL INFLUENCE TEST

Determinations regarding the status of persons who are neither specifically included nor excluded from the definition of a disqualified person will be based on all of the facts and circumstances of a particular situation. Facts and circumstances tending to show that a person has substantial influence include the following:

- The person founded the organization;
- The person is a substantial contributor to the organization;
- The person's compensation is based on revenues derived from activities of the organization;

- The person has authority to control or determine a significant portion of the organization's capital expenditures, operating budget, or compensation for employees; and
- The person has managerial authority or serves as a key adviser to a person with managerial authority.

Facts and circumstances tending to show that a person does not have substantial influence include:

- The person has taken a bona fide vow of poverty;
- The person is an independent contractor (e.g., an attorney) who would not benefit from a transaction aside from the receipt of professional fees; and
- The person is a donor who receives no more preferential treatment than other donors making comparable contributions as part of a solicitation intended to attract a substantial number of contributions.

G. ORGANIZATION MANAGERS

An individual can be liable for the 10-percent penalty on organizational managers if he or she is an officer, director, or trustee of the organization, or is a person with powers or responsibilities similar to those of officers, directors, or trustees. Attorneys, accountants, and investment advisers acting as independent contractors are not considered organizational managers. Any person who has authority merely to recommend particular administrative or policy decisions, but not to implement them without approval of a superior, also is excluded.

An organization manager will be considered to have participated in an excess benefit transaction not only by affirmative steps, but also by silence or inaction when the manager is under a duty to speak or take action. However, a manager will not be considered to have participated in a transaction when he or she has opposed it in a manner consistent with the manager's responsibilities to the organization.

Organization managers can avoid the 10-percent penalty if they can show that they did not act willfully or knowingly. They can meet this requirement if, after disclosing all facts to an attorney, they receive a reasoned written legal opinion that a transaction does not provide an excess benefit. This will protect them even if a transaction is later determined to be an excess benefit transaction.

H. ECONOMIC BENEFITS

Certain economic benefits provided to a disqualified person are disregarded for purposes of the excise tax. For example, there is no problem with paying reasonable expenses for board members to attend board meetings (this does not include luxury travel or a spouse's trip). Also excluded are benefits provided to a disqualified person solely as a member of the organization if the same benefits are given to other members in exchange for a membership fee of $75 or less per year.

The payment of a premium for an insurance policy covering a potential excise tax liability is not an excess benefit transaction if the premium is treated as compensation to the disqualified person and his or her total compensation is reasonable.

I. COMPENSATION

Compensation for services rendered will not be considered an excess benefit if it is an amount that would ordinarily be paid for similar services in a comparable situation. The fact that a government body or a court has approved a particular compensation package does not necessarily make it reasonable.

For purposes of the excise tax, compensation includes, but is not limited to, salary, fees, bonuses, severance payments, and all forms of deferred compensation that are earned and vested, whether paid under a tax-qualified plan or not. If deferred compensation is paid in one year for services performed in two or more years, then that compensation will be allocated to the years in which the services are performed.

Compensation also includes all benefits, whether or not included in income for tax purposes, such as medical, dental, life insurance, and disability benefits, and both taxable and nontaxable fringe benefits (other than job-related fringe benefits and fringe benefits of inconsequential value).

An economic benefit will not be treated as reasonable compensation unless the organization clearly indicates its intention to treat it as compensation at the time it is provided. For example, if the organization fails to include compensation or other payments to disqualified persons on a Form W-2 (for employees) or Form 1099 (for board members and other nonemployees) and does not treat the payments as compensation on its Form 990, then the payments will be automatically considered an excessive benefit.

Revenue-Sharing Arrangements

A special rule applies to arrangements that compensate a disqualified person in proportion to revenue generated by the organization. Such compensation may be considered to be an excess benefit transaction even when the proportional amount of revenue shared does not exceed the fair market value of the services provided. This can happen if, at any point, the arrangement permits a person to receive additional compensation without providing reciprocal benefits to the organization. Whether such compensation is an excess benefit will depend on the facts of the individual case, taking into account such factors as the relationship between the size of the benefit provided and the quality and quantity of the services provided, as well as the ability of the party receiving the compensation to control the activities generating the revenues.

J. AVOIDING THE 200-PERCENT TAX

To avoid the 200-percent tax, the excess benefit must be undone to the extent possible. In addition, other steps may be necessary to place the organization in the same position it would have been in if the transaction was made under the highest fiduciary standards.

An excess benefit can be corrected if the disqualified person repays the organization an amount equal to the excessive amount of the benefit received, plus an interest element for the period the excess benefit was outstanding. A correction may also be accomplished, in some situations, by returning property to the organization and taking any additional steps necessary to make the organization whole.

K. PRESUMPTION OF REASONABLENESS

An important "escape hatch" exists that every organization subject to the intermediate sanctions law should endeavor to take advantage of—a presumption that a compensation arrangement or property sale or rental does not confer an excessive benefit (referred to as the "rebuttable presumption of reasonableness" or "rebuttable presumption").

To qualify for the rebuttable presumption, an organization must satisfy three requirements.

- The compensation arrangement or property sale or rental must be approved by the organization's governing body or a committee of the governing body composed entirely of individuals who do not have a conflict of interest with respect to the transaction.
- The governing body or its committee must have obtained and relied upon appropriate data as to comparability prior to making its decision.
- The governing body or its committee must have adequately documented the basis for its decision at the time it was made.

These three requirements are discussed in further detail below.

Conflict of Interest

A member of a governing body or its committee will be treated as not having a conflict of interest if he or she:

- Is not the disqualified person benefiting from the transaction or a person related to the disqualified person;
- Is not an employee subject to the control or direction of the disqualified person;

- Does not receive compensation or other payments subject to approval of the disqualified person;
- Has no financial interest affected by the transaction; and
- Will not receive any economic benefit from another transaction in which the disqualified person must grant approval.

Appropriate Comparability Data

Appropriate comparability data includes information such as compensation levels paid by similarly situated organizations, both taxable and tax-exempt, for similar positions; independent compensation surveys compiled by independent firms; actual written offers from similar organizations competing for the services of the disqualified person; and independent appraisals of the value of the property.

There is a special relief provision for small organizations with annual gross receipts of less than $1 million. For such organizations, the organization will be automatically treated as satisfying the data requirement if it has data on compensation paid by three comparable organizations in similar communities for similar services.

Adequate Documentation

To meet this requirement, the governing body or its committee must have written or electronic records showing the terms of the transaction and the date it was approved; the members of the governing body or committee who were present during debate on the transaction and the names of those who voted on it; the comparability data obtained; and what was done about the members who had a conflict of interest. For a decision to be documented concurrently, records must be prepared before the later of the next meeting of the governing body or 60 days after the final action is taken. Records must be reviewed and approved by the governing body or committee as reasonable, accurate, and complete within a reasonable time period thereafter.

For purposes of this presumption of reasonableness, a governing body is a board of directors, board of trustees, or equivalent controlling body of the organization. A committee of the governing body may be composed of any individuals permitted under state law to serve on such a committee and may act on behalf of the governing body to the extent permitted by state law.

Organizations should note that if a committee member is not on the governing board and the presumption is utilized, then the committee member becomes an organization manager for purposes of the 10-percent penalty. In other words, committee members are treated like members of the governing body if the presumption is rebutted by the IRS.

A person will not be treated as a member of the governing body or its committee if he or she meets with other members only to answer questions and is not present during debate and voting on the transaction.

Finally, organizations subject to the intermediate sanctions law should note that this presumption of reasonableness is only a presumption. The IRS can rebut the presumption if there is additional information showing that the compensation was not reasonable or that the property transfer was not at fair market value. However, satisfying these three requirements should go a long way toward helping organizations avoid further IRS scrutiny in this area.

L. CONCLUSION

It is important to remember that if there is evidence of private inurement (if an organization is not operated exclusively for tax-exempt purposes), then the IRS still has the power to revoke the organization's tax exemption. Whether private inurement rises to a level justifying loss of tax-exempt status will depend on a number of factors, including: whether the organization has been involved in repeated excess benefit transactions; the size of the excess benefit transaction; whether, following an excess benefit transaction, the organization has implemented safeguards to prevent future recurrences; and whether there was compliance with other applicable laws. The intermediate sanctions law permits the IRS to punish nonprofit insiders without imposing the death penalty on the nonprofit organization itself.

VI

Reporting, Filing, Notice, and Disclosure Requirements

A. REPORTING AND FILING REQUIREMENTS

1. Annual Information Returns

Virtually every association exempt from taxation under section 501(c)(6) or section 501(c)(3) is required to file a version of the Form 990 annual information returns with the IRS. Although at one point, organizations were excused from this requirement if they did not normally have annual gross receipts of more than $25,000, now every organization which holds itself out as exempt must make a filing with the IRS, including organizations that have not yet filed an Application for Recognition of Exempt Status, have filed and are awaiting a determination letter, or are self-certifying. Associations exempt under section 501(c)(6) or section 501(c)(3) use IRS Form 990 as their information return. The version of the Form 990 that must be filed by the organization depends on the gross receipts and its assets. Gross receipts are an association's total receipts from all sources during its annual accounting period before subtracting any expenses. Organizations that normally have gross receipts of less than $50,000 per fiscal year are eligible to file the Form 990-N, an eight-question electronic "postcard." An association with gross receipts of less than $200,000 and total assets of less than $500,000 at the end of the fiscal year is eligible to file Form 990-EZ, a two-page return. An organization that does not fit within the threshold income and asset levels to file a Form 990-EZ must file the full

Form 990. If the organization is exempt under section 501(c)(3), it must also complete and attach Schedule A to its Form 990, to provide the IRS with greater detail as to its income, expenses, and activities.

All versions of the Form 990 have the same due date and must be filed on or before the fifteenth day of the fifth month after the close of the association's fiscal year; for associations operating on a calendar fiscal year, that due date is May 15 (unless this date falls on a legal holiday or a weekend day, in which case the due date would be the next business day). Associations can apply for an extension of time to file the return by filing IRS Form 8868 on or before the due date for the Form 990. The Form 8868 can also be filed online for a small fee (for most organizations), or for free for smaller organizations. (For a discussion of group Form 990 returns, see Section I.D.5.)

The IRS imposes significant financial penalties for late filing of returns and a failure to file for three consecutive years leads to revocation of the organization's tax-exempt status, as further explained below.

With respect to the statute of limitations for IRS enforcement purposes, generally, the statute of limitations on assessment of federal tax is three years from the date the return is filed or the last permissible day prescribed by law or regulation for the filing. If an organization (other than a would-be 501(c)(3) organization) determines in good faith that it is tax-exempt, without filing an application for recognition of tax exemption, and files an information return (e.g., Form 990), the filing of such return will initiate the running of the statute of limitations. For organizations that choose not to file an application for recognition of exempt status, the burden is on the organization of ensuring that its determination that it is tax-exempt is made in good faith. (For a discussion of the statute of limitations with respect to unrelated business income, see Section VI.A.2. below.)

Tax-exempt organizations that fail to file a Form 990 for three consecutive years will have their exempt status automatically revoked. The effective date of the revocation will be the day that the third consecutive unfiled Form 990 was due. The IRS publishes on its website a monthly auto-revocation list of the names, addresses, and taxpayer identification numbers of organizations that have been automatically revoked.

Organizations covered under a group exemption may be at risk of losing their tax-exempt status either if the parent or central organization fails to file its own information return for three consecutive years, or if the parent or central organization does not file a group return of the subordinate organizations for three consecutive years (provided that the subordinate organization does not file its own return). Of course, such subordinate organizations remain at risk of revocation if the burden of filing Form 990 rests with them and they fail to do so for three consecutive years.

If an association has its tax-exempt status revoked, it becomes a taxable entity as of the effective date of revocation and may be required to file the Form 1120, U.S. Corporation Income Tax Return, or the Form 1041, U.S. Income Tax Return for Estates and Trusts, and pay tax on its net income.

If a section 501(c)(3) entity is revoked it will also lose its ability to receive tax-deductible charitable contributions.

In order to have recognition of tax-exempt status reinstated, a revoked organization must re-apply by filing the appropriate IRS application for recognition of tax-exempt status (either a Form 1023 for organizations seeking to be exempt under section 501(c)(3) or a Form 1024 for organizations seeking to be exempt under section 501(c)(6) or section 501(c)(4)) and must pay the applicable user fee for filing such form. The Application for Recognition of Exemption must be filed even if the organization would originally have been eligible to self-certify or included as part of a group exemption. Generally, if the application is approved, the re-recognition of tax-exempt status will be retroactive only to the date of filing the Form 1023 or Form 1024 following revocation. Although the IRS initially offered a transitional relief program, under which small organizations that were revoked in the initial rounds of automatic revocation could have their exempt status restored as of the effective date of revocation, organizations now must prove they had a reasonable cause for failing to file the Form 990 returns over the entire three-year period such forms were unfiled to be eligible for retroactive reinstatement, a standard which the IRS has indicated will be narrowly interpreted.

The annual Form 990 (not the Form 990-N or Form 990-EZ) is a long form, consisting of 11 pages in its core form and 16 separate schedules. The form asks a number of questions, including some related to the governance of the filing entity. For example, Section A of Part VI requires an organization to describe the composition of its board, the delegation of certain management responsibilities, and the rights of its members. Section B of Part VI asks whether or not an organization has certain written policies in place, such as a conflict of interest policy, a whistleblower protection policy, a document retention and destruction policy, a policy for setting the compensation of key employees, and a policy to govern joint ventures with taxable entities. Although the IRS does not have specific jurisdiction to require organizations to adopt such policies (which may instead be enforced under state laws applicable to nonprofit organizations), the IRS has stated it views the lack of such policies as indicative of a possible risk of non-compliance with provisions of the Code, such as the prohibition on excess benefit payments for 501(c)(3) organizations.

2. Unrelated Business Income Tax Returns

If an association has gross taxable unrelated business income (UBI) of $1,000 or more during its fiscal year, it must file a completed IRS Form 990-T to report such income and pay any tax due. This obligation is in addition to the obligation to file the annual information return, as described above. An organization with gross taxable UBI of $10,000 or less is only obligated to complete a portion of the return. Like the Form 990, the Form 990-T is due on or before the fifteenth day of the fifth month after the close of the association's fiscal year. An automatic six-month extension can be obtained by filing IRS Form 8868 on or before the due date for the Form 990-T, so long as the estimated tax owed is paid on or before the original due date. An additional extension may be requested by filing a subsequent IRS Form 8868 with Part II completed to request an additional discretionary three-month extension. An association must make quarterly estimated tax payments if it expects its unrelated business income tax for the year (after certain adjustments) to be $500 or more.

The Form 990-T also is used to pay the proxy tax arising under the lobbying tax law (see Section IV.A.10.).

The IRS imposes significant financial penalties for late filing of returns, late payment of taxes, and underpayments of estimated tax.

With respect to the statute of limitations for IRS enforcement purposes, generally, the statute of limitations on assessment of federal tax is three years from the date the return is filed or the last day prescribed by law or regulation for the filing. With respect to unrelated business income tax specifically, the filing of Form 990-T will initiate the running of the statute of limitations with respect to sources of income identified on the form. In addition, the filing of an annual information return (e.g., Form 990) will initiate the running of the statute of limitations if sufficient information is provided to the IRS on the return upon which a tax, if owed, could be computed. In other words, in order to begin the running of the statute of limitations, sufficient information must be disclosed on the information return to alert the IRS to the existence of a potentially taxable source of income, even though the organization chooses to treat the income as tax-free.

3. Employment Tax Returns

All employers, including tax-exempt organizations, that pay wages to employees is responsible for withholding, depositing, paying, and reporting federal income tax, Social Security and Medicare (FICA) taxes, and federal unemployment tax (FUTA), unless the employer is specifically excepted by law from such requirements or if the taxes clearly do not apply.

While exemptions from FICA generally are not available to trade and professional associations or their related entities, wages paid to employees of section 501(c)(3) organizations generally are not subject to FUTA taxes.

The penalties for failure to withhold and pay employment taxes can be severe and can be imposed on individuals responsible for the tax evasion. Specifically, if any person required to collect, truthfully account for, and pay over any employment taxes willfully fails to satisfy any of these requirements or willfully tries in any way to evade or defeat them, that person will be subject to a penalty. The penalty, often referred to as the "100-percent penalty," is equal to the tax evaded, not collected, or not accounted for and paid to the IRS. The term "person" includes an officer or employee of a corporation, or a member or employee of a partnership. However, the penalty will not be imposed on any unpaid volunteer director (member of the board of directors or trustees) of a tax-exempt organization if the unpaid volunteer serves solely in an honorary capacity, does not participate in the day-to-day financial operations of the organization, and does not have actual knowledge of the failure on which the penalty is imposed. This exception does not apply if it results in no one being liable for the penalty.

4. Political Activity Returns

Political organizations (including PACs) must file Form 1120-POL, U.S. Income Tax Return for Certain Political Organizations, with the IRS, and pay the associated tax, for any year in which they incur any nonexempt function expenditures over $100 or receive any nonexempt function income over $100, subject to certain deductions. (See Section III.H.2. for definitions of exempt function expenditures and income.) Tax-exempt organizations that are not political organizations must file Form 1120-POL with the IRS, and pay the associated tax, for any year in which they incur any exempt function expenditures over $100, either directly or indirectly through another organization, subject to certain deductions. Note that the amount of such taxable exempt function expenditures by a non-political organization cannot exceed the amount of the organization's net investment income (defined broadly to include interest, dividends, rents, royalties, and the excess, if any, of gains from the sale or exchange of assets over losses from the sale or exchange of assets). In essence, non-political organizations (such as associations) are taxed on expenditures that would be nontaxable if made by a political organization (such as a PAC).

5. Report of Cash Received

A tax-exempt organization that receives, in the course of its activities, more than $10,000 cash in one transaction (or two or more related transactions) that is not a charitable contribution, must report the transaction to the IRS on Form 8300, Report of Cash Payments Over $10,000 Received in a Trade or Business.

B. NOTICE REQUIREMENTS

In addition to the requirement to notify members as to the portion of their membership dues that is nondeductible as a business expense due to the association's lobbying activities (see Section IV), non-501(c)(3) associations are subject to two other required disclosures. Note that section 501(c)(3) also are subject to the second requirement described below

1. Solicitation of Nondeductible Contributions

All non-501(c)(3) tax-exempt organizations (including section 501(c)(6) organizations) that normally have more than $100,000 in annual gross revenues must include a statement in most solicitations for contributions or other payments (i.e., those solicitations that are part of a coordinated campaign soliciting more than 10 individuals or entities during the calendar year) that payments or gifts to such organizations are not deductible as charitable contributions for federal income tax purposes. The IRS has approved several alternative disclosure statements for use.

- "Contributions or gifts to ASSOCIATION are not tax deductible as charitable contributions."
- "Contributions or gifts to ASSOCIATION are not tax deductible as charitable contributions. However, they may be tax deductible as ordinary and necessary business expenses."

The statement must be:

- in print at least the size of the soliciting message;
- in the first sentence of a paragraph or its own paragraph; and
- included on the message side of any material to be returned with the contribution.

Other rules exist for telephone, television, and radio solicitations.

The statement should be included in all membership applications, dues invoices, conference registration forms, PAC fund-raising letters, and similar documents, and must be made in a "conspicuous and easily recognizable format." The statement also must be included generally whenever an intermediary organization (that normally has annual gross revenues in excess of $100,000) solicits earmarked funds as a conduit for a non-501(c)(3) organization.

Failure by an organization to make the required statement may result in a penalty of $1,000 for each day the failure occurred, up to a maximum of $10,000 for a calendar year. No penalty will be imposed if it is shown that the failure was due to reasonable cause. If the failure was due to intentional disregard of the requirements, the penalty may be higher and is not subject to a maximum amount.

2. Sales of Information or Services Available Free from Government

Tax-exempt organizations that sell to individuals information or routine services that could be readily obtained free (or for a nominal fee) from the federal government must include a statement that the information or service can be so obtained. The statement must be made in a conspicuous and easily recognizable format when the organization makes an offer or solicitation to sell the information or service.

A penalty is provided for failure to comply with this requirement if the failure is due to intentional disregard of the requirement. The penalty is the greater of $1,000 for each day the failure occurred, or 50 percent of the total cost of all solicitations that were made by the organization the same day that it fails to meet the requirement.

C. PUBLIC DISCLOSURE REQUIREMENTS

1. Public Inspection

A tax-exempt organization must make readily available to anyone who requests (for in-person public inspection) its application for recognition of tax exemption (Form 1023 or 1024), along with all materials, such as articles of incorporation and bylaws, submitted in support of the application (with certain exceptions) and all correspondence to and from the IRS in connection with the application (including but not limited to the IRS "determination letter" affirming the organization's tax-exempt status, all questions and requests for information and documents posed to the organization by the IRS, and the organization's answers to such questions and requests for information and documents). A tax-exempt organization also must make readily available its most recent three annual information returns (Form 990 or Form 990-EZ). This includes all schedules and attachments filed with such returns. The organization need not disclose the names or addresses of its contributors when making this information available. In addition, the Form 990-T is subject to the public inspection requirements if the form is for a section 501(c)(3) organization; non-501(c)(3) exempt organizations are not required to make their Forms 990-T available for inspection. In addition, the Form 1120-POL is not subject to these disclosure requirements, nor are the tax returns of any taxable subsidiary(ies). These documents must be made available during regular business hours at the organization's principal office, and at any regional or district offices with three or more employees. Note that these disclosure requirements do not apply to applications for tax exemption (or supporting or related documents, as described above) filed before July 15, 1987, unless the organization filing the application had a copy of the application on July 15, 1987; this exception does not apply to the organization's annual information returns.

2. Requests for Copies

In addition, tax-exempt organizations must comply with requests, made in person or in writing, for copies of such documents. Individuals can request parts of such documents rather than the entire document as long as they identify the specific part they want. An organization is allowed to charge reasonable fees for copying and mailing costs. The fees cannot exceed amounts charged by the IRS (the current fees are $1 for the first page and 15 cents for each subsequent page).

If a request for copies is made in person, it must be satisfied immediately (unless unusual circumstances exist, such as the receipt of numerous in-person requests that exceed the organization's ability to process such requests on the same day, or a request received while the organization's staff are performing special duties such as attending an off-site meeting or convention).

An organization is permitted 30 days to provide the copies of such documents if the request is made in writing. Advance payment for such copies can be required (provided the copies are provided within 30 days of payment), so long as the request for advance payment is made within seven days of receiving the written request for the copies. To protect requesters from unexpected fees, when an organization receives a request in writing without advance payment, it must obtain consent before providing copies that will result in fees of over $20.

An organization must accept payment by cash or money order or by personal check, if the request is made in writing, but the organization is not required to accept other means of payment, such as credit cards. However, an organization is not required to accept personal checks if it permits payment by credit card.

3. Exceptions to Copying Requirements

There are two exceptions to these copying requirements. An organization will be relieved of its obligation to provide copies if:

- it makes the requested documents widely available to the public (e.g., if the documents are posted on the organization's website on the internet or in a similar publicly available database); or
- it receives a waiver because the IRS has determined that the organization is the subject of a harassment campaign by opponents and that a waiver would be in the public interest (i.e., where the IRS determines that the purpose of a group of requests is to disrupt the operations of the organization rather than to obtain information).

Treasury Regulations provide that an organization may, without requesting IRS approval, disregard requests for copies in excess of two per month or four per year made by a single individual or sent from a single address.

4. Subordinate Organizations Covered by Group Exemption

A tax-exempt organization that did not file its own application for tax exemption because it is a subordinate organization covered by a group exemption must, upon request, make available for public inspection, or provide copies of: (1) the application submitted to the IRS by the central organization to obtain the group exemption; and (2) the documents submitted to the IRS for the purpose of including the subordinate organization in the group exemption. If the central organization provides lists or directories of the subordinate organizations covered by the group exemption, the subordinate organization is only required to provide the application for the group exemption along with the page or pages of the list or directory that specifically refers to it.

5. Subordinate Organizations Included in Group Return

An organization that does not file its own annual information return because it is affiliated with a central organization that files a group return in which it is included must, upon request, make available for public inspection, or provide copies of, the group returns filed by the central organization. If the group return includes separate schedules with respect to each subordinate organization, schedules relating to other subordinate organizations may be omitted.

For both applications for group exemption and annual information returns of subordinate organizations, the requester has the option of requesting these documents directly from the central organization.

6. Alerting IRS of Noncompliance with Requirements

If an organization denies an individual's request for inspection or a copy of any such documents, the individual may alert the IRS to the possible need for enforcement action by sending a written statement to the IRS' central tax-exempt organizations office in Cincinnati, Ohio describing the reason why the individual believes the denial was in violation of the requirements.

7. Penalties for Noncompliance

The penalty on the organization for each willful failure to permit public inspection or provide copies of such documents is $5,000 for each information return or application for tax exemption. In addition, responsible individuals of an organization who fail to provide such documents as required may be subject to a penalty of $20 per day for as long as the failure continues. There is a maximum penalty on responsible individuals of $10,000 for each failure to provide a copy of an annual information return; there is no maximum penalty for the failure to provide a copy of a tax exemption application.

D. CHANGES IN OPERATION OR FORM

1. Changes in Operation

An organization's tax-exempt status will remain in effect as long as there are no material changes in the organization's character, purposes, or methods of operation. An organization has the burden of determining whether or not a change of this nature is material or immaterial. A material change should be communicated to the IRS in the organization's next annual information return (e.g., Form 990).

A substantial change in an organization's character, purposes, or methods of operation may result in modification or revocation of the organization's tax-exempt status. In addition, a change in the law may afford the IRS a basis for modifying or revoking an organization's tax-exempt status.

2. Changes in Form

If a tax-exempt organization changes its legal form, such as from an unincorporated association to a corporation, or through reincorporation, it should—and in the case of would-be section 501(c)(3) organizations, must—file a new tax exemption application to establish that the new legal entity qualifies for tax exemption. This is the case even where the organization's purposes, methods of operation, sources of support, and accounting method remain the same as they were in its predecessor's form.

In certain situations, however, such as the merger of one entity into another entity, if the surviving organization's purposes, methods of operation, and sources of support remain substantially the same as they were prior to the merger, a new tax exemption application generally is not required. Notifying the IRS of the merger is required, however, pursuant to the standards described in Section III.B.

If a tax-exempt organization has been liquidated, dissolved, or terminated, it must file its annual information return by the fifteenth day after the fifth month after the change and follow the applicable instructions that accompany the return.

3. Inactivity

If a tax-exempt organization becomes inactive for a period of time but does not cease being an entity under the laws of the state in which it was formed, its tax exemption will not be terminated. However, it will have to continue to file an annual information return (Form 990, Form 990-EZ, or Form 990-N, as applicable) during the period of inactivity.

E. CHANGES IN ACCOUNTING PERIOD

The procedures that an individual tax-exempt organization must follow to change its accounting period (fiscal year) are different from those for a central organization that seeks a group change for its subordinate organizations under a group exemption.

Individual organizations that seek to change annual accounting periods generally need only file an information return for the transition period (the abbreviated fiscal year immediately prior to the commencement of the new accounting period) indicating that a change is being made. However, if the organization has changed its accounting period within the previous 10 years, it must file Form 1128, Application to Adopt, Change or Retain a Tax Year, as an attachment to the transition period return.

Central organizations may obtain approval for a group change in annual accounting period for their subordinate organizations on a group basis only by filing Form 1128 with the IRS Ogden (Utah) Service Center.

Form 1128 must be filed by the fifteenth day of the fifth month following the close of the short period.

F. SUBSTANTIATION AND DISCLOSURE REQUIREMENTS

Organizations that qualify for federal income tax exemption under section 501(c)(3) of the Code have the most favorable tax status, but they also have the most restrictions on their activities. As a trade-off for this preferred status, section 501(c)(3) organizations are banned from engaging in political campaign activities, are limited in the conduct of lobbying activities, are subject to penalty taxes on certain transactions with insiders, are subject to additional reporting in connection with their annual Form 990 filings, and, as discussed below, are required to make specific written disclosures concerning and to substantiate many contributions and payments to the organization, among other requirements.

Payments to section 501(c)(3) organizations (referred to hereinafter in this section as "charities") are only deductible as charitable contributions for federal income tax purposes if they are made with donative intent and to the extent that they exceed the fair market value of any goods or services received in return for the payment. To address abuses in this area, in 1993, Congress enacted a law requiring charities to inform donors in writing of the value of benefits received in return for contributions over $75. The law also requires donors to obtain written substantiation of all charitable contributions of $250 or more. If a charity does not provide appropriate documentation to donors, its donors may lose the ability to deduct their contributions, and the charity may face penalties for failure to comply with the law. The following rules apply to all section 501(c)(3) organizations, including 501(c)(3) membership associations and the related 501(c)(3) foundations of other 501(c) organizations.

1. Donor's Substantiation Requirements

No charitable deduction is permitted for any charitable contribution of $250 or more unless the donor has contemporaneous written substantiation from the charity. In cases where the charity has provided goods or services to the donor in exchange for making the contribution, this contemporaneous written acknowledgment must include a good-faith estimate of the value of such goods or services. Thus, donors may not rely solely on a canceled check to substantiate a cash contribution of $250 or more.

The substantiation must be contemporaneous: It must be obtained by the donor no later than the date the donor actually files a return for the tax year in which the contribution was made. If the return is filed after the due date or extended due date, then the substantiation must have been obtained by the due date or extended due date. However, the substantiation does not need to be attached to the donor's return.

While the responsibility for obtaining this substantiation technically lies with the donor and the charity is not required to report this information to the IRS, the charity must comply in order to protect the charitable deductibility of its donors' contributions. Since the charity will not know when its donors will file their returns, it should consider providing the substantiation at the time of contribution. In any event, charities should endeavor to provide them by January 31 of the next year.

Charities may either provide separate acknowledgments for each contribution of $250 or more from a donor, or may furnish periodic or even annual acknowledgments substantiating all contributions of $250 or more from a donor. Separate payments are regarded as independent contributions and are not aggregated for purposes of measuring the $250 threshold (subject to anti-abuse rules designed to prevent avoidance of the substantiation requirement by taxpayers writing separate smaller checks on the same date). If donations are made through payroll deductions, the deduction from each paycheck is regarded as a separate payment.

There is no prescribed format for the written acknowledgment. For example, letters, postcards, or computer-generated forms may be acceptable. The acknowledgment does not need to include the donor's Social Security or tax identification number. It must, however, provide sufficient information to substantiate the amount of the deductible contribution. The acknowledgment should note the amount of any cash contribution. However, if the donation is in the form of property, then the acknowledgment must describe, but need not value, such property. Valuation of the donated property is the responsibility of the donor. Moreover, if the value of an item or group of similar items exceeds $5,000, the donor must obtain a qualified appraisal and submit an appraisal summary with the tax return claiming the deduction.

The substantiation also must note whether the charity provided any goods or services in consideration, in whole or in part, for the contribution. If the donor received nothing in return for the contribution, the substantiation must so state. In addition, if any goods or services were provided by the charity in consideration, in whole or in part, for the contribution, then the substantiation must provide a description and good-faith estimate of the value of the goods or services. These are referred to as quid pro quo contributions. Note that charities are required to furnish disclosure statements to donors for such quid pro quo contributions in excess of $75 (see Section VI.F.2. on the next page).

Unreimbursed Expenses of Volunteers

Unreimbursed expenses incurred while providing volunteer services to a charity are deductible as a charitable contribution. Volunteer services include unpaid service as a board member, committee member, convention delegate, researcher, etc. Volunteering expenses that may be deductible as charitable contributions include, among other expenses:

- unreimbursed commuting expenses (either the actual cost of operating the vehicle for charitable work or the flat IRS-provided per mile rate; actual costs include gas, oil, and repairs directly related to the use of the vehicle for charitable work, but not general repairs, depreciation, or insurance; parking and tolls may be deducted in addition to the costs calculated under either of the two methods);

- unreimbursed travel expenses (for overnight travel away from home to render charitable services, the unreimbursed costs for plane, train, or similar tickets, as well as lodging and meals, are deductible; however, the trip must be authorized by the charity and can have no significant element of personal pleasure, recreation, or vacation); and
- unreimbursed office expenses (such as the costs of materials and supplies such as stamps and envelopes, and the costs of telephone calls made in the course of rendering charitable services).

Note that nondeductible expenses include, among others: the value of donated services, the cost of meals not incurred while traveling or away from home overnight, expenditures made for influencing legislation, and day care expenses for your children while you volunteer. For unreimbursed expenses of $250 or more incurred by charitable volunteers in connection with the rendering of services to or on behalf of a charity, in order for such expenses to be deductible charitable contributions by the volunteer, in addition to receipts, canceled checks and similar records otherwise required, the volunteer must obtain a written statement from the charity. The statement must: (1) describe the services rendered by the volunteer; (2) state whether the volunteer received any goods or services in consideration, in whole or in part, for the unreimbursed expenses; and (3) if so, provide a good-faith estimate of the value of such goods or services.

2. Disclosure of Receipt of Quid Pro Quo Contributions

Charities are required to provide a written disclosure statement to donors who make quid pro quo contributions in excess of $75. This requirement is separate from the written substantiation for deductibility purposes described in Section VII.A.1. In certain circumstances, a charity may be able to satisfy both requirements with the same written document.

A quid pro quo contribution is a payment made partly as a contribution and partly for goods or services provided to the donor by the charity. Where a donor pays more than fair market value to a charity for goods or services, only the amount that exceeds the value of the goods or services is deductible as a charitable contribution. For example, when a donor contributes $100 to a charity and receives a banquet ticket valued at $40, $60 would be deductible to the donor as a charitable contribution. Because the donor's quid pro quo contribution exceeds $75, the disclosure statement must be furnished, even though the deductible amount does not exceed $75.

Separate payments of $75 or less made at different times of the year for separate fundraising events will not be aggregated for purposes of the $75 threshold (subject to anti-abuse rules designed to prevent the avoidance of this disclosure requirement in situations such as the writing of multiple checks for the same transaction).

The required written disclosure statement must:

- inform the donor that the amount of the contribution that is deductible as a charitable contribution for federal income tax purposes is limited to the excess of any money (and the value of any property other than money) contributed to the charity by the donor *over* the value of goods and services provided by the charity to the donor; and
- provide the donor with a good-faith estimate of the value of the goods or services that the donor received.

The charity must furnish the statement in connection with either the solicitation or the receipt of the quid pro quo contribution. If the disclosure statement is furnished in connection with a particular solicitation, it is not necessary for the charity to provide another statement when the associated contribution is actually received.

The disclosure must be in writing and must be made in a manner that is reasonably likely to come to the attention of the donor. For example, a disclosure in small print within a larger document might not meet this requirement.

Due to the requirement of donative intent (discussed above), if a charity conducts a fundraising event (such as a dinner, ball, show, sports event, or other benefit event), it must employ procedures to make clear that a gift is being solicited in addition to participation in the event. This can be accomplished through the solicitation materials for the event or as part of a payment receipt. The charity must indicate the amount properly attributable to the purchase of the benefits of the event and the total amount solicited. To do this, it will need to determine the value of the benefits in advance of the solicitation.

Any reasonable method may be used to estimate the fair market value of a benefit, so long as the method is applied in good faith. If the charity paid fair market value for the benefit, such as a catered meal, then that cost is the appropriate amount. If the benefits are donated to the charity, then the charity must estimate their fair market value and cannot assume the value is zero. When the event is reasonably comparable to events for which there are established charges for admission, valuation will be simple. In other cases, the charity will need to make a good-faith attempt to value the benefit. The fact that the full amount of the donor's payment may be used by the charity for its charitable activities is irrelevant and does not affect the valuation of the benefit or the amount qualifying as a charitable contribution.

In addition, the fact that a donor does not use the tickets or other privileges (provided in consideration, in whole or in part, for the payment) does not increase the amount eligible for charitable deductibility. The test of charitable deductibility is not whether the right to attend or participate was exercised but whether the right was accepted or rejected by the donor. If the donor desires to support an event, but does not intend to use the tickets being offered for the event, the tickets can be declined or returned. In such event, the charity's receipt or acknowledgment (required if the payment is $250 or more) should state that no benefits were provided.

In the following circumstances, among others, the quid pro quo disclosure statement is not required:

- where the only goods or services provided to a donor are token items that meet the IRS standards for items of insubstantial value (e.g., goods or services with a value of less than 2 percent of the amount of the contribution up to a defined limit, newsletters not of commercial quality, "low-cost articles" (as defined by the IRS) provided for free without an advance order), such amounts which are adjusted annually for inflation;
- where there is no donative element involved in a particular transaction with a charity, such as in sales of merchandise in a gift shop; or
- where only one or both of the following membership benefits are provided in exchange for annual membership dues payments of $75 or less: (1) free admission to members-only events with a per-person cost to the charity (excluding any allocable overhead) that is no higher than the IRS standard for low-cost articles; or (2) rights or privileges that can be exercised frequently during the membership period (e.g., free or discounted admission to the charity's facilities or events, free or discounted parking, preferred access to or discounts on the purchase of goods or services).

Note that where the exclusion for certain membership benefits (provided in exchange for annual membership dues payments to a charity of $75 or less) is not applicable, and assuming donative intent exists, membership dues paid to a charity are only deductible as a charitable contribution to the extent that such dues exceed the value of the membership benefits received in return. In the case of membership dues (over $75 per year) paid to a section 501(c)(3) professional society, for instance, the value of membership benefits may equal or exceed the amount of membership dues. The same circumstance may apply in the case of a corporate sponsorship payment made to a section 501(c)(3) organization with respect to the marketing benefits received by the sponsor. In such events, the payments would not be deductible as charitable contributions. However, the membership dues and corporate sponsorship payments may well be fully deductible to the member or sponsor as a business expense. The determination as to whether a payment qualifies as an ordinary and necessary business expense is wholly separate and distinct from the determination of charitable deductibility. This case-by-case determination is made by the member on an individual basis, and the professional society has no obligation to assist in the determination.

A penalty is imposed on charities that do not meet the quid pro quo disclosure requirements. For failure to make the required disclosure in connection with a quid pro quo contribution of more than $75, there is a penalty of $10 per contribution, not to exceed $5,000 per fundraising event or mailing. A charity may avoid the penalty if it can demonstrate that the failure was due to reasonable cause.

VII

Spouse Travel and Entertainment Expenses

In general, spouse or dependent travel expenses, club dues, and business meals and entertainment expenses paid directly, reimbursed, or advanced by an association on behalf of an employee or volunteer leader constitute taxable income to the employee or volunteer if there is no bona fide business purpose for the expenditures. In other words, if there is a bona fide purpose, no taxable income will result; if there is no such bona fide purpose, the expenses will have to be included as income on the employee's Form W-2 or on a Form 1099 for the volunteer.

A. SPOUSE TRAVEL

Associations are presented with two options concerning spouse travel expenses: (1) identify a bona fide business purpose for spousal travel and take the necessary steps to protect the association in the event of an IRS audit; or (2) concede that there is not a bona fide business purpose for spousal travel and treat these expenses as taxable income to the executive or volunteer.

1. Option One: Establishing a Bona Fide Business Purpose for Spouse Travel

This is clearly the riskier of the two options.

A long succession of court decisions has made clear that the presence of the spouse on a business trip must be necessary, not merely helpful, to establish a bona fide business purpose. Various purported services performed by spouses on business trips, such as staffing convention hospitality suites, serving as host at receptions, assisting in fraternizing or becoming acquainted with business associates, or even typing notes for the executive while on the trip, have all been held to be insufficient, by themselves, to establish a valid business purpose for the spouse's presence.

There have been some cases, however, where the courts have found that even if the spouse was not an employee of the company, there was a bona fide business purpose for the spouse's presence. Unfortunately, there are relatively few such cases where the taxpayers prevailed, and many more holding to the contrary.

For an association that maintains there is a bona fide business purpose for the attendance of executives' and/or volunteers' spouses at out-of-town meetings, the test would be whether the spouse's attendance on travel significantly furthers an important tax-exempt purpose of the association. Associations claiming this position are advised to take certain important steps: document the purpose for spousal attendance by having written requirements for the spouse (such as functions that must be attended, roles that must be served, etc.) during association meetings, and actively implement these requirements; include the spouse in business as well as social functions; reflect the spouse's mandatory presence in employment contracts and meeting minutes; and, if possible, pay the spouse some amount for his or her services (such payments would, of course, be taxable as compensation). In short, ensure that the spouse's presence adds significantly to a tax-exempt function of the association.

As noted above, most cases hold that spousal attendance at business meetings does not serve a bona fide business purpose. In addition, merely providing in the association executive's employment contract that the spouse's attendance is required at association meetings, or simply making the spouse an employee of the association, will not, by themselves, suffice to establish a bona fide business purpose. More, and in most cases much more, is needed.

2. Option Two: Treating Spouse Travel Expenses as Taxable Income

Associations not willing to risk an IRS challenge to their treatment of spouse travel expenses as nontaxable fringe benefits always have the option of treating the expenses as taxable income to the staff member or volunteer leader, including them on a Form W-2 with respect to employees, or on a Form 1099 with respect to volunteers.

Where a bona fide business purpose cannot be established for the spouse's presence at an association meeting, all of the incremental costs incurred because of the spouse's attendance at that meeting must be treated as taxable income, including, but not limited to, airfare, ground transportation costs (e.g., cab fare), the additional cost (if any) of a double hotel room, and the costs of any food, drink, entertainment, or other expenses that can be calculated on a per-person basis.

For instance, if an association is paying for a dinner or cocktail reception based on the number of meeting attendees, the total cost must be divided by the number of attendees and the appropriate amount must be attributed to the spouse. If, however, the association is not paying for a given dinner, for example, because it has been provided on a complimentary basis by the hotel, no cost should be imputed to the spouse, since no cost was incurred by the association.

If an association cannot establish a bona fide business purpose for spousal travel, but does not want the staff member or volunteer leader to pay the price for the travel by being taxed on the expenses, the financial impact can be offset by simply providing the employee or volunteer with a payment designed to compensate for the tax liability. For employees, the payment would be in the form of additional salary; for volunteers, it could be in the form of an honorarium for their services. Of course, these payments also would have to be reflected in either W-2s or 1099s, respectively. This "grossing up" approach is an effective and commonly used method of addressing this issue.

Under current IRS rules, if an association executive or volunteer has frequent-flier miles available, they can be transferred to the spouse without any tax consequences.

B. CLUB DUES AND BUSINESS MEALS AND ENTERTAINMENT

With respect to club dues and business meals and entertainment expenses paid, reimbursed, or advanced by an association on behalf of an employee or volunteer, the same basic test applies as discussed above with respect to spouse travel expenses. Fortunately, it generally is far easier to establish a bona fide business purpose (at least in part) for the payment of such expenses, and thus to avoid having to treat some or all of these expenses as taxable income to the beneficiary.

If a club is used predominantly for business purposes, then no portion of the club dues must be treated as taxable income to the executive. Dues for downtown luncheon clubs generally have a valid business purpose greater than the personal benefit to the executive; therefore, payment or reimbursement of those club dues should not generally result in income being imputed to the executive. A less convincing argument might be made for airline clubs.

Country club dues are a different matter. In an IRS-provided example, an executive provides adequate substantiation to his employer that the country club was used 40 percent for business purposes. In this instance, although 100 percent of the club dues would be nondeductible, only the 60 percent personal portion would be included in the executive's taxable income.

As far as income inclusion is concerned, the same standards apply for business meals and entertainment expenses paid, reimbursed, or advanced by an association on behalf of a staff member or volunteer.

VIII

Foreign Meeting Expenses

A. DEDUCTIBILITY OF FOREIGN MEETING EXPENSES

The Code provides generally that an individual may not claim a business tax deduction for the costs of conventions, seminars, and other meetings held outside of the "North American area," unless it is "as reasonable" to hold the meeting outside the North American area as it is to hold the meeting inside the North American area (see the discussion of "reasonable" below).

The definition of the North American area includes the United States, Canada, Mexico, Puerto Rico, Central America, and some (but not all) Caribbean and other islands near the east, west, and south of the continent. Expenses incurred in attending meetings outside of the North American area, such as the Cayman Islands, will be tax deductible to the attendee only if it is as reasonable to hold the meeting in the Cayman Islands as it would be to hold it in the North American area.

Factors that are taken into account in determining whether the "as reasonable" standard has been met include:

- Whether there are business reasons for holding the meeting abroad;
- Whether the organization has members from other countries;
- Whether some of the organization's purposes are related to the international site of the meeting; and

- Whether the organization has held or is planning to hold other meetings abroad.

These deductibility rules do not impact tax-exempt associations paying travel expenses for officers, directors, or staff, due to the association's tax-exempt status. Moreover, if the association pays for foreign travel expenses to further the purposes of the association, the cost of such travel generally is not attributable to the officers, directors, or staff as income.

These deductibility rules can have a significant impact on association members who pay the registration, travel, and related costs to attend association meetings outside of the North American area, since they may or may not be entitled to deduct such costs as a business expense. Consequently, it is incumbent upon associations to conduct proper research and planning to help ensure, if desired, that members are entitled to full business tax deductibility of their expenses incurred while attending association meetings abroad.

B. CRUISE SHIP MEETING EXPENSES

Generally, the Internal Revenue Code does not allow any deductions for expenses that are incurred by an individual relating to the attendance at a convention, seminar, or other meeting which is held on any cruise ship. However, there is an exception to this general rule if the individual is able to demonstrate that the meeting is directly related to the active conduct of his trade or business and satisfy certain reporting requirements. Additionally, the deductions are only permitted for cruises for which: (A) the cruise ship is a vessel registered in the United States; and (B) all ports of call of such cruise ship are located in the United States or in possession of the United States. Finally, with respect to cruise meetings that satisfy the requirements for deductibility, the total amount of expenses that may be deducted is limited to $2,000.

For purposes of this requirement, the term "cruise ship" means any vessel sailing within or outside of the territorial waters of the United States.

Reporting Requirements

In order to be eligible for a deduction for expenses related to a convention, seminar, or similar meeting on any cruise ship, the taxpayer claiming the deduction must attach the following information to his annual income tax return:

- A written statement signed by the individual attending the meeting which includes: (a) information with respect to the total days of the trip, excluding the days of transportation to and from the cruise ship port, and the number of hours of each day of the trip which such individual devoted to scheduled business activities, (b) a program of the scheduled business activities of the meeting, and (c) such other information as may be required in regulations prescribed by the Secretary; and

- A written statement signed by an officer of the organization or group sponsoring the meeting which includes: (a) a schedule of business activities of each day of the meeting; (b) the number of hours which the individual attending the meeting attended such scheduled business activities, and (c) any other information required by the IRS (currently none).

IX

Employees versus Independent Contractors

The employee-versus-independent contractor question is a deceivingly complicated dichotomy that invokes multiples analyses and employment-related considerations. Unfortunately for organizations, there is no one common test or definition that can be applied to the relationship, in order to determine how a worker should be properly classified. Organizations must therefore tread these murky waters with extreme caution—and likely with a dose of warranted trepidation—as an improper classification may expose an organization to multiple and even simultaneous investigations, prosecutions, or civil actions and accompanying liability under tax and workers' compensation laws; federal and state wage and hour laws; and employment discrimination laws. Additionally, state and federal governments alike have openly increased their collective focus to the national misclassification problem. This decreased tolerance precipitates increased efforts to ferret out violations, increased information-sharing between the agencies, and increased penalties for misclassifications. With this in mind, organizations should prioritize proper classification as an issue to tackle well in advance of starting a new independent contractor relationship.

While it is true that agencies may apply different tests to the independent contractor-employee inquiry, and such differences may result in a determination that the worker is an employee under one law and an independent contractor under another, there is at least some good news for organizations: these tests have more similarities than differences. Moreover, at the core, the essential inquiry is the same: how much *control* does the organization exert over the worker? Control necessarily manifests itself in different ways, which then breeds these varying tests. However, "control" is the idea that anchors each, as demonstrated by the IRS' and DOL's respective tests. As reviewed herein, these, along with other related tests, encompass a plethora of factors. However, no one factor or inquiry is dispositive or outcome-determinative. Nor is there a magic number of factors that will reveal the true identity of the relationship. Rather, courts and agencies will look to see if, overall, the facts and circumstances of the particular situation evince a traditional arm's-length relationship common between separate entities (i.e., the independent contractor and the organization), or an employment relationship, whereby the employer retains the right to control the worker who is, in turn, financially and otherwise dependent on the organization.

1. The IRS Independent Contractor Test

Following sustained external pressures from government and businesses to simplify its traditional "Twenty Factor" test, the IRS abandoned this approach for its current eleven-part test, which is essentially a regrouping of the aforementioned twenty factors into eleven tests within three categories: behavioral control; financial control; and type of relationship.

Behavioral Control

A key inquiry for the IRS, the question of behavioral control assesses whether, and to what extent, the organization has the right to direct and control how the worker does the task or service at hand. This analysis looks at facts which tend to show the type and degree of training and instruction provided to the worker. Generally speaking, the more instruction provided, the more likely it is that the worker is an employee. Again, this is because the organization is exerting a heightened level of control over the worker. Independent contractors ideally will not receive any training, and they will receive little to no work instructions related to when and where to work, what methods to utilize, what tools or equipment to use, what workers to hire or to assist with the work, where to purchase supplies and services, what work must be performed by whom, and what order or sequence to follow. However, even where the organization does not give standard, clear instructions, it may exert behavioral control over a worker by retaining the right to control the details of the work.

Financial Control

This inquiry delves into whether, and to what extent, the organization retains the right to control the business or economic aspects of the work. In evaluating this category, the IRS reviews the reimbursement and expense relationship of the parties; the extent of the worker's investment (i.e., related to the respective businesses and as evidenced by an independent contractor's investment in his or her own facilities or tools); whether the worker makes his or her services available to others in the relevant market; how the organization pays the worker (i.e., hourly or salaried, as is common in employment relationships, versus a flat fee, which is common in independent contractor scenarios); and the extent to which the worker can realize a profit or loss (e.g., an independent contractor may make a profit on the work by keeping costs lower than fees). As the independent contractor is self-employed, the ideal relationship should mirror the standard relationship found between two separate companies contracting and transacting business with one another. Each entity should be financially invested in its own operations and suffer the pitfalls and windfalls associated with the same. Conversely, employees are part of the organization and do not generally invest beyond their time or profit beyond their paychecks.

Type of Relationship

In this third and final category, the IRS reviews facts demonstrating the type of relationship between the parties, including written contracts and the details incorporated in the same; whether the worker receives traditional employee benefits, such as paid time off or health insurance; the length or permanency of the relationship (e.g., for an indefinite period or a specific project period); and the extent to which the services performed are a key aspect of the organization's regular business. The IRS, along with other agencies assessing these relationships, makes clear that a written contract is likely the least important factor among those reviewed, as it could constitute no more than window-dressing for an improperly classified relationship. Regardless, it is still very useful and advisable that every independent contractor relationship be accompanied by one. Rather than focus on the written documents, the IRS will center its focus on the actions and realities underlying the relationship. Where the organization grants benefits upon the worker, or where the worker performs tasks integral to the business of the organization, he or she is more likely to be considered an employee.

2. The "Economic Realities" Test

The DOL, along with many courts, apply what is known as the "economic realities" test to the relationship, which focuses on similar factors as the IRS test. This test is often considered to take a relatively broad view of the relationship, with the focus on elements of control and financial dependency. Although these have been described differently by courts and agencies applying them, the following factors are central to this analysis:

- the degree to which the individual's work is controlled by the organization;
- the individual's investment in facilities and equipment, if any;
- the respective opportunities for profit or loss;
- the amount of skill required to perform the job;

- the extent to which the individual uses entrepreneurial initiative and judgment in the open market;
- the permanency or length of the relationship; and
- the extent to which the work is key to the organization's primary function or purpose.

3. Hybrid Tests and Application

In addition to these two commonly used tests, courts and agencies have constructed other tests that pull factors from the IRS' and DOL's blueprint, to create new, hybrid tests. Additionally, several courts and state governments have also used a commonly known three part test, referred to as the "ABC" test: (A) the worker is free from control or direction in the performance of the work; (B) The work is done outside the usual course of the company's business and is done off the premises of the business; and (C) the worker is customarily engaged in an independent trade, occupation, profession, or business.

Regardless of the test used, as previously noted, two common threads exist. First, an examination of the respective levels of control in the relationship will be extremely important to the overall assessment. Second, no single factor is outcome-determinative. Rather, a court or agency will look to the collective whole in order to draw its conclusion. As such, and for the other reasons stated in this section, independent contractor classifications inherently come with risks and should be assessed in a comprehensive manner.

APPENDICES

A. Model Association Time Log for Exempt Employees

B. Model Royalty Agreement for Association Endorsement

C. Model Corporate Sponsorship Agreement

D. Model Affiliation Agreement between Association and Taxable Subsidiary

E. Model Affiliation Agreement between Association and Related Foundation

F. Model Chapter Affiliation Agreement

G. Model Consulting/Independent Contractor Agreement (for individuals)

H. Model Consulting/Independent Contractor Agreement (for corporations)

I. Model License of Association Logo to Members

J. Model Policy on Member Participation as Vendor to Association

APPENDIX A

Model Association Time Log for Exempt Employees

DAILY TIME LOG FOR RECORDATION OF LOBBYING ACTIVITIES UNDER CODE SECTION 162(E)

Employee Name: ______________________ Month and Year: ________

Date	Daily Hours Worked (in quarter-hour increments)			
	Lobbying	**Regulatory Non-Lobbying**	**Other**	**Total**
1				
2				
3				
4				
5				
6				
7				
8				
9				
10				
11				
12				
13				
14				
15				
16				
17				
18				
19				
20				
21				
22				
23				

(continued)

Date	Daily Hours Worked (in quarter-hour increments)			
	Lobbying	**Regulatory Non-Lobbying**	**Other**	**Total**
24				
25				
26				
27				
28				
29				
30				
31				
Total				

Signature: ______________________________ Date: __________________________

APPENDIX B

Model Royalty Agreement for Association Endorsement

THIS ROYALTY AGREEMENT (the "Agreement") is made this ________ day of __________________, ______, by and between ________________________________, a ________________ nonprofit corporation, with its principal place of business at _______ ____ ("Association"), and ____________________ ____________, a ____________________ corporation, with its principal place of business at ____________________________ ("Company").

WHEREAS, Company desires to use Association's name, logo, and membership mailing list in connection with Company's marketing and sale of ______________ ______________________________ services to members of Association and others in the _________________________________ industry/profession (the "Program"), and Association is willing to permit such use in connection with the Program, in exchange for: (i) an annual royalty to be paid to Association by Company; and (ii) certain price discounts on such ________________________ services to be provided to members of Association;

NOW THEREFORE, in consideration of the premises set forth above and the promises set forth below, the sufficiency and receipt of which are hereby acknowledged, the parties hereby agree as follows:

I. **License of Intellectual Property.**

A. **Limited License of Name, Logo, and Membership Mailing List.**

1. Association hereby licenses to Company the use of its name (to include both "[ASSOCIATION NAME]" and the "[ASSOCIATION ACRONYM]" acronym), logo, and membership mailing list in connection with Company's marketing and sale of the Program to Association members and others in the ______________________________ industry/profession.

2. Company agrees that its usage of Association's name, logo, and membership mailing list shall be restricted solely to the marketing and sale of the Program to members of Association and others in the ___________________________ industry/profession. Company further agrees that the exploitation of such right of usage shall protect the name and goodwill of Association.

3. Company agrees that it shall not use, or permit any person or entity to use, Association's name, logo, or membership mailing list, or any portion thereof, without the prior written consent of Association, except to the limited extent that such use is authorized under this Agreement. Company further agrees to keep Association's

membership mailing list in strict confidence and to not sell or disclose such mailing list or its contents to any third party in any manner, except with the prior written consent of Association.

4. Upon termination or expiration of this Agreement, Company shall: (i) immediately cease utilization of Association's name, logo, and membership mailing list in connection with the Program or for any other purpose; (ii) return forthwith to Association all originals and copies of Association's name, logo, and membership mailing list (whether in printed, electronic, recorded, or other tangible form); and (iii) discard or destroy all copies thereof.

B. **Review and Approval.** In order to protect the reputation and goodwill of Association, Company shall provide Association with the right to review and pre-approve all uses of Association's name, logo, and membership mailing list, or any portion thereof, by Company and its agents.

C. **Royalty Payments.**

1. In consideration of the right to use Association's name, logo, and membership mailing list as provided under this Agreement, Company agrees to pay Association an annual royalty equal to _____ percent of Company's annual gross income from members of Association under the Program during the Term of this Agreement.

2. The royalty payments shall be made to Association (at the address specified in Section XIX (Notice) below) on a quarterly basis, specifically, on or before January 15, April 15, July 15, and October 15 of each year during the Term of this Agreement.

3. "Annual gross income from members of Association under the Program during the Term of this Agreement," as used in Section I(C)(1) above, shall include income from members of Association who are customers/clients of Company prior to and/or during the Term of this Agreement.

4. These royalties shall constitute payment solely for the use by Company of Association's name, logo, and membership mailing list, and shall in no manner be considered compensation or reimbursement for services rendered, activities undertaken by Association on behalf of Company, or income from a partnership or joint venture.

D. **Price Discounts for Association Members.** In consideration of the right to use Association's name, logo, and membership mailing list as provided under this Agreement, Company shall provide price discounts on ________________________ services to members of Association, as set forth in Exhibit A hereto, as supplemented from time to time, which is attached hereto and incorporated by reference herein.

II. **Noncompetition.**

A. During the Term of this Agreement, Association agrees not to endorse or promote, or license its name or logo to, any competitors of Company in connection with the marketing and sale of any products or services substantially similar or related to those in the Program.

B. During the Term of this Agreement, Company agrees not to enter into any endorsement or promotional agreement or understanding (whether written or oral) with any national, regional, state, or local association or nonprofit organization whose field of membership is substantially similar to that of Association in connection with the marketing and sale of any products or services substantially similar or related to those in the Program.

III. **Reporting and Inspection.**

A. **Reporting.** During the Term of this Agreement, Company shall provide to Association written quarterly reports (at the address specified in Section XIX (Notice) below) setting forth Company's monthly gross sales of Program products and services to members of Association, including the amount of Association's entitled royalties based on such gross sales. Such reports shall be made concurrently with the quarterly royalty payments payable to Association by Company.

B. **Inspection.** During the Term of this Agreement, upon reasonable notice and during regular business hours, Association or its agent(s) shall have the right to inspect all books and records of Company relating to the subject matter of this Agreement. Upon Association's request, Company shall make and send copies to Association of the books and records of Company regarding and pertaining to the Program and this Agreement.

IV. **Confidential Information.** The parties shall maintain the confidentiality of all of the confidential and proprietary information and data ("Confidential Information") of the other party. The parties also shall take all reasonable steps to ensure that no use, by themselves or by any third parties, shall be made of the other party's Confidential Information without such other party's consent. Each party's Confidential Information shall remain the property of that party and shall be considered to be furnished in confidence to the other party when necessary under the terms of this Agreement. Upon the termination or expiration of this Agreement, each party shall: (i) deliver immediately to the other party all Confidential Information of the other party, including but not limited to all written and electronic documentation of all Confidential Information, and all copies thereof; (ii) make no further use of it; and (iii) make reasonable efforts to ensure that no further use of it is made by either that party or its officers, directors, employees, agents, contractors, or any other person or third party. Each party's confidentiality obligations under this Section shall survive any termination or expiration of this Agreement.

V. **Term and Termination.** This Agreement shall be effective as of the date and year first above written and shall remain in full force and effect for a period of _____ (__) years from such date and year (the initial "Term"). Thereafter, this Agreement shall renew automatically for successive _____ (__) year Terms unless and until terminated upon written notice given by either party to the other at least _____ (__) days prior to the end of any such Term. In the event of a material breach of this Agreement, this Agreement may be terminated by the non-breaching party immediately upon written notice to the other party, such termination which shall be contingent upon the breaching party failing to cure such breach within __________ (____) days of its receipt of such written notice from the non-breaching party. In the event of one party's insolvency, fraud, or willful misconduct, this Agreement may be terminated by the other party immediately upon written notice to the offending party.

VI. **Relationship of Parties.** The relationship of Association and Company to each other is that of independent contractors. Nothing herein shall create any association, joint venture, partnership, or agency relationship of any kind between the parties. Neither party is authorized to incur any liability, obligation, or expense on behalf of the other, to use the other's monetary credit in conducting any activities under this Agreement, or to represent that Association is in the business of providing the products and/or services provided by Company.

VII. **Indemnification and Insurance.**

A. **Indemnification.** Each party hereby agrees to indemnify, save, and hold harmless the other party, and its subsidiaries, affiliates, related entities, partners, agents, officers, directors, employees, attorneys, heirs, successors, and assigns, and each of them, from and against any and all claims, actions, demands, losses, damages, judgments, settlements, costs and expenses (including reasonable attorneys' fees and expenses), and liabilities of every kind and character whatsoever, which may arise by reason of: (i) any act or omission by the party or any of its officers, directors, employees, or agents; and/or (ii) the inaccuracy or breach of any of the covenants, representations, and warranties made in this Agreement. This indemnity shall require the payment of costs and expenses as they occur. Each party shall promptly notify the other party upon receipt of any claim or legal action referenced in this Section. The provisions of this Section shall survive any termination or expiration of this Agreement.

B. **Insurance.** In order to assure the indemnity described in this Section, Company shall, at its sole expense, carry and keep in full force and effect at all times during the Term of this Agreement a liability insurance policy with a single limit of at least _____ million dollars ($____________) to cover potential liability to Association and/or others arising under the Program. Company shall name Association as an additional insured on such insurance policy, and such insurance policy shall contain a provision by which the insurer agrees that such policy shall not be canceled except after thirty (30) days written notice to Association. Company agrees to provide to Association, within thirty (30) days of the commencement of the initial Term of this Agreement, a copy of the certificate evidencing such insurance policy. Any insurance policy carried or to be carried by Company hereunder shall be primary over any insurance policy that might be carried by Association. Company's indemnification of Association under this Section shall in no way be limited by the extent of Company's insurance coverage. The provisions of this Section shall survive any termination or expiration of this Agreement for a period of one (1) year.

VIII. **Warranties.** Each party covenants, warrants, and represents that it shall comply with all laws and regulations applicable to this Agreement, and that it shall exercise due care and act in good faith at all times in performance of its obligations under this Agreement. The provisions of this Section shall survive any termination or expiration of this Agreement.

IX. **Waiver.** Either party's waiver of, or failure to exercise, any right provided for in this Agreement shall not be deemed a waiver of any further or future right under this Agreement.

X. **Governing Law.** All questions with respect to the construction, performance, and enforcement of this Agreement, and the rights and liabilities of the parties hereunder, shall be determined in accordance with the laws of the State of __________________. Any legal action taken or to be taken by either party regarding this Agreement or the rights and liabilities of parties hereunder shall be brought only before a federal, state, or local court of competent jurisdiction located within the State of __________________. Each party hereby consents to, and agrees not to contest, the jurisdiction of the federal, state, and local courts located within the State of __________________.

XI. **Headings.** The headings of the various paragraphs hereof are intended solely for the convenience of reference and are not intended for any purpose whatsoever to explain, modify, or place any construction upon any of the provisions of this Agreement.

XII. **Assignment.** This Agreement may not be assigned, or the rights granted hereunder transferred or sub-licensed, by either party without the express prior written consent of the other party.

XIII. **Heirs, Successors, and Assigns.** This Agreement shall be binding upon and inure to the benefit of each party, its subsidiaries, affiliates, related entities, partners, agents, officers, directors, employees, heirs, successors, and assigns, without regard to whether it is expressly acknowledged in any instrument of succession or assignment.

XIV. **Counterparts.** This Agreement may be executed in one (1) or more counterparts, each of which shall be deemed an original and all of which taken together shall constitute one (1) and the same instrument.

XV. **Entire Agreement.** This Agreement: (i) constitutes the entire agreement between the parties hereto with respect to the subject matter hereof; (ii) supersedes and replaces all prior agreements, oral and written, between the parties relating to the subject matter hereof; and (iii) may be amended only by a written instrument clearly setting forth the amendment(s) and executed by both parties.

XVI. **Independent Agreement.** This Agreement is an independent agreement which is not in any way contingent upon or related to any other contractual obligations of the parties. The royalties and price discounts provided by Company herein are solely in consideration for the license of Association's name, logo, and membership mailing list.

XVII. **Severability.** All provisions of this Agreement are severable. If any provision or portion hereof is determined to be unenforceable in arbitration or by a court of competent jurisdiction, then the remaining portion of the Agreement shall remain in full effect.

XVIII. **Force Majeure.** Neither party shall be liable for failure to perform its obligations under this Agreement due to events beyond its reasonable control, including, but not limited to, strikes, riots, wars, fire, acts of God, and acts in compliance with any applicable law, regulation, or order (whether valid or invalid) of any governmental body.

XIX. **Notice.** All notices and demands of any kind or nature that either party to this Agreement may be required or may desire to serve upon the other in connection with this Agreement shall be in writing and may be served personally, by certified mail, or by commercial overnight courier (e.g., Federal Express), with constructive receipt deemed to have occurred _______ (___) calendar days after the mailing or sending of such notice, to the following addresses:

If to Association: ______________________________

____

____

Attn.: ______________________________

If to Company: ______________________________

____

____

Attn.: ______________________________

*****

IN WITNESS WHEREOF, the parties hereto have caused duplicate originals of this Agreement to be executed by their respective duly authorized representatives as of the date and year first above written.

[ASSOCIATION NAME]

By: ______________________________

______________________________ [Name]

______________________________ [Title]

[COMPANY NAME]

By: ______________________________

______________________________ [Name]

______________________________ [Title]

EXHIBIT A
SCHEDULE OF PRICE DISCOUNTS FOR ASSOCIATION MEMBERS

[list schedule content]

APPENDIX C

Model Corporate Sponsorship Agreement

THIS SPONSORSHIP AGREEMENT (the "Agreement") is made this _______ day of _________________, ________, by and between ABC Association ("ABC"), a _________________ nonprofit corporation and an organization exempt from federal income taxation under Section 501(c)(___) of the Internal Revenue Code of 1986, as the same may be amended or supplemented ("the Code"), with its principal place of business at ____________________________, and ____________________________ ("Sponsor"), a _________________ corporation with its principal place of business at _______________ _________________.

RECITALS

WHEREAS, in furtherance of its tax-exempt purposes, ABC conducts a program [or, alternatively, "an event"] whereby___________________________ ______________________________ [description of program or event] (the "Program" [or, alternatively, the "Event"]);

WHEREAS, Sponsor desires to sponsor the Program; and

WHEREAS, ABC desires to permit Sponsor to sponsor the Program on a non-exclusive [or, alternatively, "an exclusive"] basis in exchange for certain compensation.

NOW, THEREFORE, in consideration of the mutual promises and covenants contained herein, and for other good and valuable consideration, the receipt and sufficiency of which are hereby acknowledged, the parties, intending to be legally bound, hereby agree as follows:

I. **Recitals.** The foregoing recitals are made a part of this Agreement.

II. **Term.** The Term of this Agreement will commence on the date and year first set forth above and will continue for a period of one (1) year. Thereafter, the Agreement shall automatically renew for additional one (1) year Terms unless and until terminated by either party as set forth in Section X below.

III. **Sponsorship.**

A. During the Term of this Agreement, ABC hereby agrees to identify and acknowledge Sponsor as a sponsor [or, alternatively, as "the exclusive sponsor"] of the Program, as permitted in connection with qualified sponsorship payments under Section 513(i) of the Code and the Treasury regulations thereunder. Such identification and acknowledgment shall include displaying Sponsor's corporate logo and certain other identifying information (as permitted in connection with qualified sponsorship

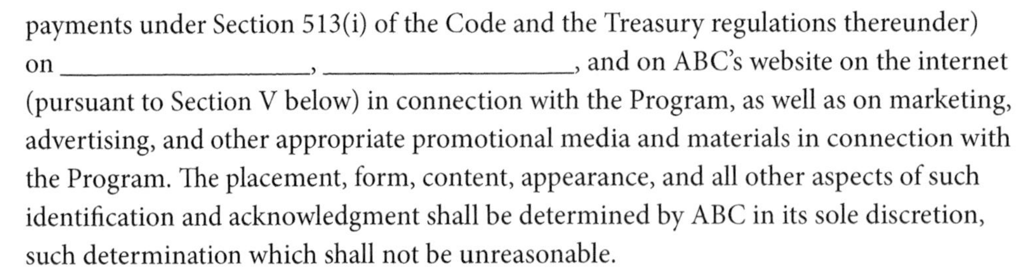

payments under Section 513(i) of the Code and the Treasury regulations thereunder) on ___________________, ___________________, and on ABC's website on the internet (pursuant to Section V below) in connection with the Program, as well as on marketing, advertising, and other appropriate promotional media and materials in connection with the Program. The placement, form, content, appearance, and all other aspects of such identification and acknowledgment shall be determined by ABC in its sole discretion, such determination which shall not be unreasonable.

B. During the Term of this Agreement, Sponsor shall be permitted to maintain an internet hyperlink on the _______________ page of ABC's website on the internet (http://www.abc.org) to the home page of Sponsor's website on the internet (http://www._______.com), pursuant to the terms and conditions of Section V below.

C. Sponsor shall provide to ABC all necessary logos and other information, content, and materials (in printed, electronic, and/or other form) for use in connection with its sponsorship of the Program; provided, however, that all uses of such logos and other information, content, and materials shall be determined by ABC in its sole discretion, such determination which shall not be unreasonable.

D. During the Term of this Agreement, Sponsor shall be permitted to utilize ABC's name, acronym, and logo for the sole purpose of promoting Sponsor's sponsorship of the Program, pursuant to the terms of Section IV below. [All uses by Sponsor of ABC's name, acronym, and logo shall be subject to the prior approval of ABC.][optional]

IV. **Mutual Intellectual Property License.**

A. **Limited License to ABC.** In connection with ABC's non-exclusive [or, alternatively, "exclusive"] grant to Sponsor to sponsor the Program, ABC is hereby granted a limited, revocable, non-exclusive license to use the name "[insert Sponsor name]," the acronym "[insert Sponsor acronym, if applicable]," and the logo of Sponsor (hereinafter collectively referred to as the "Sponsor Marks") solely to identify Sponsor as a [or, alternatively, "the"] sponsor of the Program, with the limited authority to use the Sponsor Marks solely in connection with the activities authorized under this Agreement, subject to the terms and conditions of this Agreement. Sponsor represents and warrants that it has the full right and authority to enter into this Agreement and to grant the license provided herein; that it has not previously in any manner disposed of any of the rights herein granted to ABC nor previously granted any rights adverse thereto or inconsistent therewith; that there are no rights outstanding which would diminish, encumber, or impair the full enjoyment or exercise of the rights herein granted to ABC; and that the Sponsor Marks do not and will not violate or infringe upon any patent, copyright, literary, privacy, publicity, trademark, service mark, or any other personal or property right of any third party, nor will same constitute a libel or defamation of any third party.

B. **Limited License to Sponsor.** In connection with ABC's non-exclusive [or, alternatively, "exclusive"] grant to Sponsor to sponsor the Program, Sponsor is hereby granted a limited, revocable, non-exclusive license to use the name "ABC Association" the acronym "ABC," and the logo of ABC (hereinafter collectively referred to as the

"ABC Marks") solely with the term "Sponsor" prominently displayed directly adjacent thereto (to ensure the absence of any implication that Sponsor is endorsed by ABC), with the limited authority to use the ABC Marks solely in connection with the activities authorized under this Agreement, subject to the terms and conditions of this Agreement. In no event shall Sponsor use the ABC Marks in a manner that states or implies an endorsement of Sponsor (or Sponsor's products or services) by ABC. [Notwithstanding the foregoing, all uses by Sponsor of the ABC Marks shall be subject to the prior approval of ABC.][optional] [In all uses by Sponsor of the ABC Marks, Sponsor shall ensure that, if so directed by ABC, all applicable trademark and copyright notices are used pursuant to the requirements of United States law and any other guidelines that ABC may hereafter prescribe.][optional] Any material failure by Sponsor to comply with the terms and conditions of this limited license, whether willful or negligent, may result in the immediate suspension or revocation of this license, in whole or in part, by ABC. The interpretation and enforcement (or lack thereof) of such terms and conditions, and compliance therewith, shall be made by ABC in its sole discretion.

C. **General Provisions.**

1. The Sponsor Marks and the ABC Marks are hereinafter collectively referred to as the "Marks."

2. The Marks are and shall remain at all times the sole and exclusive property of their respective owners (i.e., ABC shall be considered the "owner party" and Sponsor shall be considered the "non-owner party" with respect to the ABC Marks; Sponsor shall be considered the "owner party" and ABC shall be considered the "non-owner party" with respect to the Sponsor Marks). The respective Marks may be used by the non-owner parties if and only if such use is made pursuant to the terms and conditions of this limited license.

3. The owner parties' respective logos may not be revised or altered by the non-owner parties in any way, and must be displayed in the same form (and colors, if applicable) as provided by the owner parties.

4. The respective Marks must be used by the non-owner parties in a professional manner and solely in connection with the activities authorized under this Agreement. The respective non-owner parties shall not permit any third party or parties to use the Marks of the owner parties without the express prior written approval of the owner parties. The respective non-owner parties shall not use the Marks of the owner parties in conjunction with any third party trademark, service mark, or other mark without the express prior written approval of the owner parties. The respective non-owner parties shall not sell or trade the Marks of the owner parties without the express prior written approval of the owner parties. Notwithstanding the foregoing, the respective Marks may not be used by the non-owner parties for individual personal or professional gain or other private benefit, and the respective Marks may not be used by the non-owner parties in any manner that: diminishes their value or otherwise dilutes the Marks; discredits the owner parties or tarnishes their respective reputations and goodwill; is false, misleading, or likely to cause confusion, mistake, or deception; violates the rights

of others; violates any federal, state, or local law, regulation or other public policy; or mischaracterizes the relationship between the parties, including but not limited to the fact that Sponsor is a separate and distinct legal entity from, and is not an agent of, ABC.

5. The respective owner parties shall have the right, from time to time, to request complete samples of use of their Marks by the non-owner parties from which they can determine compliance with these terms and conditions.

6. Use of the respective owner parties' Marks by the non-owner parties shall create no rights for the non-owner parties in or to such Marks or their use beyond the terms and conditions of this limited license. All rights of usage of the respective owner parties' Marks by the non-owner parties shall terminate immediately upon the termination or expiration of this Agreement. Upon the termination or expiration of this Agreement, the respective non-owner parties shall: (i) immediately cease utilization of the owner parties' Marks for any purpose; (ii) return forthwith all originals and copies of the owner parties' Marks to the respective owner parties (whether in printed, electronic, recorded, and/or other tangible form); and (iii) discard or destroy all copies thereof. The respective non-owner parties' obligations to protect the owner parties' Marks shall survive the termination or expiration of this Agreement.

V. **Mutual Linking Agreement.**

A. During the Term of this Agreement, Sponsor shall be permitted to maintain an internet hyperlink on the _______________ page of ABC's website on the internet (http://www.abc.org) to the home page of Sponsor's website on the internet (http://www._______.com), pursuant to the terms and conditions of this Section V. ABC agrees to incorporate the exact, unaltered, graphical file image to be electronically provided by Sponsor ("Sponsor's Link Logo") into the HTML files located on the _______________ page of ABC's website. The specific placement (on the _______________ page of ABC's website), appearance, and operation of the link shall, be consistent with the terms and conditions of this Agreement, and shall be mutually agreed upon by ABC and Sponsor; provided, however, that (i) the appearance of Sponsor's Link Logo may not be altered in any manner from what is electronically provided by Sponsor; (ii) Sponsor's Link Logo may not be reduced in size beyond what is electronically provided by Sponsor; (iii) Sponsor's Link Logo shall not be displayed on ABC's website more prominently than ABC's name or logo, or than ABC's website name or logo; (iv) Sponsor's Link Logo must stand by itself and must include a minimum amount of 30 pixels of empty space around it so as to avoid unintended associations with any other objects, including but not limited to type, photography, borders, and edges; (v) users of ABC's website must be able to view Sponsor's Link Logo in its entirety without scrolling; and (vi) Sponsor reserves the right to alter or modify Sponsor's Link Logo in any manner at any time, provided such alteration or modification is otherwise consistent with the terms and conditions of this Section V. No pages from Sponsor's website may be placed in a frame on any page of ABC's website. ABC does not endorse, approve, certify, or control Sponsor's website and does not warrant, guarantee, or make any representations regarding the accuracy, completeness, efficacy, timeliness, merchantability, or fitness for a particular purpose of the content or data located on such site. Reference therein to any specific product, process, or service does not constitute or imply endorsement, recommendation, or favoring by ABC. ABC is not responsible for, and expressly disclaims all liability for, damages of any kind arising out of use, reference to, reliance on, or performance of such content or data. Sponsor reserves the right to review ABC's use of Sponsor's Link Logo, and ABC agrees to provide Sponsor with unrestricted access to ABC's website to review such use. This link shall terminate and be immediately removed from ABC's website upon the termination or expiration of the Agreement. This link, and all aspects thereof, shall be subject to the terms and conditions of Section IV above.

B. During the Term of this Agreement, ABC shall be permitted to maintain an internet hyperlink on the ______________ page of Sponsor's website on the internet (http://www._______.com) to the home page of ABC's website on the internet (http://www.abc.org), pursuant to the terms and conditions of this Section V. Sponsor agrees to incorporate the exact, unaltered, graphical file image to be electronically provided by ABC ("ABC's Link Logo") into the HTML files located on the ______________ page of Sponsor's website. The specific placement (on the ______________ page of Sponsor's website), appearance, and operation of the link shall be consistent with the terms and conditions of this Agreement and shall be mutually agreed upon by Sponsor and ABC; provided, however, that (i) the appearance of ABC's Link Logo may not be altered in any manner from what is electronically provided by ABC; (ii) ABC's Link Logo may not be reduced in size beyond what is electronically provided by ABC; (iii) ABC's Link Logo shall not be displayed on Sponsor's website more prominently than Sponsor's name or logo, or than Sponsor's website name or logo; (iv) ABC's Link Logo must stand by itself and must include a minimum amount of 30 pixels of empty space around it so as to avoid unintended associations with any other objects, including but not limited to type, photography, borders, and edges; (v) users of Sponsor's website must be able to view ABC's Link Logo in its entirety without scrolling, and (vi) ABC reserves the right to alter or modify ABC's Link Logo in any manner at any time, provided such alteration or modification is otherwise consistent with the terms and conditions of this Section V. No pages from ABC's website may be placed in a frame on any page of Sponsor's website. Sponsor does not endorse, approve, certify, or control ABC's website and does not warrant, guarantee, or make any representations regarding the accuracy, completeness, efficacy, timeliness, merchantability, or fitness for a particular purpose of the content or data located on such site. Reference therein to any specific product, process, or service does not constitute or imply endorsement, recommendation, or favoring by Sponsor. Sponsor is not responsible for, and expressly disclaims all liability for, damages of any kind arising out of use, reference to, reliance on, or performance of such content or data. ABC reserves the right to review Sponsor's use of ABC's Link Logo, and Sponsor agrees to provide ABC with unrestricted access to Sponsor's website to review such use. This link shall terminate and be immediately removed from the Sponsor's website upon the termination or expiration of this Agreement. This link, and all aspects thereof, shall be subject to the terms and conditions of Section IV above.

VI. **Contribution Schedule.**

A. In consideration for the right to sponsor the Program and to be acknowledged by ABC as a sponsor [or, alternatively, as "the exclusive sponsor"] of the Program during the Term of this Agreement, Sponsor agrees to make a cash contribution to ABC in the amount of ____________________ dollars ($__________) per year, to be paid in a single lump-sum within thirty (30) days of the commencement of each Term of the Agreement [or alternative payment arrangements].

B. Additionally, Sponsor will work with ABC to identify and provide in-kind to ABC certain of its products, services, and/or facilities, as Sponsor deems appropriate, to ABC, ABC's members, and/or in connection with ABC programs, activities, or events; provided, however, that this Agreement shall not constitute nor be construed as any limitation on the sale, distribution, availability, or use of competing products, services, or facilities in connection with ABC programs, activities, or events.

C. The contributions described in this Section VI shall constitute payment by Sponsor solely for Sponsor's right to sponsor the Program and to be acknowledged by ABC as a sponsor [or, alternatively, as "the exclusive sponsor"] of the Program. Such contributions shall in no manner be considered compensation or reimbursement for services rendered, activities undertaken by ABC on behalf of Sponsor, or income from a partnership or joint venture.

D. To the extent that any portion of a payment under this Section VI would not (if made as a separate payment) be deemed a qualified sponsorship payment under Section 513(i) of the Code, such portion of such payment and the other portion of such payment shall be deemed and treated as separate payments.

VII. Relationship of Parties. The relationship of the parties to each other is that of independent contractors. Nothing herein shall create any association, joint venture, partnership, or agency relationship of any kind between the parties. Neither party is authorized to incur any liability, obligation, or expense on behalf of the other, to use the other's monetary credit in conducting any activities under this Agreement, or to represent that ABC is in the business of providing the products and/or services provided by Sponsor.

VIII. **Indemnification.** Sponsor hereby agrees to indemnify, save and hold harmless ABC and its subsidiaries, affiliates, related entities, partners, agents, officers, directors, employees, attorneys, heirs, successors, and assigns, and each of them, from and against any and all claims, actions, demands, losses, damages, judgments, settlements, costs and expenses (including reasonable attorneys' fees and expenses), and liabilities of every kind and character whatsoever, which may arise by reason of: (i) any act or omission by Sponsor or any of its officers, directors, employees, or agents; (ii) any use of Sponsor's name, logo, website, or other information, materials, products, or services provided by Sponsor; and/or (iii) the inaccuracy or breach of any of the covenants, representations, and warranties made by Sponsor in this Agreement. This indemnity shall require the payment of costs and expenses by Sponsor as they occur. ABC shall promptly notify

Sponsor upon receipt of any claim or legal action referenced in this Section VIII. The provisions of this Section VIII shall survive any termination or expiration of this Agreement.

IX. **Confidentiality.** During the Term of this Agreement and thereafter, each party shall use and reproduce the other party's Confidential Information (as defined below) only for purposes of this Agreement and only to the extent necessary for such purposes. Each party shall restrict disclosure of the other party's Confidential Information to its officers, directors, employees, contractors, and other agents with a reasonable need to know such Confidential Information, and shall not disclose the other party's Confidential Information to any third party without the prior written consent of the other party.

Notwithstanding the foregoing, it shall not constitute a breach of this Agreement for either party to disclose the other party's Confidential Information if required to do so under law or in judicial or other governmental investigations or proceedings, provided the other party has been given prior written notice and provided the disclosing party has sought all available safeguards against widespread dissemination prior to such disclosure.

As used in this Agreement, the term "Confidential Information" refers to: (i) the terms and conditions of this Agreement; (ii) each party's trade secrets, organizational and/or operational plans, strategies, methods, and/or practices; and (iii) any other information relating to either party or its business or organization that is not generally known to the public, including but not limited to information about either party's employees, contractors, agents, products, services, members, customers, marketing strategies, or future plans. Notwithstanding the foregoing, Confidential Information does not include: (i) information that is in the public domain as of the effective date of this Agreement or that subsequently enters the public domain by publication or otherwise through no action or fault of the other party; (ii) information that is known to either party without restriction, prior to receipt from the other party, from its own independent sources as evidenced by such party's written records, and which was not acquired, directly or indirectly, from the other party; (iii) information that either party receives from any third party that is reasonably known by the receiving party to have a legal right to transmit such information and to not keep such information confidential; and (iv) information independently developed by either party's employees or agents, provided that such party can demonstrate that such employees or agents had no access to the Confidential Information received hereunder.

X. **Termination.** This Agreement shall terminate: (i) upon the occurrence of a material breach of a material provision by one (1) of the parties hereto if such breach is not cured within thirty (30) days after written notice of such breach is received by the breaching party from the non-breaching party identifying the matter constituting the material breach; (ii) upon written notice provided by one (1) party to the other party no less than sixty (60) days prior to the end of any initial or renewal Term; or (iii) at any time upon the mutual written consent of both parties.

XI. **General Provisions.**

A. **Warranties.** Each party covenants, warrants, and represents that it shall comply with all laws and regulations applicable to this Agreement and the performance of the parties' obligations hereunder, and that it shall exercise due care and act in good faith at all times in the performance of its obligations hereunder. The provisions of this Section shall survive any termination or expiration of this Agreement.

B. **Waiver.** Either party's waiver of, or failure to exercise, any right provided for in this Agreement shall not be deemed a waiver of any further or future right under this Agreement.

C. **Governing Law.** All questions with respect to the construction of this Agreement or the rights and liabilities of the parties hereunder shall be determined in accordance with the laws of the State of ________________. Any legal action taken or to be taken by either party regarding this Agreement or the rights and liabilities of parties hereunder shall be brought only before a federal, state, or local court of competent jurisdiction located within the State of ________________. Each party hereby consents to the jurisdiction of the federal, state, and local courts located within the State of ________________.

D. **Headings.** The headings of the various paragraphs hereof are intended solely for the convenience of reference and are not intended for any purpose whatsoever to explain, modify, or place any construction upon any of the provisions of this Agreement.

E. **Assignment.** This Agreement may not be assigned, or the rights granted hereunder transferred or sub-licensed, by either party without the express prior written consent of the other party.

F. Heirs, Successors, an**d Assigns.** This Agreement shall be binding upon and inure to the benefit of each party, its subsidiaries, affiliates, related entities, partners, shareholders, agents, officers, directors, employees, heirs, successors, and assigns, without regard to whether it is expressly acknowledged in any instrument of succession or assignment.

G. **Counterparts.** This Agreement may be executed in one (1) or more counterparts, each of which shall be deemed an original and all of which taken together shall constitute one (1) and the same instrument.

H. **Entire Agreement.** This Agreement: (i) constitutes the entire agreement between the parties hereto with respect to the subject matter hereof; (ii) supersedes and replaces all prior agreements, oral and written, between the parties relating to the subject matter hereof; and (iii) may be amended only by a written instrument clearly setting forth the amendment(s) and executed by both parties.

I. **Independent Agreement.** This Agreement is an independent agreement which is not in any way contingent upon or related to any other contractual obligations of the parties.

J. **Severability.** All provisions of this Agreement are severable. If any provision or portion hereof is determined to be unenforceable in arbitration or by a court of competent jurisdiction, then the remaining portion of the Agreement shall remain in full effect.

K. **Force Majeure.** Neither party shall be liable for failure to perform its obligations under this Agreement due to events beyond its reasonable control, including, but not limited to, strikes, riots, wars, fire, acts of God, and acts in compliance with any applicable law, regulation, or order (whether valid or invalid) of any governmental body.

L. **Notice.** All notices and demands of any kind or nature that either party to this Agreement may be required or may desire to serve upon the other in connection with this Agreement shall be in writing and may be served personally, by certified mail, or by commercial overnight courier (e.g., Federal Express), with constructive receipt deemed to have occurred ________ (___) calendar days after the mailing or sending of such notice, to the following addresses:

If to ABC: ______________________________

____

____

Attn.: ______________________________

If to Sponsor: ______________________________

____

____

Attn.: ______________________________

*****

IN WITNESS WHEREOF, the parties hereto have caused duplicate originals of this Agreement to be executed by their respective duly authorized representatives as of the date and year first above written.

ABC ASSOCIATION

By: ______________________________

______________________________ [Name]

______________________________ [Title]

[SPONSOR NAME]

By: ______________________________

______________________________ [Name]

______________________________ [Title]

APPENDIX D

Model Affiliation Agreement between Association and Taxable Subsidiary

THIS ADMINISTRATIVE SERVICES AGREEMENT (the "Agreement") is made and effective this ______ day of ________________, ______, by and between ABC Association, Inc., a ____________________________ nonprofit corporation, with its principal place of business at ________________________________ ("ABC"), and ABC Services Corporation, a ____________________________ corporation, with its principal place of business at______________________________ ______________________________ ("ASC") (ABC and ASC are collectively referred to hereinafter as the "Parties" and individually as a "Party").

WHEREAS, given their common interests and mutual desire to maximize the opportunities available to them and to minimize their administrative expenses, the Parties desire to enter into this Agreement, under which ABC may provide, and ASC may accept, certain staffing, office space, office equipment, office furniture, office supplies, office services, and other administrative support, and under which ABC may license, and ASC may accept, certain intellectual property, in exchange for monetary compensation to be paid by ASC to ABC.

NOW THEREFORE, in consideration of the premises set forth above and the promises set forth below, the sufficiency and receipt of which are hereby acknowledged, the Parties hereby agree as follows:

I. **Term and Termination.** This Agreement shall be effective as of the date and year first written above and shall remain in full force and effect for a period of one (1) year from such date and year. Thereafter, this Agreement shall automatically renew for successive one (1) year terms without any further action by either Party. Notwithstanding the foregoing, this Agreement may be terminated by either Party for any reason upon written notice provided by either Party to the other Party no less than ___________ (_____) days prior to the effective date of any such termination. In the event of a material breach of this Agreement, this Agreement may be terminated by the non-breaching Party immediately upon written notice to the other Party, such termination which shall be contingent upon the breaching Party failing to cure such breach within ___________ (_____) days of its receipt of such written notice from the non-breaching Party.

II. **Staffing, Office Space, Office Services, and Other Administrative Support.** During the Term of this Agreement, ABC agrees to make available and provide to ASC certain professional and administrative staffing, office space, office equipment, office furniture, office supplies, office services, and other administrative support, and to license to ASC certain intellectual property of ABC, as may be required by ASC and as agreed to by ABC in its sole discretion, subject to the following terms and conditions:

A. **Professional Services and Staffing.** ABC shall provide ASC with the services of some or all of its employees as may be required by ASC from time to time and as agreed to by ABC in its sole discretion, such agreement by ABC which may be modified or withdrawn at any time in ABC's sole discretion. All ABC employees who perform services for or on behalf of ASC shall maintain contemporaneous written daily time logs reflecting the amount of time spent by such employees on ASC programs, activities, and administration, as well as the amount and nature of all other time logged by such employees. For time spent by ABC employees on ASC programs, activities, and administration, ASC shall reimburse ABC, on a monthly basis, for the proportionate share of the relevant ABC employees' compensation, benefits, and employment taxes. Such reimbursements shall be calculated, in part, by reference to the written daily time logs maintained by ABC employees.

B. **Office Space, Equipment, Furniture, Supplies, and Services.** ABC shall provide ASC with the use of office space within ABC's offices (the "ABC Offices"), which offices are presently located at ______________________________. ABC shall provide such office space to ASC within the ABC Offices as may be required by ASC from time to time and as agreed to by ABC in its sole discretion, such agreement by ABC which may be modified or withdrawn at any time in ABC's sole discretion. ABC also shall provide ASC with the use of such office equipment, office furniture, office supplies, office services, and other administrative support as may be required by ASC from time to time and as agreed to by ABC in its sole discretion, such agreement by ABC which may be modified or withdrawn at any time in ABC's sole discretion. ASC shall reimburse ABC, on a monthly basis, for its proportionate share of the costs or fair market value of providing such office space, office equipment, office furniture, office supplies, office services, and other administrative support. The Parties may set such costs or fair market value by mutual agreement so long as the cost or fair market value so set for each item is a reasonable approximation of the arm's length procurement cost to ABC or the arm's length fair market value of the relevant item. Where possible and practical, such reimbursements should be calculated, in part, by reference to the written daily time logs maintained by ABC employees (e.g., if five percent (5%) of all ABC employee time was spent on ASC matters during a given month, then ASC should reimburse ABC five percent (5%) of the cost of ABC's mortgage/rental payment(s), utility payments, etc. for that month). Wherever the direct costs of providing such items can be easily ascertained and allocated to ASC (e.g., postage costs, overnight mail charges, courier service charges), such direct costs shall be reimbursed in full by ASC to ABC on an actual cost basis.

III. **Intellectual Property License.**

A. **Name and Logo.** During the Term of this Agreement, ABC grants to ASC a non-exclusive, limited license to use the service marks "ABC Association" and "ABC," the logo or logos of ABC, and all other marks consisting of letters, words, or graphics in which ABC may have a proprietary interest or property right (collectively, "Marks"), in the name or description of ASC and in programs and activities undertaken by ASC, pursuant to the terms and conditions of this Section.

B. **Other Intellectual Property.** During the Term of this Agreement and unless otherwise reserved in writing by ABC, ABC grants to ASC a non-exclusive, limited license to use all other names, trademarks, service marks, certification marks, copyrights, and any such other intellectual property in which ABC may have a proprietary interest or property right (collectively, "Other Property"), including but not limited to all ABC mailing, telecopying, and electronic mail lists.

C. **Sublicenses.** During the Term of this Agreement and unless otherwise reserved in writing by ABC, ASC shall have the limited right to sublicense ("Sublicense") any and all Marks and Other Property licensed to it by ABC to third parties ("Sublicensees"), provided that all such Sublicenses shall be subject to the same restrictions on use of such Marks and Other Property and the same confidentiality requirements as are imposed upon ASC under this Agreement. All Sublicenses shall require the prior written approval of ABC, such approval which may or may not be granted by ABC in ABC's sole discretion. ASC shall take all reasonable and prudent steps in order to ensure that all Sublicensees comply with the restrictions on use and confidentiality requirements imposed under this Agreement.

D. **Ownership of Marks and Other Property.** Notwithstanding any provision contained herein, ASC hereby recognizes the exclusive residual ownership by ABC of all rights, proprietary interests, and property rights in the Marks and Other Property.

E. **Restrictions on Use of Marks or Other Property.** ASC shall not use, authorize others to use, or permit the use of Marks or Other Property except in programs and activities that are consistent with this Agreement and any written reservation of rights provided by ABC. ASC shall not use, authorize others to use, or permit the use of Marks or Other Property that would materially decrease the value of such Marks and Other Property or the goodwill or reputation associated with ABC. ASC shall take all reasonable and prudent steps to ensure that any use of the Marks or Other Property pursuant to the limited license granted herein, either by themselves or by any Sublicensee, shall contain the applicable copyright, trademark, or service mark notices, pursuant to the requirements of any applicable laws or regulations and any other guidelines provided under this Agreement or that ABC may have heretofore or may hereafter prescribe in writing.

F. **Notification of Claims; Assistance in Registration; Termination.** ASC shall promptly notify ABC of any claim related to or potentially affecting the ownership or use of the Marks or Other Property. ASC shall not object to, or impede registration by, ABC of the Marks or Other Property, and shall provide all reasonable assistance requested by ABC in ABC's efforts to protect the Marks and Other Property and/or to avoid their unauthorized use. Upon any termination or expiration of this Agreement, all use by ASC and all Sublicensees of the Marks and Other Property shall cease immediately. ASC's obligations herein to protect the Marks and Other Property shall survive any termination or expiration of this Agreement.

G. **Royalty Payments.**

1. **Use by ASC.** For the use by ASC of the Marks, Other Property, and any other intellectual property or rights of ABC, ASC shall pay to ABC a royalty of ___________________ dollars ($_____________) on a monthly basis (the "Monthly License Royalty") for the first year of this Agreement. For the duration of this Agreement, in the sole discretion of ABC, the Monthly License Royalty may be increased by any amount not to exceed _____________ percent (____%) of the prior year's Monthly License Royalty on each anniversary of the effective date of this Agreement.

2. **Sublicenses.** In addition to the Monthly License Royalty set forth under Section III(G)(1) herein, ASC shall pay to ABC, for the right to Sublicense the Marks, Other Property, and any other intellectual property granted herein, an amount equal to ________________ percent (______%) of the gross receipts from all Sublicenses, if any, on a monthly basis.

IV. **Coordinated Activities.** In the event that ABC and ASC mutually determine to coordinate certain activities, the Parties shall ensure that the separateness and independence of the Parties is respected at all times with respect to finances, marketing, assets, and in all other respects. The Parties also shall ensure that there is full accountability for the use by one Party of the services and assets of the other Party.

V. **Confidential Information.** The Parties shall maintain the confidentiality of all of the confidential and proprietary information and data ("Confidential Information") of the other Party. The Parties also shall take all reasonable steps to ensure that no use, by themselves or by any third parties, shall be made of the other Party's Confidential Information without such other Party's consent. Each Party's Confidential Information shall remain the property of that Party and shall be considered to be furnished in confidence to the other Party when necessary under the terms of this Agreement. Upon the termination or expiration of this Agreement, each Party shall: (i) deliver immediately to the other Party all Confidential Information of the other Party, including but not limited to all written and electronic documentation of all Confidential Information, and all copies thereof; (ii) make no further use of it; and (iii) make reasonable efforts to ensure that no further use of it is made by either that Party or its officers, directors, employees, agents, contractors, or any other person or third party. Each Party's confidentiality obligations under this Section shall survive any termination or expiration of this Agreement.

VI. **Indemnification.** Each Party hereby agrees to indemnify, save, and hold harmless the other Party and the other Party's subsidiaries, affiliates, related entities, partners, agents, officers, directors, employees, attorneys, heirs, successors, and assigns, and each of them, from and against any and all claims, actions, demands, losses, damages, judgments, settlements, costs, and expenses (including reasonable attorneys' fees and expenses), and liabilities of every kind and character whatsoever, which may arise by reason of: (i) any act or omission of the Party or any of its officers, directors, employees, or agents in their capacity as officers, directors, employees, or agents of the Party; and/or (ii) the inaccuracy or breach of any of the covenants, representations, or warranties made by the Party under this Agreement. The indemnity under this Section shall require the payment of costs and expenses by the liable Party as they are incurred. The Party seeking reimbursement or indemnity under this Section shall promptly notify the liable (other) Party upon receipt of any claim or legal action referenced in this Section. The indemnified Party shall not at any time admit liability or otherwise attempt to settle or compromise said claim action or demand, except upon the express prior written instructions of the indemnifying Party or upon the repudiation or denial of indemnification by the indemnifying Party. For purposes of this Section, a repudiation or denial of indemnification shall be deemed to occur if the Party seeking indemnification does not receive written confirmation of indemnification from the Party from whom indemnification is sought within thirty (30) days of notice of the claim, action, or demand by the Party seeking indemnification. The Party seeking indemnification shall make all reasonable efforts to provide the Party from whom reimbursement is sought with all information that may be useful in determining whether indemnification is proper. The provisions of this Section shall survive any termination or expiration of this Agreement.

VII. **Separate Entities.** The Parties further agree that they are, and shall remain, separate entities and that no partnership, joint venture, or agency relationship shall be actually or constructively created under this Agreement.

VIII. **Warranties.** Each Party covenants, warrants, and represents that it shall comply with all laws and regulations applicable to this Agreement, and that it shall exercise due care and act in good faith at all times in performance of its obligations under this Agreement. The provisions of this Section shall survive any termination or expiration of this Agreement.

IX. **Waiver.** Either Party's waiver of, or failure to exercise, any right provided for in this Agreement shall not be deemed a waiver of that or any further or future right under this Agreement.

X. **Governing Law and Jurisdiction for Dispute Resolution.** All questions with respect to the construction of this Agreement or the rights and liabilities of the Parties hereunder shall be determined in accordance with the laws of the State of __________________. Any legal action taken or to be taken by either Party regarding this Agreement or the rights and liabilities of Parties hereunder shall be brought only before a federal, state, or local court of competent jurisdiction located within the State of __________________. Each Party hereby consents to the jurisdiction of the federal, state, and local courts located within the State of __________________.

XI. **Headings.** The headings of the various paragraphs herein are intended solely for the convenience of reference and are not intended for any purpose whatsoever to explain, modify, or place any construction upon any of the provisions of this Agreement.

XII. **Assignment.** Except as otherwise provided herein, this Agreement may not be assigned, or the rights granted herein transferred or sublicensed, by either Party without the express prior written consent of the other Party. Any attempted assignment in contravention of this Section shall be of no force or effect and shall not act to relieve either Party of any responsibility or liability under this Agreement. Any attempted assignment in contravention of this Section shall not act to convey, transfer, or assign any rights to any third party and no such rights shall inure to the benefit of any such third party.

XIII. **Heirs, Successors, and Assigns.** This Agreement shall be binding upon and inure to the benefit of each Party, its subsidiaries, affiliates, related entities, partners, agents, officers, directors, employees, heirs, successors, and assigns, without regard to whether it is expressly acknowledged in any instrument of succession or assignment, notwithstanding Section XII herein.

XIV. **Severability.** All provisions of this Agreement are severable. If any provision or portion hereof is determined to be unenforceable in arbitration or by a court of competent jurisdiction, then the remaining portion of the Agreement shall remain in full force and effect.

XV. **Entire Agreement.** This Agreement: (i) constitutes the entire agreement between the Parties with respect to the subject matter hereof; (ii) supersedes and replaces all prior agreements, oral and written, between the Parties relating to the subject matter hereof; and (iii) may be amended only by a written instrument clearly setting forth the amendment(s) and executed by both Parties.

XVI. **Force Majeure.** Neither Party shall be liable for failure to perform its obligations under this Agreement due to events beyond that Party's reasonable control, including, but not limited to, strikes, riots, wars, fire, acts of God, and acts in compliance with any applicable law, regulation, or order (whether valid or invalid) of any governmental body.

XVII. **Counterparts.** This Agreement may be executed in one (1) or more counterparts, each of which shall be deemed an original and all of which taken together shall constitute one (1) and the same instrument.

XVIII. **Notice.** All notices and demands of any kind or nature that either Party may be required or may desire to serve upon the other in connection with this Agreement shall be in writing and may be served personally, by telecopier, by certified mail, or by overnight courier, with constructive receipt deemed to have occurred on the date of the mailing, sending, or faxing of such notice, to the following addresses or telecopier numbers:

If to ABC: ABC Association, Inc.

____

____

Attention: President, ABC Association

Telecopier (_____) ______-__________

If to ASC: ABC Services Corporation

____

____

Attention: President, ABC Services Corporation

Telecopier (_____) ______-__________

*****

IN WITNESS WHEREOF, the parties hereto have caused duplicate originals of this Agreement to be executed by their respective duly authorized representatives as of the date and year first above written.

ABC ASSOCIATION

By: ______________________________

______________________________ [Name]

______________________________ [Title]

ABC SERVICES CORPORATION

By: ______________________________

______________________________ [Name]

______________________________ [Title]

APPENDIX E

Model Affiliation Agreement between Association and Related Foundation

THIS AFFILIATION AGREEMENT (the "Agreement") is made and effective this ______ day of ________________, ______, by and between ABC Association, Inc., a ___________________________ nonprofit corporation, with its principal place of business at ____________________________________ ("ABC"), and ABC Educational Foundation, Inc., a ____________________________ nonprofit corporation, with its principal place of business at ______________________________ ("AEF") (ABC and AEF are collectively referred to hereinafter as the "Parties" and individually as a "Party").

WHEREAS, ABC and AEF, while separate, distinct and independent corporate entities, have certain common goals and interests in furthering and promoting ______________________________, such goals and interests which are in furtherance of the tax-exempt purposes of both ABC and AEF;

WHEREAS, in furtherance of such common goals and interests, ABC and AEF may desire to coordinate certain complementary activities; and

WHEREAS, given such common goals and interests, the mutual desire of the Parties to maximize the opportunities available to them, and the mutual desire of the Parties to minimize their administrative expenses, the Parties desire to enter into this Agreement, under which ABC may provide, and AEF may accept, certain staffing, office space, office equipment, office furniture, office supplies, office services, and other administrative support, and under which ABC may license, and AEF may accept, certain intellectual property.

NOW THEREFORE, in consideration of the premises set forth above and the promises set forth below, the sufficiency and receipt of which are hereby acknowledged, the Parties hereby agree as follows:

I. **Term and Termination.** This Agreement shall be effective as of the date and year first written above and shall remain in full force and effect for a period of one (1) year from such date and year. Thereafter, this Agreement shall automatically renew for successive one (1) year terms without any further action by either Party. Notwithstanding the foregoing, this Agreement may be terminated by either Party for any reason upon written notice provided by either Party to the other Party no less than __________ (____) days prior to the effective date of any such termination. In the event of a material breach of this Agreement, this Agreement may be terminated by the non-breaching Party immediately upon written notice to the other Party, such termination which shall be contingent upon the breaching Party failing to cure such breach within __________ (____) days of its receipt of such written notice from the non-breaching Party.

II. **Staffing, Office Space, Office Services, and Other Administrative Support.** During the Term of this Agreement, as an in-kind donation to AEF and in furtherance of ABC's tax-exempt purposes, ABC agrees to make available and provide to AEF certain professional and administrative staffing, office space, office equipment, office furniture, office supplies, office services, and other administrative support, and to license to AEF certain intellectual property of ABC, as may be required by AEF and as agreed to by ABC in its sole discretion, subject to the following terms and conditions:

A. **Professional Services and Staffing.** ABC shall provide AEF, at no cost to AEF, with the services of some or all of its employees as may be required by AEF from time to time and as agreed to by ABC in its sole discretion, such agreement by ABC which may be modified or withdrawn at any time in ABC's sole discretion. All ABC employees who perform services for or on behalf of AEF shall maintain contemporaneous written daily time logs reflecting the amount of time spent by such employees on AEF programs, activities, and administration, as well as the amount and nature of all other time logged by such employees. The financial value of such time spent by ABC employees on AEF programs, activities, and administration (i.e., the financial value of the allocable share of the relevant ABC employees' compensation, benefits, and employment taxes, calculated, in part, by reference to the written daily time logs maintained by ABC employees) shall be treated by ABC and AEF as an in-kind donation from ABC to AEF.

B. **Office Space, Equipment, Furniture, Supplies, and Services.** ABC shall provide AEF, at no cost to AEF, with the use of office space within ABC's offices (the "ABC Offices"), which offices are presently located at ____________________________. ABC shall provide such office space to AEF within the ABC Offices as may be required by AEF from time to time and as agreed to by ABC in its sole discretion, such agreement by ABC which may be modified or withdrawn at any time in ABC's sole discretion. ABC also shall provide AEF with the use of such office equipment, office furniture, office supplies, office services, and other administrative support as may be required by AEF from time to time and as agreed to by ABC in its sole discretion, such agreement by ABC which may be modified or withdrawn at any time in ABC's sole discretion. The financial value of such office space, office equipment, office furniture, office supplies, office services, and other administrative support shall be treated by ABC and AEF as an in-kind donation from ABC to AEF. Where possible and practical, the financial value of such services and support should be calculated, in part, by reference to the written daily time logs maintained by ABC employees (e.g., if five percent (5%) of all ABC employee time was spent on AEF matters during a given month, then five percent (5%) of the cost of ABC's mortgage/rental payment(s), utility payments, etc. for that month should be treated as an in-kind donation from ABC to AEF). Wherever the direct costs of providing such services and support can be easily ascertained (e.g., postage costs, overnight mail charges, courier service charges), such direct costs of ABC should be treated as an in-kind contribution from ABC to AEF.

III. **Intellectual Property License.**

A. **Name and Logo.** During the Term of this Agreement, ABC grants to AEF a non-exclusive, limited license to use the service marks "ABC Association" and "ABC," the logo or logos of ABC, and all other marks consisting of letters, words, or graphics in which ABC may have a proprietary interest or property right (collectively, "Marks"), in the name or description of AEF and in programs and activities undertaken by AEF, pursuant to the terms and conditions of this Section.

B. **Other Intellectual Property.** During the Term of this Agreement and unless otherwise reserved in writing by ABC, ABC grants to AEF a non-exclusive, limited license to use all other names, trademarks, service marks, certification marks, copyrights, and any such other intellectual property in which ABC may have a proprietary interest or property right (collectively, "Other Property"), including but not limited to all ABC mailing, telecopying, and electronic mail lists.

C. **Sublicenses.** During the Term of this Agreement and unless otherwise reserved in writing by ABC, AEF shall have the limited right to sublicense ("Sublicense") any and all Marks and Other Property licensed to it by ABC to third parties ("Sublicensees"), provided that all such Sublicenses shall be subject to the same restrictions on use of such Marks and Other Property and the same confidentiality requirements as are imposed upon AEF under this Agreement. All Sublicenses shall require the prior written approval of ABC, such approval which may or may not be granted by ABC in ABC's sole discretion. AEF shall take all reasonable and prudent steps in order to ensure that all Sublicensees comply with the restrictions on use and confidentiality requirements imposed under this Agreement.

D. **Ownership of Marks and Other Property.** Notwithstanding any provision contained herein, AEF hereby recognizes the exclusive residual ownership by ABC of all rights, proprietary interests, and property rights in the Marks and Other Property.

E. **Restrictions on Use of Marks or Other Property.** AEF shall not use, authorize others to use, or permit the use of Marks or Other Property except in programs and activities that are consistent with this Agreement and any written reservation of rights provided by ABC. AEF shall not use, authorize others to use, or permit the use of Marks or Other Property that would materially decrease the value of such Marks and Other Property or the goodwill or reputation associated with ABC. AEF shall take all reasonable and prudent steps to ensure that any use of the Marks or Other Property pursuant to the limited license granted herein, either by themselves or by any Sublicensee, shall contain the applicable copyright, trademark, or service mark notices, pursuant to the requirements of any applicable laws or regulations and any other guidelines provided under this Agreement or that ABC may have heretofore or may hereafter prescribe in writing.

F. **Notification of Claims; Assistance in Registration; Termination.** AEF shall promptly notify ABC of any claim related to or potentially affecting the ownership or use of the Marks or Other Property. AEF shall not object to, or impede registration by, ABC of the Marks or Other Property, and shall provide all reasonable assistance requested by ABC in ABC's efforts to protect the Marks and Other Property and/or to avoid their unauthorized use. Upon any termination or expiration of this Agreement, all use by AEF and all Sublicensees of the Marks and Other Property shall cease immediately. AEF's obligations herein to protect the Marks and Other Property shall survive any termination or expiration of this Agreement.

IV. **Boards of Directors.**

A. **Election of AEF Board of Directors.** The Board of Directors of ABC, on an annual basis at a meeting of the Board of Directors of ABC, shall elect the members of the Board of Directors of AEF. Such election shall be by the affirmative vote of a majority of the Directors of ABC present at such meeting, provided a quorum (as set forth in the Bylaws of ABC) is present. The Board of Directors of ABC shall set forth procedures for the nomination of candidates for AEF's Directorships.

B. **Board of Directors Meetings.** For reasons of convenience and cost efficiency, if reasonably feasible, the Annual Meeting of the Board of Directors of AEF should be held on the same or proximate date and at the same general location as the Annual Meeting of the Board of Directors of ABC. In addition, if reasonably feasible, all other in-person regular meetings, if any, of the Board of Directors of AEF should be held on the same or proximate date and at the same general location as regular meetings, if any, of the Board of Directors of ABC. All Board of Directors meetings of AEF shall be separate and distinct from Board of Directors meetings of ABC.

V. **Coordinated Activities.** In the event that ABC and AEF mutually determine to coordinate certain activities, the Parties shall ensure that the separateness and independence of the Parties is respected at all times with respect to finances, marketing, assets, and in all other respects. The Parties also shall ensure that there is full accountability for the use by one Party of the services and assets of the other Party.

VI. **Separate Entities.** The Parties further agree that they are, and shall remain, separate entities and that no partnership, joint venture, or agency relationship shall be actually or constructively created under this Agreement.

VII. **Confidential Information.** The Parties shall maintain the confidentiality of all of the confidential and proprietary information and data ("Confidential Information") of the other Party. The Parties also shall take all reasonable steps to ensure that no use, by themselves or by any third parties, shall be made of the other Party's Confidential Information without such other Party's consent. Each Party's Confidential Information shall remain the property of that Party and shall be considered to be furnished in confidence to the other Party when necessary under the terms of this Agreement. Upon the termination or expiration of this Agreement, each Party shall: (i) deliver immediately to the other Party all Confidential Information of the other Party, including but not limited to all written and electronic documentation of all Confidential Information, and all copies thereof; (ii) make no further use of it; and (iii) make reasonable efforts to ensure that no further use of it is made by either that Party or its officers, directors, employees, agents, contractors, or any other person or third party. Each Party's confidentiality obligations under this Section shall survive any termination or expiration of this Agreement.

VIII. **Indemnification.** Each Party hereby agrees to indemnify, save, and hold harmless the other Party and the other Party's subsidiaries, affiliates, related entities, partners, agents, officers, directors, employees, attorneys, heirs, successors, and assigns, and each of them, from and against any and all claims, actions, demands, losses, damages, judgments, settlements, costs, and expenses (including reasonable attorneys' fees and expenses), and liabilities of every kind and character whatsoever, which may arise by reason of: (i) any act or omission of the Party or any of its officers, directors, employees, or agents in their capacity as officers, directors, employees, or agents of the Party; and/or (ii) the inaccuracy or breach of any of the covenants, representations, or warranties made by the Party under this Agreement. The indemnity under this Section shall require the payment of costs and expenses by the liable Party as they are incurred. The Party seeking reimbursement or indemnity under this Section shall promptly notify the liable (other) Party upon receipt of any claim or legal action referenced in this Section. The indemnified Party shall not at any time admit liability or otherwise attempt to settle or compromise said claim action, or demand, except upon the express prior written instructions of the indemnifying Party or upon the repudiation or denial of indemnification by the indemnifying Party. For purposes of this Section, a repudiation or denial of indemnification shall be deemed to occur if the Party seeking indemnification does not receive written confirmation of indemnification from the Party from whom indemnification is sought within thirty (30) days of notice of the claim, action, or demand by the Party seeking indemnification. The Party seeking indemnification shall make all reasonable efforts to provide the Party from whom reimbursement is sought with all information that may be useful in determining whether indemnification is proper. The provisions of this Section shall survive any termination or expiration of this Agreement.

IX. **Warranties.** Each Party covenants, warrants, and represents that it shall comply with all laws and regulations applicable to this Agreement, and that it shall exercise due care and act in good faith at all times in performance of its obligations under this Agreement. The provisions of this Section shall survive any termination or expiration of this Agreement.

X. **Waiver.** Either Party's waiver of, or failure to exercise, any right provided for in this Agreement shall not be deemed a waiver of that or any further or future right under this Agreement.

XI. **Governing Law and Jurisdiction for Dispute Resolution.** All questions with respect to the construction of this Agreement or the rights and liabilities of the Parties hereunder shall be determined in accordance with the laws of the State of ____________________. Any legal action taken or to be taken by either Party regarding this Agreement or the rights and liabilities of Parties hereunder shall be brought only before a federal, state, or local court of competent jurisdiction located within the State of ____________________. Each Party hereby consents to the jurisdiction of the federal, state, and local courts located within the State of ____________________.

XII. **Headings.** The headings of the various paragraphs herein are intended solely for the convenience of reference and are not intended for any purpose whatsoever to explain, modify, or place any construction upon any of the provisions of this Agreement.

XIII. **Assignment.** Except as otherwise provided herein, this Agreement may not be assigned, or the rights granted herein transferred or sublicensed, by either Party without the express prior written consent of the other Party. Any attempted assignment in contravention of this Section shall be of no force or effect and shall not act to relieve either Party of any responsibility or liability under this Agreement. Any attempted assignment in contravention of this Section shall not act to convey, transfer, or assign any rights to any third party and no such rights shall inure to the benefit of any such third party.

XIV. **Heirs, Successors, and Assigns.** This Agreement shall be binding upon and inure to the benefit of each Party, its subsidiaries, affiliates, related entities, partners, agents, officers, directors, employees, heirs, successors, and assigns, without regard to whether it is expressly acknowledged in any instrument of succession or assignment, notwithstanding Section XIII herein.

XV. **Severability.** All provisions of this Agreement are severable. If any provision or portion hereof is determined to be unenforceable in arbitration or by a court of competent jurisdiction, then the remaining portion of the Agreement shall remain in full force and effect.

XVI. **Entire Agreement.** This Agreement: (i) constitutes the entire agreement between the Parties with respect to the subject matter hereof; (ii) supersedes and replaces all prior agreements, oral and written, between the Parties relating to the subject matter hereof; and (iii) may be amended only by a written instrument clearly setting forth the amendment(s) and executed by both Parties.

XVII. **Force Majeure.** Neither Party shall be liable for failure to perform its obligations under this Agreement due to events beyond that Party's reasonable control, including, but not limited to, strikes, riots, wars, fire, acts of God, and acts in compliance with any applicable law, regulation, or order (whether valid or invalid) of any governmental body.

XVIII. **Counterparts.** This Agreement may be executed in one (1) or more counterparts, each of which shall be deemed an original and all of which taken together shall constitute one (1) and the same instrument.

XIX. **Notice.** All notices and demands of any kind or nature that either Party may be required or may desire to serve upon the other in connection with this Agreement shall be in writing and may be served personally, by telecopier, by certified mail, or by overnight courier, with constructive receipt deemed to have occurred on the date of the mailing, sending, or faxing of such notice, to the following addresses or telecopier numbers:

If to ABC: ABC Association, Inc.

____

____

Attention: President, ABC Association

Telecopier (_____) ______-__________

If to ASC: ABC Educational Foundation, Inc.

____

____

Attention: President, ABC Educational Foundation

Telecopier (_____) ______-__________

*****

IN WITNESS WHEREOF, the parties hereto have caused duplicate originals of this Agreement to be executed by their respective duly authorized representatives as of the date and year first above written.

ABC ASSOCIATION, INC.

By: ____

____ [Name]

____ [Title]

ABC EDUCATIONAL FOUNDATION, INC.

By: ____

____ [Name]

____ [Title]

APPENDIX F

Model Chapter Affiliation Agreement

THIS AFFILIATION AGREEMENT (the "Agreement"), is made this _____ day of ________, ______, by and between ______________________________ _______________________________ ("ASSOCIATION"), a _____________ nonprofit corporation, with its principal place of business at ___________________________ ___________ ____________________________, and ________________________ ("CHAPTER"), a _______________ nonprofit corporation, with its principal place of business at____.

NOW THEREFORE, in consideration of the premises set forth above and the promises set forth below, the sufficiency and receipt of which are hereby acknowledged, the parties hereby agree as follows:

I. **Grant of Charter to CHAPTER.**

A. **Charter.** ASSOCIATION hereby grants to CHAPTER a nonexclusive charter to be a chapter of ASSOCIATION. In accordance therewith, CHAPTER is authorized to use the name "[insert full name of ASSOCIATION]," "[insert acronym of ASSOCIATION]," and logo of ASSOCIATION in or in connection with CHAPTER's name, acronym, and logo, with the authority to use such marks in connection with CHAPTER's activities authorized under this Agreement, subject to the terms and conditions of this Agreement and any written guidelines attached hereto, otherwise incorporated herein, or subsequently provided to CHAPTER by ASSOCIATION.

B. **Term and Termination.** The Term of this Agreement shall commence on the effective date set forth above and shall continue until revoked by ASSOCIATION or surrendered by CHAPTER, pursuant to the terms of this Agreement for revocation and surrender.

C. **Territory.** CHAPTER shall represent ASSOCIATION as ASSOCIATION's affiliate in ____________________________ (the "Territory"), pursuant to and in accordance with ASSOCIATION's mission and purposes as set forth in ASSOCIATION's Articles of Incorporation and Bylaws or as otherwise established by ASSOCIATION's Board of Directors. CHAPTER acknowledges that this designation is non-exclusive in the Territory and that ASSOCIATION may, in its sole discretion, designate other affiliates in the Territory or may sponsor or conduct programs, accept members, and perform other activities within the Territory.

D. **Authorized Activities.** ASSOCIATION specifically authorizes CHAPTER to conduct the following activities within the Territory: _________________,

________________, ________________, ________________, ________________,
and such other activities as may be consistent with the mission and purposes of ASSOCIATION and in which ASSOCIATION may from to time to time authorize CHAPTER to engage.

II. **Membership.** Members of CHAPTER also must be members of ASSOCIATION. The terms and conditions of membership in ASSOCIATION shall be determined exclusively by ASSOCIATION. The terms and conditions of membership in CHAPTER shall be determined exclusively by CHAPTER, and shall be set forth in CHAPTER's Bylaws. [All CHAPTER and ASSOCIATION membership dues shall be collected directly from members by ASSOCIATION. ASSOCIATION shall thereafter remit CHAPTER dues to CHAPTER.]

III. **Obligations of ASSOCIATION.** ASSOCIATION's obligations under this Agreement shall include:

____.

____.

____.

____.

____.

IV. **Obligations of CHAPTER.** CHAPTER's obligations under this Agreement shall include:

A. **Corporate and Tax Status.** CHAPTER warrants that it is incorporated as a nonprofit corporation in good standing, that it shall remain in good standing, and is and shall remain exempt from federal income tax under Section 501(c)(____) of the Internal Revenue Code of 1986, as the same may be amended or supplemented. [Insert alternative requirements if CHAPTER is exempt from federal income tax pursuant to a group exemption.]

B. **Articles of Incorporation, Bylaws, and Other Requirements.** As a condition of receipt of its charter as a chapter of ASSOCIATION, CHAPTER heretofore provided to ASSOCIATION, and ASSOCIATION provided its approval to, the ARTICLES OF INCORPORATION and BYLAWS of CHAPTER. Such CHAPTER Bylaws are, and shall remain, consistent in all material respects with the Model Bylaws attached hereto as **Exhibit A** and incorporated by reference herein. Any amendments to CHAPTER's Articles of Incorporation or Bylaws must first be submitted to, and approved by, ASSOCIATION. CHAPTER shall have as its purposes those set forth in the Model Bylaws attached hereto, shall conduct its activities at all times in strict accordance with such Bylaws, and shall comply at all times with all of the requirements set forth in ASSOCIATION's Bylaws and all other chapter-related policies, procedures, handbooks, or other written guidance heretofore or hereafter promulgated by ASSOCIATION (all of which are incorporated by reference herein).

C. **Compliance with Laws.** CHAPTER warrants that it is in full compliance with all applicable laws, regulations, and other legal standards that may affect its performance under this Agreement, and shall remain in full compliance with, and otherwise conduct its activities at all times in accordance with all applicable law, regulations, and other legal standards. Further, CHAPTER warrants that it shall maintain at all times all permits, licenses, and other governmental approvals that may be required in the Territory in connection with its performance under this Agreement. Furthermore, CHAPTER warrants that it shall make all required filings, such as annual corporate reports and tax filings, that may affect its corporate or tax status.

D. **Recordkeeping, Reporting, and Inspection.** CHAPTER shall maintain all records related to its corporate and tax-exempt status and shall forward to ASSOCIATION copies of its Articles of Incorporation, Bylaws, and tax exemption determination letter from the Internal Revenue Service, as well as any adverse notices or other correspondence received from any governmental agency (e.g., Internal Revenue Service, state Secretary of State, or corresponding agency). CHAPTER shall maintain reasonable records related to all of its programs, activities, and operations. CHAPTER shall submit regular written reports, no less than once per year, to ASSOCIATION summarizing its programs, activities, and operations, including but not limited to budget and financial statements. Upon the written request of ASSOCIATION and at ASSOCIATION's expense, CHAPTER shall permit ASSOCIATION or ASSOCIATION's designated agent to review appropriate records of CHAPTER pertaining to its programs, activities, and operations. Alternatively, CHAPTER shall send to ASSOCIATION copies of such records.

E. **Programs and Activities.** CHAPTER shall endeavor to sponsor and conduct programs and activities that further the purposes and objectives of ASSOCIATION, and shall use its best efforts to ensure that such programs and activities are of the highest quality with respect to content, materials, logistical preparation, and otherwise. CHAPTER shall endeavor to use, to the extent possible, materials available through ASSOCIATION in support of such programs and activities. CHAPTER shall send to ASSOCIATION on a regular basis a schedule of upcoming meetings, conferences, and seminars, as well as other programs and activities that CHAPTER intends to sponsor or conduct. ASSOCIATION may, at its sole discretion, send representatives to observe such programs and activities.

F. **Government Affairs Efforts.** CHAPTER shall endeavor to conduct government affairs efforts within the Territory consistent with the purposes and objectives of ASSOCIATION. In performing this function, CHAPTER shall work with ASSOCIATION in order to ensure national consistency in these efforts.

G. **Other Obligations:**

1. ______________________________.
2. ______________________________.
3. ______________________________.
4. ______________________________.
5. ______________________________.

V. **Intellectual Property and Confidential Information.**

A. **Limited License.** In accordance with ASSOCIATION's non-exclusive grant to CHAPTER to be a chapter of ASSOCIATION in the Territory, CHAPTER is hereby granted a limited, revocable, non-exclusive license to use (i) the name "[insert full name of ASSOCIATION]," acronym "[insert acronym of ASSOCIATION]," logo of ASSOCIATION, and other ASSOCIATION trademarks, service marks, trade names, and logos (hereinafter collectively referred to as the "Marks"), (ii) ASSOCIATION's membership mailing, telephone, telecopier, and electronic mail lists with respect to past, current, and prospective members of ASSOCIATION located within the Territory (hereinafter collectively referred to as the "Mailing List"), and (iii) all copyrighted or proprietary information and materials provided by ASSOCIATION to CHAPTER during the Term of this Agreement (hereinafter referred to as the "Proprietary Information") (the Marks, Mailing List, and Proprietary Information are hereinafter collectively referred to as the "Intellectual Property") in or in connection with CHAPTER's name, acronym, and logo and for other official CHAPTER-related purposes, with the limited authority to use the Intellectual Property solely in connection with the activities authorized under this Agreement, subject to the terms and conditions of this Agreement and any written guidelines attached hereto, otherwise incorporated herein, or subsequently provided to CHAPTER by ASSOCIATION.

1. The Intellectual Property is and shall remain at all times the sole and exclusive property of ASSOCIATION. The Intellectual Property may be used by CHAPTER of ASSOCIATION if and only if such use is made pursuant to the terms and conditions of this limited and revocable license. Any failure by CHAPTER to comply with the terms and conditions contained herein, whether willful or negligent, may result in the immediate suspension or revocation of this license, in whole or in part, by ASSOCIATION. Failure to comply, whether willful or negligent, also may result in the suspension or revocation of the charter of CHAPTER by ASSOCIATION. The interpretation and enforcement (or lack thereof) of these terms and conditions, and compliance therewith, shall be made by ASSOCIATION in its sole discretion.

2. ASSOCIATION's logo may not be revised or altered in any way, and must be displayed in the same form as produced by ASSOCIATION. The Marks may not be used in conjunction with any other trademark, service mark, or other mark without the express prior written approval of ASSOCIATION.

3. The Intellectual Property must be used by CHAPTER in a professional manner and solely for official CHAPTER-related purposes. CHAPTER shall not permit any third party to use the Intellectual Property without ASSOCIATION's express prior written approval. CHAPTER shall not sell or trade the Intellectual Property without ASSOCIATION's express prior written approval. Notwithstanding the foregoing, the Intellectual Property may not be used for individual personal or professional gain or other private benefit, and the Intellectual Property may not be used in any manner that, in the sole discretion of ASSOCIATION, discredits ASSOCIATION or tarnishes its reputation and goodwill; is false or misleading; violates the rights of others; violates any law, regula-

tion or other public policy; or mischaracterizes the relationship between ASSOCIATION and CHAPTER, including but not limited to the fact that CHAPTER is a separate and distinct legal entity from ASSOCIATION.

4. CHAPTER shall maintain the confidentiality of the Mailing List and shall not sell, trade, transmit, or otherwise disseminate the Mailing List, in whole or in part, to any third party without the express prior written approval of ASSOCIATION.

5. In any authorized use by CHAPTER of the Intellectual Property, CHAPTER shall ensure that the applicable trademark and copyright notices are used pursuant to the requirements of United States law, the laws of the Territory, and any other guidelines that ASSOCIATION may prescribe.

6. ASSOCIATION shall have the right, from time to time, to request samples of use of the Intellectual Property from which it may determine compliance with these terms and conditions. ASSOCIATION reserves the right to prohibit use of any of the Intellectual Property, as well as to impose other sanctions, if it determines, in its sole discretion, that CHAPTER's usage thereof is not in strict accordance with the terms and conditions of this limited and revocable license.

7. Use of the Intellectual Property shall create no rights for CHAPTER in or to the Intellectual Property or its use beyond the terms and conditions of this limited and revocable license. All rights of usage of the Intellectual Property by CHAPTER shall terminate immediately upon the revocation, surrender, or other termination of this Agreement. CHAPTER's obligations to protect the Intellectual Property shall survive the revocation, surrender, or other termination of this Agreement.

B. **Confidential Information.** The parties shall maintain the confidentiality of all of the confidential and proprietary information and data ("Confidential Information") of the other party. The parties also shall take all reasonable steps to ensure that no use, by themselves or by any third parties, shall be made of the other party's Confidential Information without such other party's consent. Each party's Confidential Information shall remain the property of that party and shall be considered to be furnished in confidence to the other party when necessary under the terms of this Agreement. Upon any revocation, surrender, or other termination of this Agreement, each party shall: (i) deliver immediately to the other party all Confidential Information of the other party, including but not limited to all written and electronic documentation of all Confidential Information, and all copies thereof; (ii) make no further use of it; and (iii) make reasonable efforts to ensure that no further use of it is made by either that party or its officers, directors, employees, agents, contractors, or any other person or third party. Each party's confidentiality obligations under this Section shall survive any revocation, surrender, or other termination of this Agreement.

VI. **Relationship of Parties.** The relationship of ASSOCIATION and CHAPTER to each other is that of independent contractors. Nothing herein shall create any association, joint venture, partnership, or agency relationship of any kind between the parties. Unless expressly agreed to in writing by the parties, neither party is authorized to incur any liability, obligation, or expense on behalf of the other, to use the other's monetary credit in conducting any activities under this Agreement, or to represent to any third party that CHAPTER is an agent of ASSOCIATION.

VII. **Indemnification.** CHAPTER shall indemnify, save, and hold harmless ASSOCIATION, and its subsidiaries, affiliates, related entities, partners, agents, officers, directors, employees, members, shareholders, attorneys, heirs, successors, and assigns, and each of them, from and against any and all claims, actions, suits, demands, losses, damages, judgments, settlements, costs and expenses (including reasonable attorneys' fees and expenses), and liabilities of every kind and character whatsoever (a "Claim"), which may arise by reason of (i) any act or omission by CHAPTER or any of its subsidiaries, affiliates, related entities, partners, officers, directors, employees, members, shareholders or agents, or (ii) the inaccuracy or breach of any of the covenants, representations, and warranties made by CHAPTER in this Agreement. This indemnity shall require CHAPTER to provide payment to ASSOCIATION of costs and expenses as they occur. CHAPTER shall promptly notify ASSOCIATION upon receipt of any Claim and shall grant to ASSOCIATION the sole conduct of the defense to any Claim. The provisions of this Section shall survive any revocation, surrender, or other termination of this Agreement.

VIII. **Revocation or Surrender of Charter.**

A. **Revocation of Charter.** The charter granted by ASSOCIATION to CHAPTER hereunder shall remain in full force and effect unless and until revoked by ASSOCIATION or surrendered by CHAPTER in accordance with the provisions of this Agreement. ASSOCIATION, through its Board of Directors, shall have the authority to revoke the charter of CHAPTER if the Board of Directors determines that the conduct of CHAPTER is in breach of any provision of this Agreement. Any decision by ASSOCIATION to revoke CHAPTER's charter shall be initiated by sending written notice to CHAPTER specifying the grounds upon which the revocation is based; provided, however, that ASSOCIATION shall provide CHAPTER with __________ (___) days from the date of such notice to cure any alleged breach of this Agreement. In the event that ASSOCIATION determines, in its sole discretion, that CHAPTER has not corrected the condition leading to ASSOCIATION's decision to revoke CHAPTER's charter, ASSOCIATION shall so notify CHAPTER in writing. ASSOCIATION's decision shall become final unless, within ________ (___) days of its receipt of written notice from ASSOCIATION, CHAPTER delivers to ASSOCIATION a written notice to appeal such determination. Upon the filing of such an appeal notice, CHAPTER shall have the opportunity to present its case, by written communication or in person, to the Board of Directors of ASSOCIATION pursuant to the applicable rules or procedures prescribed by ASSOCIATION's Board of Directors. The decision of ASSOCIATION's Board of Directors upon such appeal shall be final and not subject to further appeal.

B. **Surrender of Charter.** CHAPTER may surrender its charter by delivering to ASSOCIATION written notice of its intention to do so no less than ________ (____) days prior to the effective date of such surrender.

IX. **Miscellaneous.**

A. **Entire Agreement**. This Agreement: (i) constitutes the entire agreement between the parties hereto with respect to the subject matter hereof; (ii) supersedes and replaces all prior agreements, oral and written, between the parties relating to the subject matter hereof; and (iii) may be amended only by a written instrument clearly setting forth the amendment(s) and executed by both parties.

B. **Warranties.** Each party covenants, warrants, and represents that it shall comply with all laws, regulations, and other legal standards applicable to this Agreement, and that it shall exercise due care and act in good faith at all times in performance of its obligations under this Agreement. The provisions of this Section shall survive any revocation, surrender, or other termination of this Agreement.

C. **Waiver.** Either party's waiver of, or failure to exercise, any right provided for in this Agreement shall not be deemed a waiver of any further or future right under this Agreement.

D. **Arbitration.** Any and all disputes arising under this Agreement shall be subject to mandatory and binding arbitration. Said arbitration shall take place in the State of ______________________. Neither party shall have any right to bring an action relating to this Agreement in a court of law, except insofar as to either enforce or appeal the results of any such arbitration. In any such arbitration, and subsequent court action, the prevailing party shall be entitled to collect its fees and costs associated therewith from the non-prevailing party.

E. **Governing Law.** All questions with respect to the construction of this Agreement or the rights and liabilities of the parties hereunder shall be determined in accordance with the laws of the State of __________________. Any legal action taken or to be taken by either party regarding this Agreement or the rights and liabilities of parties hereunder shall be brought only before a federal, state, or local court of competent jurisdiction located within the State of __________________. Each party hereby consents to the jurisdiction of the federal, state, and local courts located within the State of

____________________.

F. **Assignment.** This Agreement may not be assigned, or the rights granted hereunder transferred or sub-licensed, by either party without the express prior written consent of the other party.

G. **Heirs, Successors, and Assigns.** This Agreement shall be binding upon and inure to the benefit of each party, its subsidiaries, affiliates, related entities, partners, agents, officers, directors, employees, heirs, successors, and assigns, without regard to whether it is expressly acknowledged in any instrument of succession or assignment.

H. **Headings.** The headings of the various paragraphs hereof are intended solely for the convenience of reference and are not intended for any purpose whatsoever to explain, modify, or place any construction upon any of the provisions of this Agreement.

I. **Counterparts.** This Agreement may be executed in one (1) or more counterparts, each of which shall be deemed an original and all of which taken together shall constitute one and the same instrument.

J. **Severability.** All provisions of this Agreement are severable. If any provision or portion hereof is determined to be unenforceable in arbitration or by a court of competent jurisdiction, then the remaining portion of the Agreement shall remain in full effect.

K. **Force Majeure.** Neither party shall be liable for failure to perform its obligations under this Agreement due to events beyond its reasonable control, including, but not limited to, strikes, riots, wars, fire, acts of God, and acts in compliance with any applicable law, regulation, or order (whether valid or invalid) of any governmental body.

L. **Notice.** All notices and demands of any kind or nature that either party may be required or may desire to serve upon the other in connection with this Agreement shall be in writing and may be served personally, by telecopier, by certified mail, or by overnight courier, with constructive receipt deemed to have occurred on the date of the mailing, sending, or faxing of such notice, to the following addresses or telecopier numbers:

If to ASSOCIATION: ______________________________

____

____

Attn.: ______________________________

Telecopier (_____) ______-__________

If to CHAPTER: ______________________________

____

____

Attn.: ______________________________

Telecopier (_____) ______-__________

*****

IN WITNESS WHEREOF, the parties hereto have caused duplicate originals of this Agreement to be executed by their respective duly authorized representatives as of the date and year first above written.

[NAME OF ASSOCIATION]

By: ______________________________

______________________________ [Name]

______________________________ [Title]

[NAME OF CHAPTER]

By: ______________________________

______________________________ [Name]

______________________________ [Title]

EXHIBIT A
MODEL CHAPTER BYLAWS

[list chapter bylaws]

APPENDIX G

Model Consulting/Independent Contractor Agreement

(FOR USE WHEN CONSULTANT IS AN INDIVIDUAL)

THIS CONSULTING AGREEMENT (the "Agreement") is made this ____ day of ________, ____, by and between ABC Association ("ABC"), a __________________ nonprofit corporation, and _________________ ("Consultant"), a natural person, and sets forth the terms of the Consultant's consulting relationship with ABC as follows:

1. **Consulting Services.** Effective __________, ____, ABC shall retain Consultant and Consultant shall provide ABC with consulting services (hereinafter described as the "Consulting Services" or "Consulting Relationship"), which shall include, without limitation, [describe consulting services here]. The nature of the Consulting Services may be modified by ABC in writing at any time, with the written agreement of Consultant.

2. **Term.** This Agreement shall remain in effect from __________ until _________________ (the "Term" or "Consulting Period"), unless terminated earlier by one (1) or both of the parties as set forth herein.

3. **Fee.** In consideration of the performance of the Consulting Services, ABC shall pay Consultant a fee of $_________ per month during the Consulting Period, payable by the ___ of each month during the Term of this Agreement [or set forth alternative fee arrangement agreed to by the parties].

4. **Termination.** ABC or Consultant may terminate this Agreement with or without cause (i) by the written agreement of both parties, or (ii) with ___ days' written notice to the other party. Upon termination of the Agreement, ABC's obligation to pay the fees described in Paragraph 3 herein and to reimburse Consultant for the expenses described in Paragraph 6 herein shall cease, effective as of the date of termination; provided, however, that ABC shall remain obligated to pay such fees and/or reimburse such expenses as have already been incurred or obligated prior to the date of termination.

5. **Control.** Consultant has the right to control and direct the means, manner, and method by which the Consulting Services are performed.

6. **Equipment and Materials, Expenses, and Insurance.** Consultant shall furnish all equipment, materials, and labor used to perform the Consulting Services. Consultant shall pay all ordinary and necessary expenses arising from its performance of the Consulting Services. [ABC shall, however, upon the submission by Consultant of appropriate written substantiation as set forth below and pursuant to the following terms and conditions, reimburse Consultant for ordinary and necessary business expenses,

including travel and communication costs (e.g., phone, fax, computer, printer) and other materials and equipment costs, reasonably incurred by Consultant in connection with the provision of Consulting Services, as reasonably allocable to the provision of Consulting Services. As a precondition to reimbursement of any such expenses, Consultant shall provide ABC with detailed documentation regarding such expenses, including receipts, itineraries, reasons for the expenses, and such other documentation as ABC may require. Notwithstanding the foregoing, no expenses incurred by Consultant in connection with the provision of Consulting Services shall be reimbursed by ABC if and when such expenses exceed $__________ per ___________, unless reimbursement in excess of such limit is approved by the ABC Executive Director in writing.]* ABC shall not provide insurance coverage of any kind for Consultant or name Consultant as an additional insured on any of its insurance policies.

7. **Independent Contractor Status.** The Parties agree and acknowledge that Consultant is an independent contractor. Nothing herein shall be construed to create any partnership, joint venture, or agency relationship of any kind between the parties. Consultant has no authority to enter into any agreements or contracts on behalf of ABC, or to bind ABC in any way, and shall not represent, either explicitly or implicitly, that he possesses any such authority. Consultant is not, nor shall be, deemed to be, for any purpose, an employee or agent of ABC. ABC shall not be responsible to Consultant, or to any governmental authority, for the payment or withholding of any federal, state, or local income, unemployment or other employment-related taxes in connection with the performance of the Consulting Services. It is understood that ABC shall not withhold from Consultant's compensation any amount that would normally be withheld from an employee's pay and Consultant warrants and agrees to pay all federal, state, and local taxes incurred and chargeable to him in connection with the performance of the Consulting Services. Consultant further warrants and agrees to file all required forms and make all federal, state, or local tax payments appropriate and necessary to Consultant's tax status as an independent contractor and shall not claim any other status. Consultant further warrants and agrees to file all other required forms, registrations, reports, and other filings, and to pay all corresponding fees or other charges, as may be required of Consultant, at the federal, state, and/or local levels, as a consequence of activities being conducted by Consultant for or on behalf of ABC.

8. **Indemnification.** Consultant agrees to indemnify, save, and hold harmless ABC and its officers, directors, employees, and agents from and against any and all losses, expenses (including, but not limited to, payroll and income taxes and attorneys' fees), damages, claims, suits, demands, judgments, and causes of action of any nature arising from or as a result of (i) the performance of Consultant's obligations under this Agreement, (ii) the failure of Consultant to comply with any term or condition (including but not limited to all warranties and representations) of this Agreement, and/or (iii) the reclassification or attempted reclassification of Consultant as an employee of ABC.

---

* This bracketed passage is not required. ABC may wish to modify or delete some or all of this passage depending upon the type of consulting work performed.

9. **Property of ABC.** During the course of performing Consulting Services, Consultant may, independently or in conjunction with ABC, develop information, produce work product, or achieve other results for ABC in connection with the Consulting Services it performs for ABC. Consultant agrees that such information, work product, or other results, systems, and information developed by the Consultant and/or ABC in connection with such Consulting Services (hereinafter collectively referred to as the "Work Product") shall vest with ABC and shall remain the sole and absolute property of ABC. Consultant hereby assigns all right, title, and interest in all intellectual property rights and all other property rights in the Work Product, including all extensions and renewals thereof, to ABC. Consultant further agrees to provide all assistance reasonably requested by ABC, both during and subsequent to the Term of this Agreement, in the establishment, preservation, and enforcement of ABC's' rights in the Work Product. Upon the termination of this Agreement, Consultant agrees to promptly deliver to ABC all printed, electronic, audio-visual, and other tangible manifestations of the Work Product, including all originals and copies thereof. Consultant also agrees to waive any and all moral rights relating to the Work Product, including but not limited to, any and all rights of identification of authorship and any and all rights of approval, restriction, or limitation on use, and subsequent modifications.

10. **Reporting and Inspection.** During the Term of this Agreement, Consultant shall report in writing to ABC with whatever frequency and regarding whatever subject matter ABC shall hereinafter require of Consultant in order for ABC to stay apprised of Consultant's activities under this Agreement. Furthermore, during the Term of this Agreement, upon reasonable notice and during regular business hours, ABC shall have the right to inspect all books and records of Consultant relating to the subject matter of this Agreement.

11. **Conflict of Interest.** Consultant represents and warrants that it has no business, professional, personal, or other interest, including but not limited to the representation of other clients, that would conflict in any manner or degree with the performance of its obligations under this Agreement. If any such actual or potential conflict of interest arises during the Term of this Agreement, Consultant shall immediately inform ABC in writing of such conflict. If, in the reasonable judgment of ABC, such conflict poses a material conflict to and with the performance of Consultant's obligations under this Agreement, then ABC may terminate the Agreement immediately upon written notice to Consultant; such termination of the Agreement shall be effective upon the receipt of such notice by Consultant. Nothing herein shall preclude Consultant from engaging in other business activities, so long as such other activities do not violate or are not inconsistent with the terms and conditions of this Agreement, or do not otherwise pose a conflict of interest with Consultant's obligations under this Agreement.

12. **Nondisclosure of Confidential and Proprietary Information.**

a. Through its Consulting Relationship with ABC, Consultant may have access to confidential and proprietary information concerning ABC's organization, employees, members, and otherwise, including but not limited to, information concerning

ABC's organization and structure, business and marketing plans, financial data, the identity of present and prospective members of ABC, ABC's current and prospective contracts, and policies, standards, procedures, and practices of ABC (hereinafter referred to as "Confidential Information"). The use of Confidential Information for the benefit of any person or entity other than ABC and the disclosure of such information to any person outside of ABC would cause severe competitive and financial damage to ABC.

b. Unless expressly authorized by ABC, both during and after the Term of this Agreement, Consultant will not use Confidential Information for his own benefit or for the benefit of anyone other than ABC, or disclose such information to anyone outside of ABC, except in the proper course of ABC's business. Consultant shall use all reasonable efforts to keep this information confidential.

c. Upon the termination of the Consulting Relationship, or at any time upon the request of ABC, Consultant shall return to ABC all printed, audio-visual, and electronic documents, data, and other materials, including all originals, copies, and extracts thereof, containing or referencing any Confidential Information or otherwise relating to ABC's organization or operations, and all other property of ABC then in Consultant's possession.

13. **Miscellaneous.**

a. This Agreement contains the entire understanding between the parties and supersedes any prior written or oral agreements between them. This Agreement shall not be modified or waived except by written instrument signed by both parties.

b. In the event that any part of this Agreement shall be declared unenforceable or invalid, the remaining parts shall continue to be valid and enforceable.

c. This Agreement shall inure to the benefit of and be binding upon the parties and their respective executors, administrators, personal representatives, heirs, assigns, and successors in interest.

d. This Agreement may not be assigned by Consultant or the rights granted to or obligations imposed upon Consultant transferred or sublicensed by Consultant, without the express prior written consent of ABC.

e. Either party's waiver of, or failure to exercise, any right provided for herein shall not be deemed a waiver of any further or future right under this Agreement.

f. This Agreement may be executed in one (1) or more counterparts, each of which shall be deemed an original and all of which taken together shall constitute one (1) and the same instrument.

g. Consultant covenants, warrants, and represents that Consultant shall comply with all laws and regulations applicable to this Agreement, and that Consultant shall exercise due care and act in good faith at all times in performance of Consultant's obligations under this Agreement.

h. All notices and demands of any kind or nature which either party may be required or desire to serve upon the other in connection with this Agreement shall be in writing and may be served personally, by telecopier, by certified mail, or by commercial overnight delivery (e.g., Federal Express), with constructive receipt deemed to have occurred one (1) calendar day after the mailing, sending, or transmitting of such notice, to the following addresses or telecopier numbers:

If to ABC: ______________________________

____

____

Attn.: ______________________________

Telecopier (_____) ______-__________

If to Consultant: ______________________________

____

____

Attn.: ______________________________

Telecopier (_____) ______-__________

i. Consultant acknowledges that this Agreement was made by the parties in the State of _______________ and shall be governed and enforced in accordance with the laws of the State of _______________. Consultant acknowledges that the state and federal courts of the State of _______________ shall be the exclusive forums for the resolution of any disputes concerning this Agreement or Consultant's provision of Consulting Services to ABC, and Consultant agrees to submit to the jurisdiction of such courts.

j. Consultant acknowledges that, if Consultant breaches any provision of this Agreement, ABC would be irreparably harmed, that monetary damages alone may not be sufficient to adequately protect ABC from or compensate ABC for such breach, and that, in addition to any other remedy, ABC shall be entitled to recover all expenses incurred in enforcing these provisions, including but not limited to attorneys' fees and expenses, court costs, and to a preliminary and permanent injunction enjoining such breach.

k. Both parties have read the foregoing Agreement in its entirety and voluntarily agree to each of its terms with full knowledge thereof.

*****

IN WITNESS WHEREOF, the parties hereto have caused duplicate originals of this Agreement to be executed by their respective duly authorized representatives as of the date and year first above written.

ABC ASSOCIATION	**[CONSULTANT]**
By: ______________________	By: ______________________
[Name] ______________________	
[Title] ______________________	
Dated: ______________________	Dated: ______________________

APPENDIX H

Model Consulting/Independent Contractor Agreement

(FOR USE WHEN CONSULTANT IS A CORPORATE ENTITY)

THIS CONSULTING AGREEMENT (the "Agreement") is made this ____ day of ________, ____, by and between ABC Association ("ABC"), a ____________ nonprofit corporation, and _________________ ("Consultant"), a ____________ corporation, and sets forth the terms of the Consultant's consulting relationship with ABC as follows:

1. **Consulting Services.** Effective __________, ____, ABC shall retain Consultant and Consultant shall provide ABC with consulting services (hereinafter described as the "Consulting Services" or "Consulting Relationship"), which shall include, without limitation, [describe consulting services here]. The nature of the Consulting Services may be modified by ABC in writing at any time, with the written agreement of Consultant.

2. **Term.** This Agreement shall remain in effect from __________ until _________________ (the "Term" or "Consulting Period"), unless terminated earlier by one (1) or both of the parties as set forth herein.

3. **Fee.** In consideration of the performance of the Consulting Services, ABC shall pay Consultant a fee of $_________ per month during the Consulting Period, payable by the ___ of each month during the Term of this Agreement [or set forth alternative fee arrangement agreed to by the parties].

4. **Termination.** ABC or Consultant may terminate this Agreement with or without cause (i) by the written agreement of both parties, or (ii) with ___ days' written notice to the other party. Upon termination of the Agreement, ABC's obligation to pay the fees described in Paragraph 3 herein and to reimburse Consultant for the expenses described in Paragraph 6 herein shall cease, effective as of the date of termination; provided, however, that ABC shall remain obligated to pay such fees and/or reimburse such expenses as have already been incurred or obligated prior to the date of termination.

5. **Control.** Consultant has the right to control and direct the means, manner, and method by which the Consulting Services are performed. This right of control includes, but is not limited to, the selection and supervision of any employees retained by Consultant to assist in the provision of Consulting Services to ABC. "Consultant," as used in this Agreement, shall mean the corporation (or other business entity) and all directors, officers, employees, and other representatives thereof.

6. **Equipment and Materials, Expenses, and Insurance.** Consultant shall furnish all equipment, materials, and labor used to perform the Consulting Services.

Consultant shall pay all ordinary and necessary expenses arising from its performance of the Consulting Services. [ABC shall, however, upon the submission by Consultant of appropriate written substantiation as set forth below and pursuant to the following terms and conditions, reimburse Consultant for ordinary and necessary business expenses, including travel and communication costs (e.g., phone, fax, computer, printer) and other materials and equipment costs, reasonably incurred by Consultant in connection with the provision of Consulting Services, as reasonably allocable to the provision of Consulting Services. As a precondition to reimbursement of any such expenses, Consultant shall provide ABC with detailed documentation regarding such expenses, including receipts, itineraries, reasons for the expenses, and such other documentation as ABC may require. Notwithstanding the foregoing, no expenses incurred by Consultant in connection with the provision of Consulting Services shall be reimbursed by ABC if and when such expenses exceed $__________ per ___________, unless reimbursement in excess of such limit is approved by the ABC Executive Director in writing.]* ABC shall not provide insurance coverage of any kind for Consultant or name Consultant as an additional insured on any of its insurance policies.

7. **Independent Contractor Status**. The Parties agree and acknowledge that Consultant is an independent contractor. Nothing herein shall be construed to create any partnership, joint venture, or agency relationship of any kind between the parties. Consultant's directors, officers, employees, and other representatives shall have no authority to enter into any agreements or contracts on behalf of ABC, or to bind ABC in any way, and they shall not represent, either explicitly or implicitly, that they possess any such authority. Consultant's directors, officers, employees, and other representatives are not, nor shall they be, deemed to be, for any purpose, employees or agents of ABC. ABC shall not be responsible to Consultant, its directors, officers, employees, or other representatives, or to any governmental authority, for the payment or withholding of any federal, state, or local income, unemployment, or other employment-related taxes in connection with the performance of the Consulting Services. It is understood that ABC shall not withhold from Consultant's compensation any amount that would normally be withheld from an employee's pay and Consultant warrants and agrees to pay all federal, state, and local taxes incurred and chargeable to it in connection with the performance of the Consulting Services. Consultant further warrants and agrees to file all required forms and make all federal, state, or local tax payments appropriate and necessary to the status of Consultant and its directors, officers, employees, and other representatives as an independent contractor and shall not claim any other status. Consultant further warrants and agrees to file all other required forms, registrations, reports, and other filings, and to pay all corresponding fees or other charges, as may be required of Consultant, at the federal, state, and/or local levels, as a consequence of activities being conducted by Consultant for or on behalf of ABC.

---

* This bracketed passage is not required. ABC may wish to modify or delete some or all of this passage depending upon the type of consulting work performed.

8. **Indemnification.** Consultant agrees to indemnify, save, and hold harmless ABC and its officers, directors, employees, and agents from and against any and all losses, expenses (including, but not limited to, payroll and income taxes and attorneys' fees), damages, claims, suits, demands, judgments, and causes of action of any nature arising from or as a result of (i) the performance of Consultant's obligations under this Agreement, (ii) the failure of Consultant or any of its directors, officers, employees, or other representatives to comply with any term or condition (including but not limited to all warranties and representations) of this Agreement, and/or (iii) the reclassification or attempted reclassification of any director, officer, employee, or other representative of Consultant as an employee of ABC.

9. **Property of ABC.** During the course of performing Consulting Services, Consultant's directors, officers, employees, or other representatives may, independently or in conjunction with ABC, develop information, produce work product, or achieve other results for ABC in connection with the Consulting Services it performs for ABC. Consultant agrees that such information, work product, or other results, systems, and information developed by the Consultant and/or ABC in connection with such Consulting Services (hereinafter collectively referred to as the "Work Product") shall vest with ABC and shall remain the sole and absolute property of ABC. Consultant hereby assigns all right, title, and interest in all intellectual property rights and all other property rights in the Work Product, including all extensions and renewals thereof, to ABC. Consultant further agrees to provide all assistance reasonably requested by ABC, both during and subsequent to the Term of this Agreement, in the establishment, preservation, and enforcement of ABC's rights in the Work Product. Upon the termination of this Agreement, Consultant agrees to promptly deliver to ABC all printed, electronic, audio-visual, and other tangible manifestations of the Work Product, including all originals and copies thereof. Consultant also agrees to waive any and all moral rights relating to the Work Product, including but not limited to, any and all rights of identification of authorship and any and all rights of approval, restriction, or limitation on use, and subsequent modifications.

10. **Reporting and Inspection.** During the Term of this Agreement, Consultant shall report in writing to ABC with whatever frequency and regarding whatever subject matter ABC shall hereinafter require of Consultant in order for ABC to stay apprised of Consultant's activities under this Agreement. Furthermore, during the Term of this Agreement, upon reasonable notice and during regular business hours, ABC shall have the right to inspect all books and records of Consultant relating to the subject matter of this Agreement.

11. **Conflict of Interest.** Consultant represents and warrants that it has no business, professional, personal, or other interest, including but not limited to the representation of other clients, that would conflict in any manner or degree with the performance of its obligations under this Agreement. If any such actual or potential conflict of interest arises during the Term of this Agreement, Consultant shall immediately inform ABC in writing of such conflict. If, in the reasonable judgment of

ABC, such conflict poses a material conflict to and with the performance of Consultant's obligations under this Agreement, then ABC may terminate the Agreement immediately upon written notice to Consultant; such termination of the Agreement shall be effective upon the receipt of such notice by Consultant. Nothing herein shall preclude Consultant's directors, officers, employees, or other representatives from engaging in other business activities, so long as such other activities do not violate or are not inconsistent with the terms and conditions of this Agreement, or do not otherwise pose a conflict of interest with Consultant's obligations under this Agreement.

12. **Nondisclosure of Confidential and Proprietary Information.**

a. Through its Consulting Relationship with ABC, Consultant and its directors, officers, employees, or other representatives may have access to confidential and proprietary information concerning ABC's organization, employees, members, and otherwise, including but not limited to, information concerning ABC's organization and structure, business and marketing plans, financial data, the identity of present and prospective members of ABC, ABC's current and prospective contracts, and policies, standards, procedures, and practices of ABC (hereinafter referred to as "Confidential Information"). The use of Confidential Information for the benefit of any person or entity other than ABC and the disclosure of such information to any person outside of ABC would cause severe competitive and financial damage to ABC.

b. Unless expressly authorized by ABC, both during and after the Term of this Agreement, neither Consultant nor its directors, officers, employees, or other representatives shall use Confidential Information for their own benefit or for the benefit of anyone other than ABC, or disclose such information to anyone outside of ABC, except in the proper course of ABC's business. Consultant shall use all reasonable efforts to keep this information confidential.

c. Upon the termination of the Consulting Relationship, or at any time upon the request of ABC, Consultant shall return to ABC all printed, audio-visual, and electronic documents, data and other materials, including all originals, copies, and extracts thereof, containing or referencing any Confidential Information or otherwise relating to ABC's organization or operations, and all other property of ABC then in its possession or in the possession of its directors, officers, employees, or other representatives.

13. **Miscellaneous.**

a. This Agreement contains the entire understanding between the parties and supersedes any prior written or oral agreements between them. This Agreement shall not be modified or waived except by written instrument signed by both parties.

b. In the event that any part of this Agreement shall be declared unenforceable or invalid, the remaining parts shall continue to be valid and enforceable.

c. This Agreement shall inure to the benefit of and be binding upon the parties and their respective executors, administrators, personal representatives, heirs, assigns, and successors in interest.

d. This Agreement may not be assigned by Consultant or the rights granted to or obligations imposed upon Consultant transferred or sublicensed by Consultant, without the express prior written consent of ABC.

e. Either party's waiver of, or failure to exercise, any right provided for herein shall not be deemed a waiver of any further or future right under this Agreement.

f. This Agreement may be executed in one (1) or more counterparts, each of which shall be deemed an original and all of which taken together shall constitute one (1) and the same instrument.

g. Consultant covenants, warrants, and represents that it shall comply with all laws and regulations applicable to this Agreement, and that it shall exercise due care and act in good faith at all times in performance of its obligations under this Agreement.

h. All notices and demands of any kind or nature which either party may be required or desire to serve upon the other in connection with this Agreement shall be in writing and may be served personally, by telecopier, by certified mail, or by commercial overnight delivery (e.g., Federal Express), with constructive receipt deemed to have occurred one (1) calendar day after the mailing, sending, or transmitting of such notice, to the following addresses or telecopier numbers:

If to ABC: ______________________________

____

____

Attn.: ______________________________

Telecopier (_____) ______-__________

If to Consultant: ______________________________

____

____

Attn.: ______________________________

Telecopier (_____) ______-__________

i. Consultant acknowledges that this Agreement was made by the parties in the State of ______________ and shall be governed and enforced in accordance with the laws of the State of ______________. Consultant acknowledges that the state and federal courts of the State of ______________ shall be the exclusive forums for the resolution of any disputes concerning this Agreement or Consultant's provision of Consulting Services to ABC, and Consultant agrees to submit to the jurisdiction of such courts.

j. Consultant acknowledges that, if it or any of its directors, officers, employees, or other representatives breaches any provision of this Agreement, ABC would be irreparably harmed, that monetary damages alone may not be sufficient to adequately protect ABC from or compensate ABC for such breach, and that, in addition to any other remedy, ABC shall be entitled to recover all expenses incurred in enforcing these provisions, including but not limited to attorneys' fees and expenses, court costs, and to a preliminary and permanent injunction enjoining such breach.

k. The individual executing this Agreement on behalf of Consultant hereby represents and warrants to ABC that he or she is duly authorized to bind Consultant to the terms and conditions of this Agreement.

l. Both parties have read the foregoing Agreement in its entirety and voluntarily agree to each of its terms with full knowledge thereof.

*****

IN WITNESS WHEREOF, the parties hereto have caused duplicate originals of this Agreement to be executed by their respective duly authorized representatives as of the date and year first above written.

ABC ASSOCIATION	[CONSULTANT]
By: ______________________	By: ______________________
[Name] ______________________	
[Title] ______________________	
Dated: ______________________	Dated: ______________________

APPENDIX I

Model License of Association Logo to Members

The attached logos are the property of the ABC Association ("ABC") but may be used by ABC members in good standing in accordance with the terms and conditions set forth below. Use of one or more of the logos shall constitute consideration for, agreement to, and acceptance of the following terms and conditions of this license by the user:

1. The attached logos are the sole and exclusive property of ABC. These logos may be used only by ABC members in good standing if and only if such use is made pursuant to the terms and conditions of this limited and revocable license. Any failure by a user to comply with the terms and conditions contained herein may result in the immediate revocation of this license, in addition to any other sanctions imposed by ABC. The interpretation and enforcement (or lack thereof) of these terms and conditions, and compliance therewith, shall be made by ABC in its sole discretion.

2. As set forth on the Attachment, the logos are made available to ABC members in good standing in camera-ready, printed form in color and/or black [modify accordingly for electronic media]. The logos may not be revised or altered in any way, and must be displayed in the same form as produced by ABC. The logos are a single color. The logos must be printed in their official color or in black.

3. The logos may be used in a professional manner on the user's business cards, stationery, literature, advertisements, store-front window, or in any other comparable manner to signify the user's membership in ABC. The logo may never be used independent of the term "MEMBER," as set forth on the Attachment. Notwithstanding the foregoing, the logos may not be used in any manner that, in the sole discretion of ABC: discredits ABC or tarnishes its reputation and goodwill; is false or misleading; violates the rights of others; violates any law, regulation, or other public policy; or mischaracterizes the relationship between ABC and the user, including but not limited to any use of the logos that might be reasonably construed as an endorsement, approval, sponsorship, or certification by ABC of the user, the user's business or organization, or the user's products or services, or that might be reasonably construed as support or encouragement to purchase or utilize the user's products or services.

4. Use of the logos shall create no rights for users in or to the logos or their use beyond the terms and conditions of this limited and revocable license. The logos shall remain at all times the sole and exclusive intellectual property of ABC. ABC shall have the right, from time to time, to request samples of use of the logos from which it may determine compliance with these terms and conditions. Without further notice, ABC reserves the right to prohibit use of the logos if it determines, in its sole discretion, that a

user's logo usage, whether willful or negligent, is not in strict accordance with the terms and conditions of this license, otherwise could discredit ABC or tarnish its reputation and goodwill, or the user is not an ABC member in good standing.

5. Any questions concerning use of the logos or the terms and conditions of this license should be directed to ___________________ at ABC at (_____) _____-_________.

ATTACHMENT

(Association Logo(s))

APPENDIX J

Model Policy on Member Participation as Vendor to Association

[Note: The following model policy is designed to apply whenever an officer, director, committee member, or member of the association desires to offer goods or services to the association for a fee. This policy is designed as a corollary to any existing association conflict of interest policy, and is designed to ensure association compliance with laws and rules concerning conflicts of interest, private inurement, and private benefit.]

The following rules and restrictions shall apply whenever a member of the association desires to offer goods or services to the association in exchange for monetary compensation. Members can participate in the Request for Proposal (RFP) process and otherwise offer goods or services to the association for a fee only in the event of full compliance with this policy.

1. **Full disclosure.** If a member or any related party* of such member has an interest in a proposed transaction with the association in the form of a (direct or indirect) personal financial interest or other personal interest in the transaction, or in any entity involved in the transaction (or holds a position as a director, officer, or employee of any such entity), he or she must make full disclosure of such interest before any discussion or negotiation of such transaction.

2. **Would-be vendor must be "in the business."** The member/would-be vendor must be "in the business" of providing the goods or services which such member seeks to provide to the association.

3. **No role in the decision-making process.** Any member who has such an interest in the proposed transaction shall not be present at any Board of Directors or committee meeting for any discussion of or vote in connection with the proposed transaction. Moreover, such member shall not participate, directly or indirectly, as an advocate on his or her own behalf, either formally at Board or committee meetings or informally through private contact, communication, and discussion, except to the extent permitted for non-member vendors to the association.

4. **No role in the post-award evaluation process.** If a member of the association becomes a vendor to the association, such member shall not participate,

* "Related party" is defined as members of your immediate family, which includes your spouse, minor children, and all other dependents; estates, trusts and partnerships in which you or your immediate family has a present or vested future beneficial interest; and a corporation or entity in which you or your immediate family is a beneficial owner of more than five percent (5%) of the voting interests.

directly or indirectly, in any process by which the member's performance as a vendor to the association is evaluated, either formally at Board or committee meetings or informally through private conduct, communication, and discussion, except to the extent permitted for non-member vendors to the association.

5. **Transaction must be in the best interests of the association.** The transaction must be fair to and in the best interests of the association. To this end, to ensure a competitive evaluative process, the standard RFP process must be utilized whenever one of the would-be vendors is a member of the association. Further, the following questions must be considered by the Board of Directors and/or other governing body making such decisions:

a. Is the association paying more than it would pay to a non-interested seller, or receiving less than it would receive from a non-interested buyer, for comparable goods or services?

b. What efforts have been made to develop "comparables" to help establish "fairness" (e.g., surveys, competitive bids)?

c. Will the vendor provide the best quality goods or services at the most competitive price?

6. **No special advantages in marketing or promotion.** If a member of the association becomes a vendor to the association, such member cannot use his or her membership in the association to market or promote his or her business, except to the extent permitted for non-member vendors to the association (e.g., advertisements in magazines at standard advertising rates, booths at trade shows at standard booth rates, corporate sponsorships), and provided that such marketing and promotion may highlight the fact that he or she is a vendor to and member of the association.

INDEX

T

U

V–Z